Systems Approach to Curriculum and Instructional Improvement

Middle School—Grade 12

C. Jennie Casciano–Savignano

Villanova University

Charles E. Merrill Publishing Co.
A Bell & Howell Company
Columbus   Toronto   London   Sydney

This book was set in Times Roman and Kabel.
The production editor was Jan Hall.
The cover was designed and prepared by Gene Hite.

Published by Charles E. Merrill Publishing Co.
A Bell & Howell Company
Columbus, Ohio 43216

Library of Congress Catalog Card Number: 77–087847

International Standard Book Number: 0–675–08394–X

1 2 3 4 5 6 7 8 9—83 82 81 80 79 78

Printed in the United States of America

To the Honor and Glory of God—

in Memory of My Departed Parents

Foreword

Whenever I see the term *systems approach* in the title of a book, I brace myself for a disappointment. Upon reading the book, I find very little application of systems principles. There may be one or two illustrations that resemble a flow chart and some terms borrowed from the systems discipline; however, the basic systems framework is rarely present.

I must admit that I approached the reading of this book with the same trepidation. Much to my surprise, I found that this author has, indeed, organized her book around systems concepts. She discusses feedback and systems regulation, servomechanism principles, entropy; she has flow charts and models. She has, also, carefully assisted the reader in making appropriate connections between these systems ideas and the task of curriculum and instructional improvement.

To be very honest with the reader, I really approach all curriculum books with the same trepidation. Having spent a major portion of my career as a curriculum coordinator and as an assistant superintendent for instruction, I have read many books that promised to help me to do my job better. I was often very disappointed. Again, I think that this author has delivered a text that offers considerable help to the practicing curriculum worker.

Finally, as a classroom teacher at the university level, I have another set of concerns regarding Education textbooks in general. Often they are either heavily slanted towards practice applications, slighting the development of a conceptual framework, or highly theoretical, offering no connections to practice. Again, this author has written a text that presents a theoretical framework within which the reader is helped to guide his or her practice.

In summary, this text discusses the extremely difficult task of curriculum and instructional improvement within a systems framework. The college student and the practitioner will benefit from this exposition. The practitioner needs the conceptual framework and the suggestions for practice; the college student needs to see the connection between theory and practice as well. Dr. Casciano—Savignano has succeeded in writing a text that is a systems approach to curriculum and instructional improvement.

WILLIAM L. KORBA
Associate Professor and Coordinator of Educational Administration
Villanova University

Preface

Systems analysis is an outgrowth of technology. Popularized through its use in business, industrial, and defense organizations, systems analysis is viewed by some educators as a promising technique for solving pervasive educational problems.

A system is a grouping of events, activities and/or processes that are treated as a unit. All kinds of organizations can be viewed as systems. Today a widely held point of view describes almost anything, education included, as a system that may have subsystems while being a part of a suprasystem. The main objective of systems theory is to promote better comprehension of complex interactions by relating elements into a comprehensive pattern or structure. Systems analysis is the process of analyzing systems; it is a technique for dealing with complex organizational problems, and seeing such problems as a whole, as well as in detail. However, systems theory and systems analysis must not be regarded as a panacea for all problems, regardless of where they exist.

Today educational organizations—like business and industry—face many difficulties because of increased size, new technology, extended services, and so on. Attempts by schools to renew curriculum and instruction have produced only minimal benefits. Increasingly, educators are becoming aware of the need for system-wide decision-making organization and process (as have been introduced into business and industry). It is interesting to note that, although schools have traditionally been referred to as systems, they have not been managed according to systems concepts. As is characteristic of systems, however, schools have inputs, processes, and outputs. School systems have subsystems, or interdependent parts, and they are part of a suprasystem—viz., society. These particular concepts regarding school systems are expanded upon in this book.

Since a system is considered to be a set of components that are related and organized to attain the ends for which the system is established, a curriculum and instructional program can be referred to as a system. The set of components of this particular system consists of the plan for providing and implementing teaching-learning situations. The ends of this particular system consist of the general and specific objectives that have been formulated as the goals for the specific school population.

The use of the systems concept offers advantages in planning for curriculum and instructional improvement. With a systems approach, objectives are central in decision-making activities, and pursuant planning includes a consideration of all relevant factors to the steps that are taken in the achievement of the goals. Without a regulated systems approach, curriculum and instructional planning tends to lose sight of the integral relationship of goals and teaching-learning activities, and to be piecemeal and fragmentary. The book explains the concept of "regulation" as used within the systems context.

This book is a guide for improving the curriculum and instructional program of middle schools, junior high schools, and senior high schools. It is designed fundamentally as a text for courses that involve the process of curriculum and instructional program improvement. However, it should serve, also, as a reference to professional school personnel who participate in curriculum and instructional improvement programs. The purpose of this book is to illustrate the use of the systems approach for improving curriculum and instruction.

The book is divided into nine chapters. The first chapter introduces the reader to basic systems theory—and input-output systems models—and preliminary extension of concepts into the area of curriculum and instructional programs (all to be explicated further, throughout the book). Chapter 2 presents a systems approach to curriculum and instructional improvement, and chapter 3 explains the roles and the responsibilities of all who should participate in the improvement program. Chapter 4 focuses on input into the system with an exploration of the needs, interests, and abilities of the students—and the needs and demands of the school community. Chapters 5 through 7 present, discuss, and illustrate the thruput process stage. Successively, these chapters explore the components of the thruput process stage—viz., (1) the formulation of the school philosophy and objectives; (2) the selection and organization of curriculum content for middle schools, junior high schools, and senior high schools; and (3) the selection of teaching methods and materials for middle schools, junior high schools, and senior high schools. Chapter 8 explores the importance and the various means for assessing, measuring, and evaluating the outputs of the system; and chapter 9 concentrates on basic principles and considerations for conversion to a systems approach. These nine chapters are divided into three parts: (1) Systems Theory, (2) Curriculum as a System, and (3) Conversion to a Systems Approach.

A workbook section is included at the end of each chapter. Each workbook section includes a variety of possible learning experiences, such as: (1) short-answer quizzes; (2) library reference work that requires synthesis of readings, study of models, interpretations, evaluations, and note-taking for pursuant class dialogue; (3) school visits that provide for attendance at curriculum and instructional improvement meetings, examination of curriculum and instructional materials, observation of curriculum and instructional improvement procedures; (4) interviews and polls of professional personnel, students, parents, community —for gathering data for curriculum and instructional improvement; (5) assignments that require arranging for a class speaker, conducting a symposium, using curriculum and instructional materials, and writing a school philosophy, school objectives, and a curriculum.

The workbook section of each chapter helps, among other things, to promote (1) class dialogue, (2) activity-oriented classes, (3) understanding of the concepts that are presented in each chapter, and (4) involvement in practical experiences that are based on the concepts that are presented in the chapter.

Space is provided in the workbook section for student responses to learning activities. Students should feel free to use notebook paper whenever additional space is needed. Pages are perforated and three-hole punched, so that they can be torn out easily and placed in a binder. The book is conceived to serve as the beginning of what should be a lifelong file for use in curriculum and instructional improvement. The write-in answers, reports, and independent research findings, when coupled with the printed portion of the book, provide the beginning of such a personalized resource.

The book is the result of the education and the experience of the author. In preliminary form, it was used in the graduate Curriculum and Methods classes of the author. In present form, the book is the product of refinements prompted by evaluation of its effectiveness in the classroom. It is further based on such resources as:

1. Personal observation of—and participation in—experimental and innovative programs.
2. Research studies and professional readings regarding curriculum and instructional improvement.
3. Learnings gleaned from participation in conferences and workshops.
4. Points of view and recommendations—gathered in dialogue—with the professional personnel of middle schools, junior high schools, and senior high schools.

Appreciation is expressed to Dr. William L. Korba, who diligently read the manuscript, and conscientiously reacted to the author. Appreciation is also expressed to my sister, Louise, the power of whose prayers was felt in insight—and in unbounded energy; and to the many persons, too numerous to mention, who helped in more ways than they will ever know. Special gratitude is felt to my departed parents, to whom I owe all that I am—and all that I will ever be. Their ideals, sacrifices, love, and inspiration have been the threads that have woven a life for me that, otherwise, would never have been. For all of this, I am thankful to God.

Dr. Casciano—Savignano

Contents

PART
I

SYSTEMS THEORY

1

Systems Concepts: Their Application to Curriculum and Instructional Improvement

For several years schools in the United States have felt the need for reform in curriculum, in grouping students, in scheduling learning activities, in individualizing and equalizing educational opportunities, in utilizing teaching methods and media, in rendering accountability, and so forth. However, too often efforts for improvement have been sporadic and unrelated. Too often, efforts have been based on whim, rather than a systematic evaluation of alternatives, and on inadequate data of what might be better than the already existent situation. Too often, efforts for improvement have been attempted in school organizations only to cause ill effects in other parts of the school organization. Also, the results of testing and evaluation have not been used systematically to improve system performance.

Nevertheless, demands continue to be made for expanded service. Today schools are called upon to provide services and programs far beyond the demands of the past. The nation looks to education as one of the ingredients in building national defense, increasing economic opportunity, helping developing countries, and alleviating poverty, crime, and juvenile delinquency. Most schools have tried to cope with growing demands within a traditional administrative and organizational framework that continues into the present. Doubt is increasing as to whether or not schools can efficiently educate children and serve society adequately, in the seventies and eighties, within the traditional administrative and organizational framework. It appears that changes in organizational structure and processes must be made if schools are to capitalize fully from revolutionary

3

proposals for curriculum and instructional improvement and, ultimately, for improvement of conditions in society.

The systems approach, grounded in modern organization theory, is advanced with the prospect that it can break impasses existent in schools today, for example, the impasse that impedes curriculum and instructional improvement. This chapter introduces prospects for curriculum and instruction. This book builds upon this first chapter with explications of sequential concepts, and their implementation, for a comprehensive and unified curriculum and instructional improvement program.

Systems Defined

Systems have been defined in a variety of ways. A. D. Hall and R. E. Fagen have offered this succinct definition: "A system is a set of objects together with relationships between the objects and between their attributes." [1] F. H. Allport has presented this comprehensive definition:

> . . . any recognizably delimited aggregate of dynamic elements that are in some way interconnected and interdependent and that continue to operate together according to certain laws and in such a way as to produce some characteristic total effect. A system, in other words, is something that is concerned with some kind of activity and preserves a kind of integration and unity; and a particular system can be recognized as distinct from other systems to which, however, it may be dynamically related. Systems may be complex; they may be made up of interdependent subsystems, each of which, though less autonomous than the entire aggregate, is nevertheless fairly distinguishable in operation. [2]

Daniel Griffiths has made the simple statement that a system is "a complex of elements in mutual interaction." [3] According to Roy Grinker, a system is "some whole form in structure or operation, concepts or function, composed of united and integrated parts." [4] James Miller reasons that systems may vary as to size, complexity, abstractness, or concreteness. [5] Feyereisen, Fiorino, and Nowak define a system as "a set of components organized in such a way as to constrain action toward the accomplishment of the purposes for which the system exists." [6]

This author depicts a system as a unit characterized by defined boundaries and an array of interrelated parts, purposed to achieve stated objectives. This is the definition that is adopted for use in this book. Emphasis is placed on interrelations with an awareness that a change in one part or element will have an effect on the other parts or elements of the system. In simplest form, a system consists of input, process (thruput), and output. A regulated system consists of input, process, output, and feedback.

Systems Illustrated

Gordon Hearn views it possible that all forms of animate and inanimate matter may be represented as systems that are governed by certain constant principles that have been discovered by scientists in fields such as biology, gestalt psychology, or economics. [7] An examination of the environment reveals that it contains systems that can be categorized as either natural or developed by human beings. The begonia plant would be an example of a natural system. A begonia plant receives as its input: nutrients and water from the soil, heat and light from the sun, and, by a process, produces flowers as one output. The oil lamp is an example of a system developed by human beings. An oil lamp receives oil as its input, and, by a process, transforms it into light as its output.

Systems developed by human beings may be subdivided into machine-to-machine, person-to-machine, and person-to-person systems. The following are given in illustration. An electric lamp that is turned on or off by an automatic timer would be an example of a machine-to-machine system because the process is produced by machine, and the input-output is machine. Operation of a´ cash register by a person would be considered a person-to-machine system. In a school district, the process is performed by persons, and the input-output is persons. A school district is, therefore, considered a person-to-person system. Systems developed by human beings are most frequently referred to as behavioral systems. The words, *scheme, network,* and *organism,* are sometimes used as synonyms for system.[8]

Historical Background

A short discussion of the historical antecedents and the derivation of the systems approach would promote understanding of the concepts being presented in this chapter. The application of systems procedures in education is a relatively recent development. However, historical antecedents date back to the beginnings of recorded history.[9] For example, the Egyptians used a system of measurement for the construction of their pyramids. The Phoenicians devised a system of navigation that was based on the stars. In third-century China, principles synthesizing laws, methods, and authority were derived in an attempt to systematize management.[10] Systems, as we know them today, can be traced to the work of engineers, particularly electrical engineers, in their development of what is called automation. The systems approach has evolved from engineering, to the biological sciences, and, finally, to the social sciences. Many of the terms originated by engineers in their work with automation have been retained in this evolution of the systems approach.

Properties

All systems except the very basic have subsystems, and all systems except the most inclusive have a suprasystem. A school system may be subdivided into any number of subsystems, four of which could be the following: (1) students and personnel, (2) finance, (3) buildings and grounds, and (4) curriculum and instruction. At the same time, a school system is part of the total educational system of the state, or country, which entities constitute the suprasystem.

Glenn Immegart has observed, further, that systems have the following additional properties:

1. All systems exist in time-space.
2. All systems tend toward a state of randomness and disorder, the ultimate of which is entropy, or inertia.
3. All systems have boundaries, which are more or less arbitrary demarcations of that included within and that excluded from the system.

4. All systems have environment, which is everything external to (without the boundary of) the system.

5. All systems have factors that affect the structure and function of the system. Factors within the system are variables; factors in the system's environment are parameters.[11]

In simplest form, a system consists of input, process, and output. In a school system, input consists, among other things, of the incoming students to be educated, teachers' knowledges and skills, the regulations that stipulate the courses that must be (or may be) taught, the regulations that require that certain types of programs be offered, the regulations that allow experimental programs to be introduced, the demands of parents, the needs of students, and the needs of the community. The output is the product of the system, i.e., educated individuals. The process consists of subprocesses which act upon the input to transform it into output. See figure 1 for illustrative basic models of the input-process-output concept.

Systems may be viewed as open or closed. An open system is related to—and makes exchanges of matter, energy, and information with—its environment. A

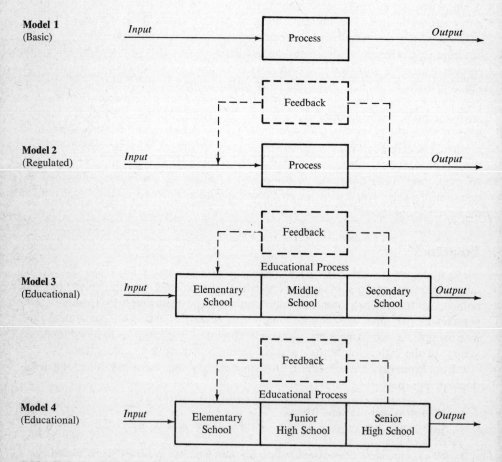

FIGURE 1.   Models: Input-Process-Output Concept

closed system, on the other hand, is not related to—and does not make these exchanges with—its environment. In this regard the school is an open system.

Open systems have the already-discussed properties of systems in general, but they also have the following characteristics that distinguish them from closed systems:

1. Open systems have a tendency to maintain themselves in a steady state through self-regulating mechanisms. A steady state does not necessarily mean a static state; it might mean a constant state of growth and change. Nevertheless, illustratively, a curriculum coordinator trying to provide leadership in curriculum improvement—and, thereby, disrupting some of the steady states of others in the school—would sense the relevance of the principle of steady state in his attempts to provide leadership. In further illustration, a school may respond to external or internal modifications in objectives or procedures, yet retain a condition of equilibrium.

2. Open systems display equifinality, i.e., identical (or, equally desirable) outcomes can be derived from initial conditions or circumstances that may be quite different. In curriculum and instructional improvement, this principle of equifinality calls attention to alternative processes—wherein any process or combination of processes may lead to equally desirable results.

3. Open systems display progressive segregation by dividing into a hierarchy order of subsystems that gain a certain independence of each other. The school, for example, is characteristically segregated in terms of subsystems termed departments or units, which, of themselves, consist of classroom subsystems. Articulation among subsystems is crucial if the system is to operate smoothly.

4. If open systems are to operate effectively, feedback processes are essential. Feedback may be external or internal. Feedback is the process of comparing a sample of the output to the input. It consists of either information or evaluative data that are useful to the total system and to the units of the system. Feedback affects future system performance because it serves as a control over changes in system and subsystem processes. In general, feedback refers to that part of output that is fed back to input and affects succeeding outputs. Feedback refers to the property of adjusting future conduct by reference to past performance.[12]

An understanding of feedback is important to the concept of this book. If the reader is still confused, he or she might think about the home thermostat. The room air temperature is sampled. If the temperature is too low, the thermostat "directs" the furnace to supply heat. The air temperature is monitored until it reaches the desired temperature, at which time the thermostat "directs" the furnace to stop supplying heat. When the room cools, the process is repeated. The heating system is regulated through this feedback process.

Systems Analysis Defined

Guy Black and C. J. Hitch explain that systems analysis is a method of analyzing a situation or a problem by identifying objectives and available resources, and determining alternatives, including the optimal one, in using resources to attain objectives.[13]

Stephen Knezevich proposes that systems analysis enhances decision making by framing problems, so that appropriate objectives and relevant important environments are presented sharply, "by collecting and arranging data significant to the decision, by stipulating the alternatives and how each might be tested, and by outlining possible costs and benefits of alternative actions." [14]

According to Donald Meals, systems analysis consists of viewing the whole as an integration and interaction of its parts and identifying problems.[15] In education, "systems analysis calls upon the educator . . . to see his activity as a whole—not only the whole child but also the curriculum and the media and the teacher and the management system for putting these and other resources together in a functional system." [16] Charles Blaschke attaches significance to systems analysis for education in that systems analysis ". . . forces the individual manager to define the problem precisely, note the alternatives available and their cost, and choose the most efficient alternative according to performance criteria." [17]

Some authorities argue that all problems can be attacked in purely quantitative terms that will dictate the solution decision to be made in a particular situation. Others, however, caution that systems analysis will not automatically lead to the most prudent decision.

The systems approach has been defined in various ways in educational writings. Roger Kaufman divides the systems approach into two major categories: system analysis and system synthesis.[18] System analysis includes the following steps: (1) identifying the problem and (2) determining solution requirements and alternatives. System synthesis, on the other hand, involves the three remaining steps: (3) choosing a solution strategy from alternatives, (4) implementing the solution strategy, and (5) determining performance effectiveness. System design (or system modeling) includes all five steps. Figure 2 illustrates these categories and steps.

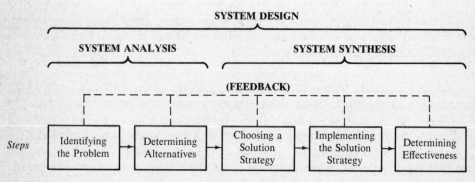

FIGURE 2.   Model: System Design (Categorized as to System Analysis and System Synthesis, and These Categories Divided into Steps)

SOURCE: Adapted from Roger A. Kaufman, "System Approaches to Education: Discussion and Attempted Integration," in Philip K. Piele, Terry L. Eidell, and Stuart C. Smith, eds., *Social and Technological Change: Implications for Education* (Eugene: Center for Advanced Study of Educational Administration, University of Oregon, 1970), pp. 143, 168; cited in James M. Lipham and James A. Hoeh, *The Principalship: Foundations and Functions* (New York: Harper and Row, 1974), p. 35. Reprinted by permission.

A third activity, system regulation, consists of the collection of feedback. This is accomplished through sampling the output and comparing it to the input. Changes observed are the result of the action of the system. Discrepancies in desired output are reduced (or eliminated) through system modification.

It is to be noted that Kaufman uses the term *system* (singular) *analysis,* rather than *systems* (plural) *analysis.* Edwin Read clarifies the meanings of these two terms and the term, *problem analysis.*[19] Each of these terms implies a systems approach to educational problem solving, planning, and decision making. This approach views each educational system or subsystem as an integrated whole that consists of interdependent parts that act together to accomplish a predetermined objective. Read defines systems (plural) analysis as:

> . . . a quantitative approach to decision-making that seeks to offer the decision-maker a set of alternative solutions representing a variety of costs and benefits. Its procedures include six major elements: (1) the objective, (2) data, (3) alternative solutions, (4) costs nad benefits, (5) models, and (6) the decision rule.[20]

Alternative systems are analyzed and evaluated in terms of cost, time, and effectiveness. A decision is reached on the basis of comparative data. System (singular) analysis is much less complex and sophisticated than systems (plural) analysis. System analysis may be thought of as:

> . . . a designing process which is used to build "from scratch" a single system for implementing one of several alternative solution strategies that meets previously established performance requirements. System analysis is an approach to problem-solving that begins with a need assessment and moves systematically to define the problem and the objective, specify the requirements of a solution, identify alternate solutions and finally, design a single system for meeting the requirements of a solution.[21]

It has already been suggested above that Kaufman views system analysis as "the first of a two-part planning and problem-solving technique; the second part is referred to as system synthesis." [22] Problem analysis is:

> . . . an essential, yet distinct, part of system analysis that should be performed prior to the identification of solution strategies. Its purpose is to provide the problem-solver with a more comprehensive insight into the problem and its several components. By analyzing a problem into its component parts, the educational planner has a much better chance of identifying and conceptualizing appropriate and creative solutions.[23]

This author's definition of systems analysis incorporates Read's definitions of system (singular) analysis and systems (plural) analysis.

Tools and Techniques

Logical and quantifiable tools and techniques are available for analyzing school programs, monitoring educational projects, collecting feedback (evaluating educational outcomes), and making educational decisions. The following are but a few of these tools and techniques: standardized testing, task analysis, diagnostic or prescriptive teaching, behavioral objectives, criterion-referenced performance, management by objectives (MBO), planning-programming-budgeting system (PPBS), program evaluation review technique (PERT), and operations research (OR). It is not the purpose of this book to teach the use of these tools and techniques and the situations under which they are most pertinent. The reader is, therefore, referred to the following references for detailed information:

1. Alioto, Robert F., and Jungherr, J. A. *Operational PPBS for Education.* New York: Harper and Row, 1971.

2. Anderson, Scarvia B.; Ball, Samuel; Murphy, Richard T.; and associates. *Encyclopedia of Educational Evaluation.* San Francisco: Jossey-Bass, 1975.

3. Evarts, Harry F. *Introduction to PERT.* Boston: Allyn and Bacon, 1964.

4. Hacker, Thorne. "Management by Objectives for Schools," *Administrator's Notebook* 20 (November 1971): 1-4.

5. Odiorne, George S. *Management Decisions by Objectives.* Englewood Cliffs, N.J.: Prentice-Hall, 1969.

6. Van Dusseldorp, Ralph; Richardson, Duane E.; and Foley, Walter J. *Educational Decision-Making through Operations Research.* Boston: Allyn and Bacon, 1971.

Models: Decision-Making Models in Curriculum and Instruction

A model is a symbolic, simplified representation of a system. In systems analysis, models are used to help the analyst visualize components of a system and their relationship. Figure 3 symbolizes the basic responsibility of a school system to its students (in regard to curriculum and instruction).

A decision-making model is illustrative of the process by which a decision is made within a particular organization. Since processes of decision making within organizations differ, decision-making models differ, also.

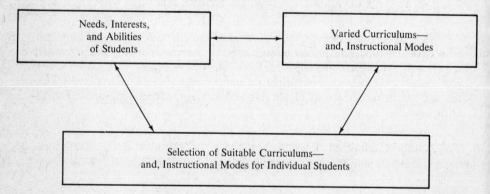

FIGURE 3.   Basic Responsibility of a School System to Its Students (in Regard to Curriculum and Instruction)

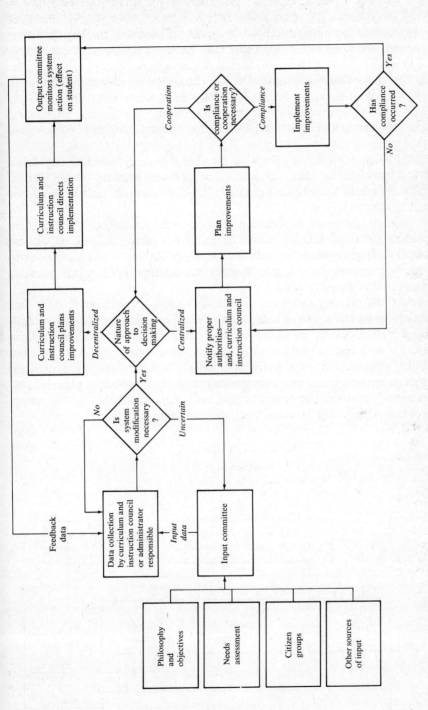

FIGURE 4. Model: Basic System for Decision Making in Curriculum and Instruction

Figure 4 presents a proposed, basic system design for decision making in curriculum and instruction. The reader will note that provision has been made for either a centralized or a decentralized approach to decision making. In some school systems, the centralized approach may be the primary approach taken. Whereas, in other school systems, the decentralized approach may be the choice. This writer suggests that the nature of the approach taken should be dependent upon the *type* of decision to be made, rather than upon other factors. It is recognized, however, that the degree of centralization is probably primarily a result of the leadership style of the superintendent and the traditions of the school board.

The model is self-explanatory except for possible confusion regarding the person or agency responsible for data collection, for deciding whether or not system modification is necessary, and whether the approach to decision making should be centralized or decentralized.

If the primary approach to decision making were centralized, an assistant superintendent (or other official) would serve as the person who is responsible for collecting and comparing the information from the input and output committees. He or she would also decide how the subsequent steps towards planning and implementation would occur.

If, however, the primary approach to decision making were decentralized, data collection would be the responsibility of the curriculum and instruction council. This council (which will be discussed in detail later in this text) would, in turn, compare input data and feedback data and make the determination as to whether or not system modification is necessary. In addition, in most cases, the curriculum and instruction council would continue the decentralized approach to planning and implementation. However, the council could, on occasion, decide that the nature of the problem is such that a centralized follow-through is best.

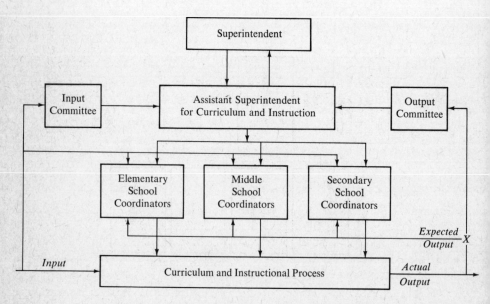

FIGURE 5.   Alternative System for Centralized Decision Making (in Curriculum and Instruction) in a School Organization Comprised of an Elementary School, Middle School, and Secondary School

Consistent with sound systems-design principles, the basic decision-making paradigm in figure 4 illustrates the interrelation of components, decision points, alternatives, and regulation through feedback.

This author feels that the systems approach can be applied to centralized—as well as decentralized—decision-making situations. Figure 5 presents an alternative system to centralized decision making. This figure presents a model symbolizing centralized decision making (in curriculum and instruction) in a school organization that is comprised of an elementary school, middle school, and secondary school. An explanation of the decision-making process symbolized in the model follows. Greater breadth and depth of discussion of the process will be given in subsequent chapters of this book. Succinctly, explanations of the process symbolized in figure 5 are as follows:

1. The function of the input committee (or person) is to gather, analyze, and organize information about the environment needed by the system for curriculum and instructional improvement. The input committee gathers, for example, information to answer such a question as: Are the needs, interests, and abilities of students who are entering the system changing?

2. The output committee (or person) compares actual output with expected output and reports variances to the superintendent (feedback). The output committee reports, for example, a comparison of the reading achievement scores (of students entering the middle school of the system) with national norms.

3. In a rather bureaucratic, traditional system, key administrators, e.g., assistant superintendent for instruction or director of curriculum, would analyze the reports from the input committee and the output committee. These reports, when compared, would indicate the effects of the system. If the effects were not those desired, the discrepancies would be reduced by system modification. In this type of organizational pattern, it would not be unusual for these administrators to take appropriate steps to modify the system—either through directives or some other means at their disposal. Throughout the rest of this text, this approach will be referred to as the *centralized approach.*

There is a tendency in modern school administrative structures to move from centralized decision making to a decentralized structure. There is a growing recognition of the fact that directives from above may result in little real improvement and that there is a need to involve those responsible for implementation in the decision-making process itself. Such involvement results in wider "ownership" of the decision and a greater tendency to cooperate, rather than merely to comply.

In a school system operating within these administrative philosophies, the reports of the input and the output committees would be delivered to an organizational structure, such as a curriculum and instruction council. The curriculum and instruction council would do the analysis and develop any policies or procedures that would be necessary to modify the system. Throughout the rest of this text, this approach will be referred to as the *decentralized approach.*

4. The curriculum coordinators (sometimes called curriculum directors) in a centralized system take the orders or directives received from the assistant superintendent for curriculum and instruction, and initiate and expedite changes in the curriculum and instructional process.

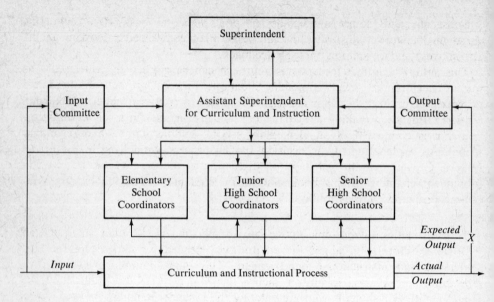

FIGURE 6.   Alternative System for Centralized Decision Making (in Curriculum and Instruction) in a School Organization Comprised of an Elementary School, Junior High School, and Senior High School

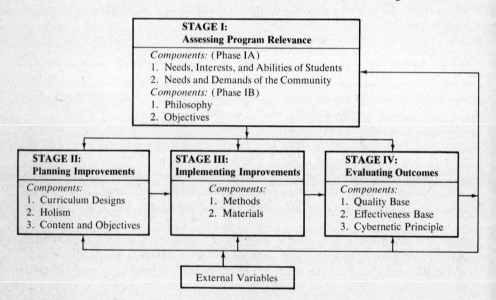

FIGURE 7.   Model: System for Curriculum and Instructional Improvement

5. The superintendent of schools (or some duly assigned person) is constantly kept informed by the output committee (or some person acting in this capacity), so that the system can be redesigned, if necessary, to function more effectively.

A model for decision making (in curriculum and instruction) in a school organization comprised of an elementary school, junior high school, and senior high school is comparable to the model in figure 5. The model of an organization comprised of an elementary school, junior high school, and senior high school is presented in figure 6. The explanations of this particular model are the same as those for the model in figure 5.

Systems Model for a Curriculum and Instructional Improvement Program

Figure 7 presents a model symbolizing a system for a curriculum and instructional improvement program. The rest of the chapters of this book will explicate this symbolized system for curriculum and instructional improvement.

Summary

The systems approach can be divided into three major categories: system analysis, system synthesis, and system regulation. System analysis includes the following steps: (1) identifying the problem and (2) determining solution requirements and alternatives. System synthesis, on the other hand, involves the three remaining steps: (3) choosing a solution strategy from alternatives, (4) implementing the solution strategy, and (5) determining performance effectiveness. System design (or system modeling) includes all five steps. System regulation consists of collecting feedback, i.e., monitoring output, and comparing it to input.

A distinction can be made between systems (plural) analysis and system (singular) analysis. Systems (plural) analysis is a quantitative approach to decision making that seeks to offer the decision maker a set of alternative solutions representing a variety of costs and benefits. System (singular) analysis, on the other hand, is a designing process that is used to build "from scratch" a single system for implementing one of several alternative solution strategies that meets previously established performance requirements.

Some authorities argue that all problems can be attacked in purely quantitative terms that will dictate the solution decision to be made in a particular situation. Others, however, caution that systems analysis will not automatically lead to the most prudent decision.

The systems approach has evolved from engineering, to the biological sciences, and, finally, to the social sciences. In some part, its beginnings can be traced, for all practical purposes, to the team efforts of scientists and military experts in attempting to solve the problem of warfare in the early years of World War II. Operations research (basically, a multidisciplinary task-force approach to problem solving based on scientific procedures) produced outstanding successes during World War II.

A system is a unit characterized by defined boundaries and an array of interrelated parts purposed to achieve stated objectives. Emphasis is placed on interrelations with an awareness that a change in one part or element will have an effect on the other parts or elements of the system. In simplest form, a system consists of input, process (thruput), and output. In a school system, input consists of, among other things, teachers, incoming students to be educated, regulations that stipulate the courses that must be (or may be) taught, regulations that require that certain types of programs be offered, regulations that allow experimental programs to be introduced, demands of parents, and needs of the community. The output is the product of the system, i.e., educated individuals. The process consists of subprocesses that act upon the input to transform it into output. Such a concept portrays a school system as a network of interrelated parts, each responsible for accomplishing part of the task of transforming inputs into desired outputs. This particular concept is in contrast to the concept that portrays a school system as a conglomeration of separate parts. Supporters of the latter concept imply that a school system can be reformed by changing only one part included in the system. However, supporters of the contrasting view (that a school system is a network of interrelated parts) are not partisan to this implication.

Systems have certain properties. The following are among the properties: (1) All systems except the very basic have subsystems, and all systems except the most inclusive have a suprasystem. (2) Systems may be viewed as open or closed. An open system is related to—and makes exchanges of matter, energy, and information with—its environment. A closed system is not related in this way, and it does not make these exchanges.

Logical and quantifiable tools and techniques are available for analyzing school programs, monitoring educational projects, evaluating educational outcomes, and making educational decisions. The chapter presents some of these tools and techniques. Systems analysis is not to be confused with computer-based data processing.

A model is a symbolic, simplified representation of a system. A decision-making model is illustrative of the process by which a decision is made within a particular organization. Models play an important part in systems studies. They portray situations being studied, thus aiding the analyst to expedite his study.

Systems concepts are used to design a self-regulating system that redirects itself to ensure that the objectives of the system are accomplished. This chapter presents and discusses models that this author has designed, regarding the basic responsibility of a school system to its students (concerning curriculum and instruction), and decision making (in curriculum and instruction) in a school organization.

Chapter 2 explicates the concepts that are introduced in chapter 1, relative to the application of a systems approach to the curriculum and instructional improvement program.

NOTES

1. A. D. Hall and R. E. Fagen, "General Systems," in *Yearbook of the Society for General Systems Research,* eds. L. von Bertalanffy and A. Rapoport (Ann Arbor: Braun-Brumfield, 1956), p. 18.

2. F. H. Allport, *Theories of Perception and the Concept of Structure* (New York: John Wiley and Sons, 1955), p. 469. Reprinted by permission of the publisher.

3. Daniel Griffiths, "Nature and Meaning of Theory," *Behavioral Science and Educational Administration,* in *63rd Yearbook of the National Society for the Study of Education* (Chicago: University of Chicago Press, 1964), p. 116.

4. From *Toward a Unified Theory of Human Behavior, An Introduction to General Systems Theory,* Second Edition, p. 370, edited by Roy R. Ginker, Sr., with the assistance of Helen MacGill Hughes © 1956, 1967 by Basic Books, Inc., Publishers, New York.

5. James G. Miller, "Living Systems: Basic Concepts," *Behavioral Science* 10 (July 1965): 201-9.

6. K. V. Feyereisen, A. J. Fiorino, and A. T. Nowak, *Supervision and Curriculum Renewal: A Systems Approach* (New York: Appleton-Century-Crofts, 1970), p. 38. All material in this text relating to Feyereison, Fiorino, and Nowak is from *Supervision and Curriculum*

Renewal, © 1970. Reprinted by permission of Prentice-Hall, Inc., Englewood Cliffs, New Jersey.

7. Gordon Hearn, *Theory Building in Social Work* (Toronto: University of Toronto Press. 1958), p. 38.

8. Stephen J. Knezevich, *Administration of Public Education* (New York: Harper and Row, 1969), p. 542.

9. James M. Lipham and James A. Hoeh, *The Principalship: Foundations and Functions* (New York: Harper and Row, 1974), p. 19.

10. Ibid., pp. 19–20.

11. Glenn L. Immegart, "Systems Theory and Taxonomic Inquiry into Organizational Behavior in Education," in *Developing Taxonomies of Organizational Behavior in Educational Administration,* ed. Daniel E. Griffiths (Chicago: Rand McNally, 1969), p. 167. Reprinted by permission.

12. Hearn, *Theory Building,* pp. 38–49.

13. Guy Black, *The Application of Systems Analysis to Government Operations* (Washington, D.C.: National Institute of Public Affairs, 1966), p. 3. Reprinted by permission from C. J. Hitch, "Plans, Programs and Budgets of the Department of Defense," *Operations Research* (January–February 1963): 8. Copyright 1963, ORSA. No futher reproduction permitted without consent of the copyright owner.

14. Knezevich, *Administration,* p. 546.

15. Donald W. Meals, "Heuristic Models for Systems Planning," *Phi Delta Kappan* 48 (January 1967): 200.

16. Ibid., p. 200.

17. Charles L. Blaschke, "The DOD: Catalyst in Educational Technology," *Phi Delta Kappan* 48 (January 1967): 211.

18. Roger A. Kaufman, "System Approaches to Education: Discussion and Attempted Integration," in *Social and Technological Change: Implications for Education,* eds. Philip K. Piele, Terry L. Eidell, and Stuart C. Smith (Eugene: Center for Advanced Study of Educational Administration, University of Oregon, 1970), pp. 143, 168; cited in James M. Lipham and James A. Hoeh, *The Principalship: Foundations and Functions* (New York: Harper and Row, 1974), p. 35. Reprinted by permission.

19. Edwin A. Read, "Distinguishing among Systems Analysis, System Analysis, and Problem Analysis," *Educational Technology* 14 (May 1974): 35–39. Reprinted by permission.

20. Ibid., p. 39.

21. Ibid., pp. 36, 39.

22. Ibid., p. 36.

23. Ibid., pp. 37, 39.

Related Readings

Allport, F. H. *Theories of Perception and the Concept of Structure.* New York: John Wiley and Sons, 1955.

Banghart, F. W. *Educational Systems Analysis.* New York: Macmillan, 1969.

Chapanis, A. "On Some Relations between Human Engineering, Operations Research, and Systems Engineering." In *Systems: Research and Design,* edited by Donald P. Eckman. New York: John Wiley and Sons, 1961.

Corrigan, R. E., and Corrigan, B. O. *Systems Approach for Education.* Anaheim, Calif.: R. E. Corrigan, 1970.

Feyereisen, K. V.; Fiorino, A. J.; and Nowak, A. T. *Supervision and Curriculum Renewal: A Systems Approach.* New York: Appleton-Century-Crofts, 1970.

Griffiths, Daniel. "Nature and Meaning of Theory." In *Behavioral Science and Educational Administration, 63rd Yearbook of the National Society for the Study of Education.* Chicago: University of Chicago Press, 1964.

Grinker, Roy R. *Toward a Unified Theory of Human Behavior.* New York: Basic Books, 1956.

Hall, A. D., and Fagen, R. E. "General Systems." In *Yearbook of the Society for General Systems Research,* edited by L. von Bertalanffy and A. Rapoport. Ann Arbor: Braun-Brumfield, 1956.

Hayman, John L., Jr. "The Systems Approach and Education." *The Educational Forum* 38 (May 1974): 493–501.

Hearn, Gordon. *Theory Building in Social Work.* Toronto: University of Toronto Press, 1958.

Immegart, Glenn L. "Systems Theory and Taxonomic Inquiry into Organizational Behavior in Education." In *Developing Taxonomies of Organizational Behavior in Educational Administration,* edited by Daniel E. Griffiths. Chicago: Rand McNally, 1969.

Kaufman, R. A. *Educational System Planning.* Englewood Cliffs, N.J.: Prentice-Hall, 1972.

Knezevich, Stephen J. *Administration of Public Education.* New York: Harper and Row, 1969.

Lipham, James M., and Hoeh, James A. *The Principalship: Foundations and Functions.* New York: Harper and Row, 1974.

Miller, James G. "Living Systems: Basic Concepts." *Behavioral Science* 10 (July 1965): 201–209.

Read, Edwin A. "Distinguishing among Systems Analysis, System Analysis, and Problem Analysis." *Educational Technology* 14 (May 1974): 35–39.

Thompson, James D. *Organizations in Action.* New York: McGraw-Hill, 1967.

von Bertalanffy, Ludwig. *General System Theory: Foundations, Development, Applications.* New York: G. Braziller, 1973.

Work Sheet 1A
Questions for Class Dialogue

Student's Name _____

Date _____

Directions: Study chapter 1 with the following questions in mind. Prepare responses for each question, so that you can intelligently participate in class dialogue. Space is provided with each question, so that you can record any notes that will aid you in the dialogue.

1. What is a system?

2. What is systems analysis?

3. Distinguish among the following: system (singular) analysis, systems (plural) analysis, problem analysis.

4. Discuss the rationale upon which is based the proposal that the systems approach holds prospect for breaking impasses existent in schools today—as a case in point: the impasse that impedes curriculum and instructional improvement.

5. (a) What is the distinction that is made between a natural system and a system developed by human beings?

(b) Give examples of each.

6. (a) Into what subdivisions can systems developed by human beings be placed?

(b) Give examples of each of these subdivisions of systems developed by human beings.

7. (a) Give the properties of systems.

(b) Explain each.

8. What quantifiable tools or techniques are available for use in a systems approach to school situations or problems?

9. (a) What is a model?

(b) What is the value of models in systems analysis?

10. (a) Give the components of a model that would symbolize decision making (in curriculum and instruction) in a school organization that is comprised of an elementary school, middle school, and secondary school.

(b) Explain the decision-making process that the model would symbolize.

Work Sheet 1B
Library Reference

Student's Name _____

Date _____

Directions:
1. Obtain a copy of the following book from the library:
    Immegart, Glenn L., and Pilecki, Francis J. *An Introduction to Systems for the Educational Administrator.* Reading: Addison-Wesley Publishing, 1973.
2. Read the section of the book that is entitled "The Essence of the Systems Movement," pp. 4–8.
3. Synthesize your learnings from this section of this book with your learnings from chapter 1 in your text.
4. Give written evidence of your synthesis in the space that is provided below.

Work Sheet 1C
Chart Study

Student's Name _____

Date _____

Directions:

1. Refer to:

    Immegart, Glenn L., and Pilecki, Francis J. *An Introduction to Systems for the Educational Administrator.* Reading: Addison-Wesley Publishing, 1973.

2. On page 12 in the above-mentioned book, the authors present a chart that depicts the systems movement in a chronological perspective. Reproduce the chart in the space that is provided below. Pages 8-13, in the book, explain the chart. Read these pages. Be prepared to explain the chart in class.

Work Sheet 1D
Reactions to a School Principal's Statements Regarding Open-System and Closed-System Strategies

Student's Name _____

Date _____

Directions:

1. Consider the following statements by a school principal:

   I view the open-system strategy and the closed-system strategy to represent theoretical extremes. They do not present a complete view of organization in the light of reality. I am not certain that school organizations can continue to regard outside forces as predictable. It appears, to me, that a focus on organizational coping with uncertainty would be a major advance.

2. Refer to:

   Thompson, James D. *Organizations in Action.* New York: McGraw-Hill, 1967, pp. 4-10.

3. In the space below, present your reactions to the school principal's statements that appear above.

Work Sheet 1E
Research Findings Regarding the Open-Closed Systems Dilemma

Student's Name _____

Date _____

Directions:
1. Consider the following observation:
    There is a search for a way out of the open-system versus closed-system dilemma. A stream of research that views organizations as problem-facing, problem-solving entities may provide leadership in such a search.
2. Refer to:
    a. Simon, Herbert A. *Administrative Behavior.* New York: Macmillan, 1957.
    b. March, J. G., and Simon, Herbert A. *Organizations.* New York: John Wiley and Sons, 1958.
    c. Cyert, R. M., and March, J. G. *A Behavioral Theory of the Firm.* Englewood Cliffs, N.J.: Prentice-Hall, 1963.
3. Evaluate the observation (above) in light of the research that is given in the above-listed three references. In the space provided below, discuss the implications (for curriculum and instructional improvement) of the research findings regarding the open-closed systems dilemma.

Work Sheet 1F
Independent Study

Student's Name _____

Date _____

Directions:
1. Note: The steps of the systems approach merit independent study for a complete understanding of the execution of each step.
2. Refer to:

   Lipham, James M., and Hoeh, James A. *The Principalship: Foundations and Functions.* New York: Harper and Row, 1974, pp. 34-45.
3. In the space that is provided below, succinctly report the process by which each step is executed. Be prepared to elaborate in class.

Work Sheet 1G
Illustration of the Systems Approach in Curriculum and Instructional Improvement

Student's Name _____

Date _____

Directions:
1. Study the following illustration of the systems approach in curriculum and instructional improvement.

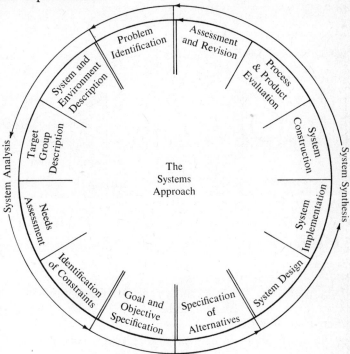

2. Refer to:
   Hayman, John L., Jr. "The Systems Approach and Education," *The Educational Forum* 38 (May 1974): 493-501. (The above illustration is taken from this reference.)
3. In the space below, explain the preceding illustration in terms of secondary school curriculum and instructional improvement.

Work Sheet 1H
Network of Decision Making

Student's Name _____
Date _____

Directions:
1. Study the following model. The model depicts the network of decisions that must be made in a program of curriculum and instructional improvement.

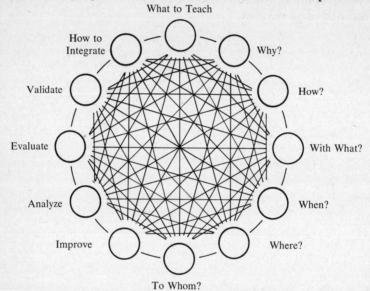

2. Refer to:
> Banathy, B. H. "Information Systems for Curriculum Planning," *Educational Technology* 10 (November 1970): 25-28. (The model above is taken from this reference.)

3. Discuss the model above in light of your learnings from the above-given reference. Record your discussion below.

Work Sheet 1I
Evaluation

Student's Name _____

Date _____

Directions:
1. Read the following statement:
    In curriculum and instructional improvement, "a multi-disciplinary approach" should be more productive than "a one-specialist approach."
2. Refer to:
    a. Feyereisen, Kathryn V.; Fiorino, A. John; and Nowak, Arlene T. *Supervision and Curriculum Renewal: A Systems Approach.* New York: Appleton-Century-Crofts, 1970, pp. 31–32.
    b. Taylor, W. Sidney. "Full Spectrum Management Improvement." In *The Management of Improvement,* edited by Robert N. Lehrer. New York: Reinhold Publishing, 1965, pp. 125–26.
3. Evaluate the above statement on the basis of your learnings in the above references. Do your learnings support (or not support) the above statement? Explain. Record your notations in the space below.

Work Sheet 1J
Model Construction

Student's Name _____

Date _____

Directions:
1. Visit a school where a systems analysis approach exists for curriculum and instructional improvement.
2. On this work sheet, construct a model that illustrates decision making for curriculum and instructional improvement in that school. Be prepared to discuss your model in class.

Work Sheet 1K
School Report

Student's Name _____

Date _____

Directions:
1. Visit a school that does not use a systems analysis approach to curriculum and instructional improvement.
2. (a) Describe the process of curriculum and instructional improvement in that school.
   (b) If possible, draw a diagram to illustrate the process.
3. Compare the process in the school that you have visited with the process that is symbolized in the pertinent model in chapter 1 in the text.

Work Sheet 1L
Extension of Learning

Student's Name _____

Date _____

Directions:
1. Choose one of the following readings (or one of the readings at the end of chapter 1) to extend the learnings that you have attained from the chapter.
2. Read critically.
3. Synthesize your learnings for class dialogue.
4. Space is provided at the end of this work sheet for notes that you may want to make.

Readings:
1. Banghart, F. W. *Educational Systems Analysis*. New York: Macmillan, 1969.
2. Corrigan, R. E., and Corrigan, B. O. *Systems Approach for Education*. Anaheim, Calif.: R. E. Corrigan, 1970.
3. Eastmond, J. N. *System Analysis for Educational Planning*. Salt Lake City: Utah State Board of Education, 1968.
4. Egbert, R. L., and Cogswell, J. F. *System Design for a Continuous Process School*, Part I. Santa Monica: System Development Corp., 1964.
5. Hills, R. J. *The Concept of System*. Eugene, Ore.: CASEA, 1967.
6. Kaufman, R. A. *Educational System Planning*. Englewood Cliffs, N.J.: Prentice-Hall, 1972.
7. Stufflebeam, Daniel I. et al. *Educational Evaluation and Decision Making*. Itasca, Ill.: F. E. Peacock Publishers, 1971.

PART II

CURRICULUM AS
A SYSTEM

2

Systems Approach to Curriculum and Instructional Improvement

The preceding chapter introduced the reader to basic systems theory—with a brief extension of the concepts into the area of curriculum and instruction. This particular chapter explicates the application of a systems approach to the curriculum and instructional improvement program.

Curriculum Defined

Educators define curriculum in a variety of ways. Some educators define it as a body of subjects or subject matters that are to be covered by the teachers and the students. This definition, which reflects a traditional concept of curriculum, was especially prevalent, and already long-standing, at the beginning of the twentieth century. Other educators define curriculum as all of the experiences that a learner has under the guidance of the school. The latter definition was introduced with great prominence in the late 1930s. Arthur Foshay maintains that this particular definition "stood unchallenged for a generation." [1] It is to be noted that the latter definition views curriculum as a *process,* but the former definition views curriculum as an *accumulated body of knowledge to be transmitted.*

In contrast to those educators who regard curriculum as accumulated knowledge or a process are those educators who consider curriculum to be an *instructional plan.* Illustrative is the definition of Hilda Taba that specifies that "a curriculum is a plan for learning." [2] George Beauchamp similarly defines curriculum as "a document designed to be used as a point of departure for instructional planning." [3] It is to be noted that the terms included in these aforementioned definitions (viz., plan for learning or document for instructional planning) may also be a lesson plan or a unit plan, but these two particular plans constitute instruments of a curriculum.[4] It is to be further noted that these definitions imply that the instructional processes by which such plans are implemented are outside the realm of curriculum.

In fact many educators maintain that instruction is separate from curriculum. W. James Popham and Eva I. Baker are among these educators. Their view is reflected in their definition of curriculum that follows. A further study of their definition shows that they take the concept of curriculum as a plan (forwarded by Taba and Beauchamp) and extend it. Popham and Baker regard curriculum to be "all planned learning outcomes for which the school is responsible [or] . . . the desired consequences of instruction." [5]

There are those educators who see curriculum as a production system. Those who speak in terms of activity or job analysis, behavioral objectives, and systems analysis are among those who should be included here. Job analysis and, more popularly, activity analysis are the advocations of Franklin Bobbitt and W. W. Charters, dating back to the start of the twentieth century.[6] According to Bobbitt, life consists of the performance of specific activities; if education is preparation for life, it must prepare for these specific activities; these activities can be taught; these activities should be considered the objectives of the curriculum.[7] Corresponding to this, Bobbitt regarded the curriculum to be the series of experiences that students should have in order to attain these objectives. Charters, on the other hand, viewed the curriculum as involving "the analysis of definite operations, to which the term job analysis is applied, as in the analysis of the operations involved in running a machine." [8]

According to Popham, curriculum revolves around "objectives [that] an educational system hopes its learners will achieve." [9] Popham sees curriculum as a production process that leads to a measurable product called terminal behavior.[10] According to him, curriculum revolves around ends, rather than means to ends. He separates curriculum from instruction. Like Popham, B. F. Skinner, as well as other behaviorists, views curriculum as a technological production process.[11] In addition, Skinner and these behaviorists see the student as a kind of mechanical learning unit in the production process.

With the introduction of accountability and performance contracting in the late 1960s and early 1970s, curriculum has been defined as a component of a production process called *educational engineering*.[12] The learner is treated as raw material (input), and the product (output). Effectiveness of teaching and learning is assessed by quantitative input-output measures.

Systems analysis is an outgrowth of technology. Systems analysis, when applied to education, identifies curriculum as a technological process that contains many subprocesses. In this perspective, curriculum is conceived as a transmitting system that is intended to convert raw material (students) into products. In this conception, curriculum is separated from instruction.

Curriculum as a System

In chapter 1, a system was defined as a unit characterized by defined boundaries and an array of interrelated parts purposed to achieve stated objectives. This particular chapter presents the definition of curriculum that the author has chosen, for use in this book, to be all of the learning experiences that are provided the learner under the guidance and the direction of the school through which it expects to achieve its objectives. The author views instruction as a means for implementing curriculum, but not necessarily extricably apart and separate. It is obvious that a similarity exists between the definition of system and the definition of curriculum. The learning experiences that are mentioned in the definition of curriculum are viewed as comparable to the interrelated parts of the system. The guidance and the direction that are provided by the school suggest the aspect of defined boundaries or organization in the system. Both definitions include mention of objectives. Similarity of definitions allows for the curriculum of the school to be conceptualized as a system.

A system implies organization and interaction between components, integration of all activities, mutual dependence between components, and achievement of purpose. These aspects are discussed below.

Purpose. The reason for the existence of a system is the achievement of its purpose. The components of a system are related and organized to attain the ends for which the system is established.

The components of a system for a curriculum and instructional improvement program consist of the plan for providing and implementing teaching-learning situations. With a systems approach, objectives are central in decision-making activities, and pursuant planning includes a consideration of all relevant factors to the steps that are taken in the achievement of the goals. The ends of this particular system consist of the general and specific objectives that have been formulated as the goals for the specific school population.

The components of the curriculum should relate to long-term or general goals and short-term or specific goals. For example, a currently advocated goal of curriculum planning is to develop educational programs that help learners to become self-learners. To reflect this goal, curriculum plans would need to include curriculum designs and learning activities that would extend over an entire period of schooling. Furthermore, evaluative means would need to assess growth as self-learners over an extended period of time as well as for short-term instructional activities.

Certain principles underlie the relation that should exist between goals and programs. First, there should be a continuous focus on goals if a relevant curriculum is to exist. Programs should be relevant to a rapidly changing society. The nature and the needs of learners change. Social conditions change. The needs and demands of communities change. Educational goals and curriculum objectives should change in correspondence to these sources. A second principle is that the curriculum should be based on dynamic and realistic goals and objectives. Finally, a curriculum should lack the rigidity of providing a sequence of learning activities for a class of students, but, rather, possess the flexibility of providing a set of suggested alternate programs and activities that may be chosen by individual students.

Organization and Interaction.   Organization is a necessary characteristic of a system. Organization in a system denotes "the arrangement of the components of the system into interdependent parts which function in a manner that allows the system to achieve its objectives." [13] The components or parts, considered as a whole, constitute the organization. The components, however, must interact because, if there is no interaction, there is no organization but simply a collection of components. When there is interaction between the components of a system, there is an exchange of information, i.e., communication or dialogue. The exchange of information results in organization. For example, a school consists of a number of professional personnel. If there were no communication or exchange of information among the various members of this professional staff, they would simply be a collection of individuals engaged in executing school duties. They would not, however, be an organized professional staff.

The loss of equilibrium in a system is described by the concept of entropy, a measure of the degree of organization of a system.[14] Feyereisen, Fiorino, and Nowak add clarity thus:

> Entropy can be conceptualized as a continuum. When a system is at the maximum-entropy end of the continuum, it is disorganized to the extent that it would have great difficulty producing a minimum output or achieving the objectives of the system. At the negentrophy, or zero entropy, end of the continuum, the system would be so well organized that it would have little difficulty producing a maximum output and achieving the objectives of the system.[15]

Energy must be applied to a system to order it. As the ratio of energy to entropy increases, order increases. As the ratio of entropy to energy increases, disorder increases.

Considering the entropy concept in light of school curriculums today, it is expected that the negentrcpy-entropy continuum is covered. It is expected, for example, that in any particular subject area there is interaction between the lessons and the programs for each year. It is further expected, however, that interaction between related subject areas is minimal. In illustration, interaction between mathematics and science is probably at a minimum. Extension of these examples to include all of the subject areas offered in any school would approach a state of maximum entropy, rather than negentropy. Realistically, a state of negentropy is an ideal, especially in systems that are living systems.

Integration.   Integration in a system denotes that the components of the system are unified; they constitute a whole. In curriculum, integration is promoted if a synthesis of learning occurs. Fragmentation of learning taught in isolation defeats integration. An interdisciplinary approach is one way by which integration should be accomplished. It is to be noted that the principle of integration, like all systems principles and concepts, should be extended to all dimensions and levels of

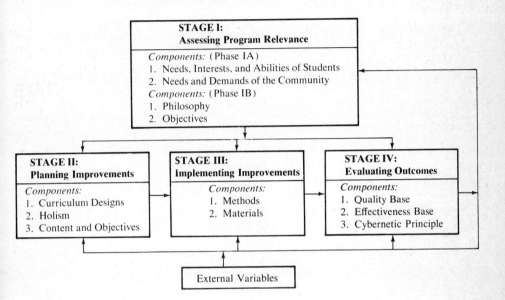

FIGURE 8. Model: System for Curriculum and Instructional Improvement

curriculum. This is to say that, not only is subject matter involved, but also curriculum design, methods, materials, and evaluation (i.e., components of a system for curriculum and instructional improvement, as symbolized in figures 7 and 8).

Dependence.   A mutual dependence exists between a system and the components and/or subsystems of that system. The processes that take place within each component and/or subsystem are dependent on the processes of each other component and/or subsystem. The attainment of the objectives of the system is dependent on the processes that occur in each other component and/or subsystem.

The preceding principle is illustrative in curriculum. The curriculum system consists of subsystems that can be classified as vertical or horizontal subsystems. In a traditional curriculum, the vertical subsystems would be referred to as grade levels, and the horizontal subsystems would be referred to, individually, as courses —e.g., mathematics, English, science, and so on.

Each subsystem is dependent on the other subsystems to accomplish its own objectives—and the objectives of the system. To illustrate, a student's success in creative writing is dependent upon his or her ability to compose with attention to unity, coherence, and emphasis. And his or her ability to compose with unity, coherence, and emphasis is dependent upon his or her knowledge of grammar, punctuation, and spelling. The system itself, for the accomplishment of its objectives, is dependent upon all of these abilities and those attained in the other subsystems of the system.

System for Curriculum and Instructional Improvement

Figure 8 presents a model symbolizing a system for a curriculum and instructional improvement program. The model elaborates on the input, process, and output stages of the system as illustrated in figures 4, 5, and 6. The model presented in figure 8 is the same as the model in figure 7 in chapter 1. The model is repeated here for easy reference by the reader. Subsequent chapters of this book add explanations of greater breadth and depth. Succinctly, explanations of the system symbolized in figures 7 and 8 are these:

1. Curriculum and instructional improvement is viewed in terms of a systems approach including four major stages. The first stage assesses program relevance, necessitating an examination of the curriculum and instructional program in light of the needs, interests, and abilities of the students; the needs and demands of the school community; the school philosophy and objectives; and some measure of current system performance. The second stage (planning program improvements) involves the choosing of program modifications or changes that will satisfy the particular needs. The third stage consists of an implementation of program improvements. The fourth and last stage is an evaluation of program outcomes. The system that is described is suitable for both a new school system and a school already in operation. Chapters 4 and 5 will explicate the first stage depicted above; chapter 6, the second stage; chapter 7, the third stage; and, chapter 8, the fourth.

2. Input into the system is derived from an exploration of the needs, interests, and abilities of the students; the needs and demands of the school community; and an objective measure of current system performance. The components of the process stage are these: (a) the formulation of the school philosophy and objectives; (b) the selection and organization of curriculum content; and (c) the selection of teaching methods and materials. The output stage consists of assessing, measuring, and evaluating the products of the system.

3. The model consists of "boxes" that represent variables, or forces. The variables are of two kinds—external and internal.[16] The external variables are depicted by the upper part of the top box and the very bottom box in the model. The lower part of the top box and the rest of the boxes represent internal variables. Variables within the system are considered to be internal; those outside the system, external. Internal variables have a functional relationship with each other and are controllable in the accomplishment of the objectives of the system. External variables, on the other hand, affect curriculum decision but are not controllable in the accomplishment of the objectives of the system. Examples of internal variables are materials, methods, curriculum content, and so forth. Examples of external variables include state curriculum regulations, accreditation requirements, teacher certification requirements, special interest groups, and changes in the economy. A further distinction is that an internal variable interacts with the rest of the internal variables of the system and must be organized and integrated with the rest of the internal variables. For example, such conditions exist between what is offered (scope) and the order in which the offerings are placed (sequence). An external variable could be adopted as part of the system, or used as a guide in making a curriculum decision. For

example, the teaching-learning materials of some special interest group could be adopted for use in a particular curriculum and instructional program, or used as an illustration for other materials that might be produced.

4. In the model, it will be noticed that the internal variables—philosophy and objectives—are placed above the other internal variables. It will also be noticed that two external variables (needs, interests, and abilities of students, and needs and demands of the community) are placed above the philosophy and objectives. Position indicates relationship among variables in a system. Variables placed above others are regarded to be determining variables. Consequently, it is to be noted that the needs, interests, and abilities of students, and the needs and demands of the community, determine philosophy and objectives. It is to be noted further that the philosophy and objectives determine the other internal variables (curriculum design, methods, materials, and evaluation). These internal variables (also referred to as internal influencing variables) are affected by each other and by the external influencing variables. These external influencing variables are depicted by the very bottom box in the schema. (Earlier in this discussion, they were explained as representing state curriculum regulations, accreditation requirements, teacher certification requirements, special interest groups, changes in the economy, and so on.) These external influencing variables, plus the internal influencing variables, affect the philosophy and objectives.

5. The philosophy and objectives are the factors that determine content selection. Only that content that contributes directly to the achievement of one or more objective can justifiably be included in a curriculum. Content so selected is subsequently validated by being checked against the external influencing variables. The advocations of professional associations, subject-matter specialists, philosophers of education, state departments of education, accrediting associations, and other educators are but a few of the variables that may influence the selection of content. If some content really seems to be desirable and needed, but does not directly contribute to some stated objective, it might be prudent to consider the objectives for revision or extension to cover the desired content. It can be concluded that the use of systems analysis makes content selection relatively easy. Content is intended to mean anything that can be learned, e.g., facts, concepts, generalizations, values, skills, and competencies.

6. The curriculum design is the pattern for the learning opportunities that will be provided. It anticipates the range of learning opportunities that will be available, and bespeaks how the curriculum content will be organized. The design may be the subject discipline pattern, the traditional subject pattern, the correlated curriculum pattern, the broad fields pattern, the core curriculum pattern, or the experience curriculum pattern. Design concepts are not referred to by the same name by all educators. It is important to know the concepts and be able to recognize them by any name. The philosophy and objectives should determine the curriculum design. If, for example, an objective of the system is application, analysis, or synthesis of knowledge, the curriculum design or pattern should promote application, analysis, or synthesis.

7. Methods and materials provide for implementation of curriculum design or

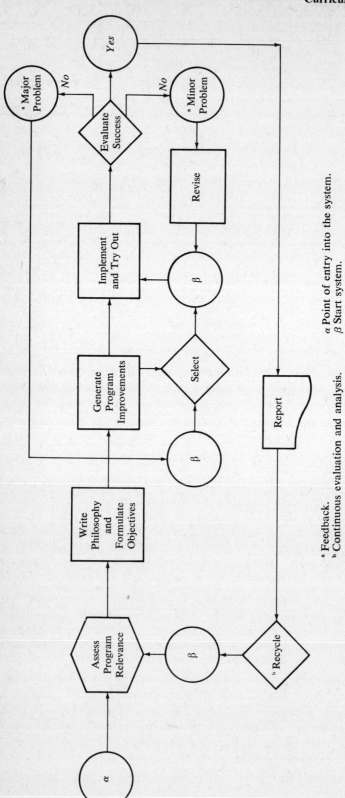

FIGURE 9. Model: Process for Modifying the Designed Curriculum and In-structional System Based on Deficiencies in Meeting the Objectives as Determined through Evaluation

ᵃ Point of entry into the system.
β Start system.

ᵃ Feedback.
ᵇ Continuous evaluation and analysis.

SOURCE: Adapted from James R. Marks, Emery Stoops, and Joyce King-Stoops. *Handbook of Educational Supervision* (Boston: Allyn and Bacon, 1971), p. 487. Reprinted by permission.

program improvements. Methods are long-range procedures. Examples are as follows: recitation method, lecture method, socialized recitation method, and case method. Some educators distinguish methods from techniques and strategies. Techniques may be defined as short-range procedures. Examples are these: going on a field trip, writing on the blackboard, asking questions, or taking a test. Strategies may be defined as specialized means for teaching a particular thing, e.g., strategies for teaching the making of maps, or the conducting of a particular experiment in the science laboratory. Though disagreement exists as to definitions of methods, techniques, and strategies, and examples thereof, the importance is to know the possibilities that exist for implementation of curriculum designs or program improvements, so that stated objectives can be achieved. The objectives constitute the determining variable. Learning experiences are intended to achieve objectives.

8. Feedback and evaluation constitute a major contribution of the systems model for curriculum and instructional improvement, and they constitute the major basis for continuing curriculum and instructional improvement. Feedback from each step in the system, and from learners in each instructional situation, is inherent in the system. Evaluation is in terms of the goals or objectives. Evaluation is both formative and summative.[17] Formative evaluative procedures are the feedback arrangements that make it possible for implementers of the curriculum to make adjustments and improvements throughout the implementing process. The summative evaluation comes at the end and deals with the total curriculum design. This particular evaluation constitutes feedback for the curriculum planners for their use in deciding whether to modify, negate, or repeat the curriculum design that has been implemented and evaluated. The final step in a systems analysis approach to curriculum and instructional improvement involves the process of modifying the designed curriculum and instructional system based on deficiencies in meeting the objectives as determined through evaluation. Figure 9 presents a model that represents a process for modifying the designed curriculum and instructional system based on deficiencies in meeting the objectives as determined through evaluation.

Summary

Educators define curriculum in a variety of ways. Some educators define curriculum as a body of subjects or subject matters that is to be covered by the teachers and the students. Some educators view curriculum as all of the experiences that a learner has under the guidance of the school. Some educators regard curriculum to be an instructional plan. Other educators see curriculum as a production system, a production process or technological process, or a component of a production process called educational engineering. Systems analysis, when applied to education, identifies curriculum as a technological component that contains many subcomponents. In some definitions, curriculum is separated from instruction; in others, it is not.

In chapter 1, a system was defined as a unit characterized by defined boundaries and an array of interrelated parts, purposed to achieve stated objectives. This particular chapter presents the author's definition of curriculum to be all of the learning experiences that are provided the learner under the guidance and the direction of the school through which it expects to achieve its objectives. It is obvious that similarity exists between the definition of system and the definition of curriculum. Similarity of definitions allows for the curriculum of the school to be conceptualized as a system. This author views instruction as a means for implementing curriculum, but not necessarily extricably apart and separate.

Certain aspects implicit in the concept of a system apply to the school curriculum conceptualized as a system. Specifically:

1. The reason for the existence of a system is the achievement of its purpose. The components of a system are related and organized to attain the ends for which the system is established. The components of a system for a curriculum and instructional improvement program consist of the plan for providing and implementing teaching-learning situations. With a systems approach, objectives are central in decision-making activities, and pursuant planning includes a consideration of all relevant factors to the steps that are taken in the achievement of the goals.

2. Organization is a necessary characteristic of a system. The components or parts of a system, considered as a whole, constitute the organization. The components, however, must interact because if there is no interaction, there is no organization but simply a collection of components. The loss of equilibrium in a system is described by the concept of entropy, a measure of the degree of organization of a system. A system that is in a state of maximum entropy is disorganized to the extent that it has great difficulty producing a minimum output or achieving the objectives of the system. On the other hand, if a system is in a state of negentropy, or zero entropy, it is so well organized that it has little difficulty producing a maximum output and achieving the objectives of the system. Considering the entropy concept as a negentropy-entropy continuum, and considering the entropy concept in light of school curriculums today, it is expected that any school approaches a state of entropy, rather than negentropy.

3. Integration in a system denotes that the components of the system are unified; they constitute a whole. In curriculum, integration is promoted if a synthesis of learning occurs.

4. A mutual dependence exists between a system and the components and/or subsystems of that system. The chapter illustrates this principle in regard to curriculum.

This chapter presents and discusses a model that the author has designed for symbolizing a system for a curriculum and instructional improvement program. The final step in a systems analysis approach to curriculum and instructional improvement involves the process of modifying the designed curriculum and instructional system based on deficiencies in meeting the objectives as determined through evaluation. The chapter closes with a model of a process for modifying the designed curriculum and instructional system based on deficiencies in meeting the objectives as determined through evaluation. Chapter 3 presents and discusses the roles and responsibilities of the various persons who are essential in a system for curriculum and instructional improvement.

NOTES

1. Arthur W. Foshay, "Curriculum," in *Encyclopedia of Educational Research,* ed. Robert L. Ebel (New York: Macmillan, 1969), p. 275; cited in Daniel Tanner and Laurel N. Tanner, *Curriculum Development: Theory into Practice* (New York: Macmillan, 1975), p. 17.

2. Hilda Taba, *Curriculum Development: Theory and Practice* (New York: Harcourt Brace Jovanovich, 1962), p. 11. Reprinted by permission.

3. George A. Beauchamp, "Basic Components of a Curriculum Theory," *Curriculum Theory Network* (Fall 1972): 19; cited in Tanner and Tanner, *Curriculum Development,* p. 25. Reprinted by permission.

4. Tanner and Tanner, *Curriculum Development,* p. 25.

5. W. James Popham and Eva I. Baker, *Systematic Instruction* (Englewood Cliffs, N.J.: Prentice-Hall, 1970), p. 48. Reprinted by permission.

6. Franklin Bobbitt, *The Curriculum* (Boston: Houghton Mifflin, 1918), p. 42. W. W. Charters, "Activity Analysis and Curriculum Construction," *Journal of Educational Research* 5 (May 1922): 359; cited in Tanner and Tanner, *Curriculum Development,* p. 27. Reprinted by permission.

7. Ibid., p. 42.

8. Charters, "Activity Analysis," p. 359.

9. W. James Popham et al., *Instructional Objectives* (Chicago: Rand McNally, 1969), p. 34. Copyright 1969, American Educational Research Association, Washington, D.C.

10. Ibid., p. 41.

11. B. F. Skinner, *The Technology of Teaching* (New York: Appleton-Century-Crofts, 1968), pp. 256–58.

12. Leon M. Lessinger, "Accountability for Results," in *Accountability in Education,* eds. Leon M. Lessinger and Ralph W. Tyler (Worthington, Ohio: Charles A. Jones, 1971), p. 10.

13. K. V. Feyereisen, A. J. Fiorino, and A. T. Nowak, *Supervision and Curriculum Renewal: A Systems Approach* (New York: Appleton-Century-Crofts, 1970), p. 43. Reprinted by permission.

14. Ibid., p. 43.

15. Ibid.

16. Ibid., p. 137.

17. J. Galen Saylor and William M. Alexander, *Planning Curriculum for Schools* (New York: Holt, Rinehart and Winston, 1974), p. 41. Reprinted by permission.

Related Readings

Bobbitt, Franklin. *The Curriculum.* Boston: Houghton Mifflin, 1918.

Churchman, C. West. "On the Design of Educational Systems." *Audiovisual Instruction* 10 (May 1965): 361–65.

Doll, Ronald C. *Curriculum Improvement: Decision Making and Process.* Boston: Allyn and Bacon, 1974.

Feyereisen, K. V.; Fiorino, A. J.; and Nowak, A. T. *Supervision and Curriculum Renewal: A Systems Approach.* New York: Appleton-Century-Crofts, 1970.

Foshay, Arthur W. "Curriculum." In *Encyclopedia of Educational Research,* edited by Robert L. Ebel. New York: Macmillan, 1969.

Inlow, Gail M. *The Emergent in Curriculum.* New York: John Wiley and Sons, 1973.

Lessinger, Leon M. "Accountability for Results." In *Accountability in Education,* edited by Leon M. Lessinger and Ralph W. Tyler. Worthington, Ohio: Charles A. Jones, 1971.

Popham, W. James, and Baker, Eva I. *Systematic Instruction.* Englewood Cliffs, N.J.: Prentice-Hall, 1970.

Popham, W. James et al. *Instructional Objectives.* Chicago: Rand McNally, 1969.

Saylor, J. Galen, and Alexander, William M. *Planning Curriculum for Schools.* New York: Holt, Rinehart and Winston, 1974.

Skinner, B. F. *The Technology of Teaching.* New York: Appleton-Century-Crofts, 1968.

Taba, Hilda. *Curriculum Development: Theory and Practice.* New York: Harcourt Brace Jovanovich, 1962.

Tanner, Daniel, and Tanner, Laurel N. *Curriculum Development: Theory into Practice.* New York: Macmillan, 1975.

Tyler, Ralph W. *Basic Principles of Curriculum and Instruction.* Chicago: University of Chicago Press, 1971.

Wooton, L. M. "Systems Approach to Education as Viewed from the Classroom." *Education* 95 (February 1971): 215–19.

Work Sheet 2A
Questions for Class Dialogue

Student's Name _____

Date _____

Directions: Study chapter 2 with the following questions in mind. Prepare responses for each question, so that you can intelligently participate in class dialogue. Space is provided with each question, so that you can record any notes that will aid you in the dialogue.

1. (a) Discuss the variety of definitions that are given to curriculum.

   (b) Give the definition of curriculum that is given by the author for use in this book.

2. Why can the curriculum of the school be conceptualized as a system? Be complete in your answer incorporating the following: purpose, organization and interaction, integration, and dependence.

3. Curriculum and instructional improvement, viewed in terms of a systems approach, includes four major stages. Explain each stage.

4. (a) Discuss the derivation of input into a system for curriculum and instructional improvement.

(b) What are the components of the process (thruput) stage?

(c) Of what does the output stage consist?

5. Distinguish between external variables and internal variables.

6. (a) What are the factors that determine content selection?

(b) What content can justifiably be included in a curriculum?

7. (a) What is meant by curriculum design?

(b) What are the determinants of curriculum design?

8. What is the relationship of methods and materials to implementation of curriculum design or program improvements?

9. (a) Discuss the role of feedback and evaluation in a system for curriculum and instructional improvement.

(b) Distinguish between formative evaluation and summative evaluation.

10. Give the components of a model that would symbolize a process for modifying the designed curriculum and instructional system based on deficiencies in meeting the objectives as determined through evaluation.

Work Sheet 2B
Discussion of Input and Output Model

Student's Name _____

Date _____

Directions:

1. Examine the matrix below, which illustrates only a few of the inputs and outputs of a typical school district.

Partial Input/Output Model of a School System

Output → Input ↓	R & D	Communi-cations	Skills & Knowledge	Attitudinal Changes
Curriculum				
Instruction				
Personnel				

2. Refer to:

> Wooton, L. M. "Systems Approach to Education as Viewed from the Classroom." *Education* 95 (February 1971): 215–19. (The above matrix is taken from this reference.)

3. In the space below, discuss the theory that lies behind this model. In your discussion, give specific examples of inputs and outputs in both curriculum and instruction.

Work Sheet 2C
Examination of a Curriculum Management Model

Student's Name _____

Date _____

Directions:

1. Examine the following model, which provides an identification of, and illustrates the relationships among, the components of a curriculum management system.

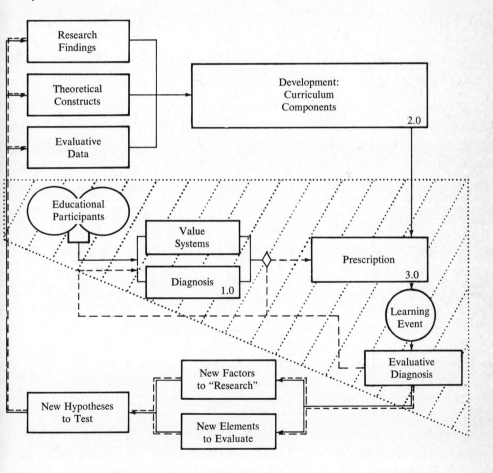

2. Refer to:
    a. Prentice, Marjorie. "Management: Curse, Cure-All, or Workable Concept?" *Educational Leadership* 30 (January 1973): 310–12. (The above model is taken from this reference.)
    b. Chapter 2 in the text.
3. For class dialogue be prepared to identify the components of the system that is illustrated, and to explain the relationships of the components. Use the space below for any notes you would like to make to guide you in class dialogue.

Work Sheet 2D
Comparison of Two Models for Curriculum and Instructional Improvement

Student's Name _____

Date _____

Directions:
1. Examine the following model, which illustrates one possible breakout of the curriculum component development process (identified by 2.0 in the model of the preceding work sheet).

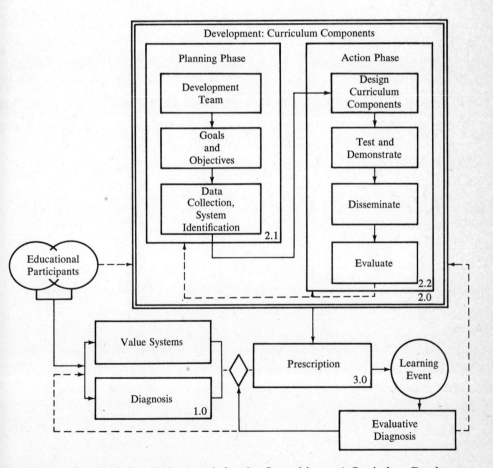

2. Refer to:
   a. Prentice, Marjorie. "Management: Curse, Cure-All, or Workable Concept?" *Educational Leadership* 30 (January 1973): 310–12. (The above model is taken from this reference.)
   b. Chapter 2 in your text.
3. For class dialogue, be prepared to:
   a. Explain the system that is symbolized in the model above.
   b. Compare the system that is symbolized in the model above with the system that is symbolized in figure 8 in chapter 2 in the text.
   Use the space below to record notes that will aid you in class dialogue.

Work Sheet 2E
Theories of Curriculum and Instructional Improvement

Student's Name _____

Date _____

Directions:

1. Consider the following statements:

> One philosophy insists that the thinker begin with the simple parts, understand them thoroughly, perfect them if he can, and then begin building the parts together into an edifice that eventually becomes the entire structure. The opposite philosophy holds that we must begin with a concept of the whole; otherwise we shall never know how to identify the parts, much less how to improve them.

2. Refer to:

   Churchman, C. West. "On the Design of Educational Systems." *Audiovisual Instruction* 10 (May 1965): 361–65. (The above statements are taken from this reference.)

3. These two philosophies may be said to have representatives in the theories of curriculum and instructional improvement. Explain. Record your explanation below.

Work Sheet 2F
Responses to Stress

Student's Name _____

Date _____

Directions:

1. Study the model below. The model represents one way that living or open systems respond to stress.

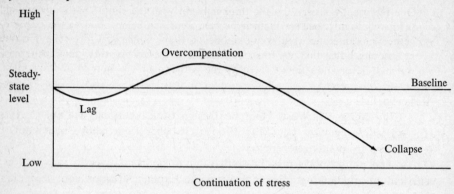

2. Refer to:

    Immegart, Glenn L., and Pilecki, Francis J. *An Introduction to Systems for the Educational Administrator.* Reading, Mass.: Addison-Wesley, 1973, pp. 70–72.

3. Define stress. Explain the response to stress that is illustrated above. In what other ways may living or open systems respond to stress? Make applications to a system for curriculum and instructional improvement. Use the space below to note your explanations.

Work Sheet 2G
Identification and Evaluation of Limitations of Systems Analysis

Student's Name _____

Date _____

Directions:

1. Note that Harry J. Hartley, in an issue of *Phi Delta Kappan,* has drawn some limitations of systems analysis.
2. Refer to:

   Hartley, Harry J. "Limitations of Systems Analysis." *Education Digest* 50 (October 1969): 28–31.
3. List the limitations that Hartley gives in the above-mentioned article. Which limitations seem to be significant in a systems approach to curriculum and instructional improvement? Explain. Record your responses in the space that is provided below.

Work Sheet 2H
Derivation of Curriculum Definitions from Teachers

Student's Name _____

Date _____

Directions:
1. Ask 3 middle school teachers for their respective definitions of curriculum.
2. What are the similarities in the definitions? Differences?
3. Repeat the exercise with 3 junior high school teachers and, subsequently, with 3 senior high school teachers.
4. Compare definitions derived from the 3 groups for similarities and differences among the groups.
5. What definition have you derived most frequently?
6. Record all of your answers in the space that is provided below.

Work Sheet 2I
Derivation of Curriculum Definitions from Administrators

Student's Name _____

Date _____

Directions:

1. Derive the definition of curriculum from an administrator in a school where there is a systems approach to curriculum and instructional improvement.
2. Derive the definition of curriculum from an administrator in a school where there is *no* systems approach to curriculum and instructional improvement.
3. Are there differences in the definitions? How can you explain possible reasons for the differences?
4. Record your responses in the space below.

Work Sheet 2J
Views Regarding the Nature of Curriculum

Student's Name _____

Date _____

Directions:

1. Note that the last 3 books in the following list are relatively recent writings in the field of curriculum, and that the first 3 books are much earlier writings.
   a. Bobbitt, Franklin. *The Curriculum.* Boston: Houghton Mifflin, 1918.
   b. Caswell, Hollis L., and Campbell, Doak S. *Curriculum Development.* New York: American Book, 1935.
   c. Dewey, John. *The Child and the Curriculum.* Chicago: University of Chicago Press, 1902.
   d. Doll, Ronald C. *Curriculum Improvement: Decision Making and Process.* Boston: Allyn and Bacon, 1974.
   e. Inlow, Gail M. *The Emergent in Curriculum.* New York: John Wiley and Sons, 1973.
   f. Saylor, J. Galen, and Alexander, William M. *Planning Curriculum for Schools.* New York: Holt, Rinehart and Winston, 1974.

2. In each book, read the author's views of the nature of curriculum. Are there differences between the earlier views and the more recent views? If so, what are they? Record your responses in the space that is provided below.

Work Sheet 2K
Challenging Messages

Student's Name _____
Date _____

Directions:
1. Over the years, certain writers have presented challenging messages to the schools and their curriculums. The following are numbered among such writings.
    a. Bestor, Arthur. *The Restoration of Learning.* New York: Alfred A. Knopf, 1956.
    b. Hutchins, Robert M. *The Higher Learning in America.* New Haven: Yale University Press, 1936.
    c. Neill, A. S. *Summerhill.* New York: Hart Publishing, 1960.
    d. Rickover, Hyman G. *Education and Freedom.* New York: E. P. Dutton, 1959.
    e. Silberman, Charles E. *Crisis in the Classroom.* New York: Random House, 1970.
2. Select one of the above-listed books and react to the author's challenging remarks. Record your reactions below. If you wish to select some book that is not listed above, ask the professor for permission.

Work Sheet 2L
Extension of Learning

Student's Name _____

Date _____

Directions:
1. Choose one of the following readings, or one of the readings at the end of chapter 2, to extend the learnings that you have attained from the chapter.
2. Read critically.
3. Synthesize your learnings for class dialogue.
4. Space is provided at the end of this work sheet for notes that you may want to make.

Readings:
1. Briggs, Leslie. *Handbook of Procedures for the Design of Instruction.* Pittsburgh: American Institute for Research, 1970.
2. Frymier, Jack. *A School for Tomorrow.* Berkeley: McCutchan Publishing, 1973.
3. Goodlad, John I. *School Curriculum Reform in the United States.* New York: The Fund for the Advancement of Education, 1964.

3

Roles in a Curriculum
and Instructional
Improvement Program

Chapter 1 introduced the reader to basic systems theory—with a brief extension of the concepts into the area of curriculum and instruction. The preceding chapter explicated the application of a systems approach to the curriculum and instructional improvement program. This particular chapter explains the roles and the responsibilities of all who should participate in the improvement program. In keeping with the purpose of this book, as specified in the preface, emphasis is given to curriculum and instructional improvement in the senior high school, junior high school, and middle school, rather than the elementary school and pre-elementary school.

Levels

Efforts at curriculum and instructional improvement occur at a variety of levels—national, interstate, state, and local.

National and Interstate. National and interstate efforts have been varied and extensive. Projects funded by the national government and various national organizations have produced, and are still producing, a variety of curriculum and instructional materials that can be, and are, adapted for local school use. Some of these materials are not adapted, but are adopted for use without any change.

State. At the state level, the most common influence is for the state department of education to stipulate the courses or subjects that must be offered, those that may be offered, and those that are required for graduation—with specifications of units of credit in each instance. Efforts in curriculum and instructional improvement vary among states. Some states still have control over the textbooks that are used. State accreditation standards give regulations regarding a school's academic program, cocurricular program, library, and so forth. And, in some states, effort for curriculum and instructional improvement is exerted through state examinations and state investigations, inspections, and required reports.

Local.   The local level can be specified as a particular school district, a particular school, a group of teachers, or an individual teacher. A school district may engage in such curriculum and instructional activities as planning the program of studies of the school; in a traditional setting, determining the courses that will be taught at the various levels; recommending time allocations for the courses that will be taught; specifying graduation credit; conducting experimental programs with means for their evaluation; providing special programs for certain groups of students; and selecting and providing teaching materials, be they hardware or software. Any of these listed activities may also be the preoccupations of an individual school. An individual school will also engage in such curriculum and instructional activities as identifying and resolving the use of community resources in the school curriculum; endorsing a cocurricular program that is based on constant evaluation as to its suitability to student interests, needs, and abilities; and organizing and scheduling courses and instructional activities.

In an individual school, the plans for the aforementioned activities may be the responsibility of a group of teachers. Teachers working as groups may produce or agree to the contents and emphasis of teaching-learning units, resource units, courses of study, learning activity packages (LAPs), and so forth, and the teaching methods to be incorporated. In so doing, they come to agreement not only in regard to content and learning activities, but also in regard to objectives and procedures for evaluating the attainment of the objectives.

In some instances, the individual teacher may very well be given the opportunity to formulate the plans that are discussed above. Nevertheless, it is the individual teacher who reduces the above-given plans to periodic and daily plans in the subject area(s) that he or she teaches to groups of students and the individual student.

Cooperative Action

If a curriculum and instructional improvement program is to be effective, it must be characterized by cooperative action. This is true at all operational levels—national, interstate, state, and local. Whatever the level, the common purpose of all who are involved in curriculum and instructional improvement is the provision of optimal and suitable learning opportunities for the students that are involved. The education of the students is the single most important consideration. Local curriculum and instructional improvement is especially close, important, and relevant to the actual teaching-learning situation. For this reason, this chapter deals primarily with roles and responsibilities at the local level, i.e., school district, school, teacher groups, and individual teacher.

Model for Cooperative Action

Currently, various groups are making demands for input into educational decision making. There is no reason why motivation for involvement cannot be channeled into constructive roles for improving curriculum and instruction with shared control and responsibility.

Figure 10 presents a model of a system that is self-regulating and adaptive. It is to be noted that the concept depicted in figure 10 is extended in figure 5 to incorporate coordinators of the elementary school, middle school, and secondary school, respectively. In addition, the concept depicted in figure 10 is extended in figure 6 to incorporate coordinators of the elementary school, junior high school, and senior high school, respectively. A self-regulating and adaptive system has "the capacity to adjust and adapt to compensate for internal stresses and tensions, and maintain its equilibrium within a tolerable range through systematic responses, despite internal and external influences toward equilibrium change." [1] In a school, there is little or no control over input. School attendance is required by law. Courses and staffing are regulated by state departments of education. Reactions are made by parents and various pressure groups. The represented system is designed so that it will act upon these inputs through a series of sequential processes to achieve the desired output.

Except in small school systems, there are often at least three levels of management in a system for curriculum and instructional improvement. At the top level is the curriculum administrator who might be an assistant superintendent. At the middle level are the curriculum coordinators of the subsystems—e.g., middle

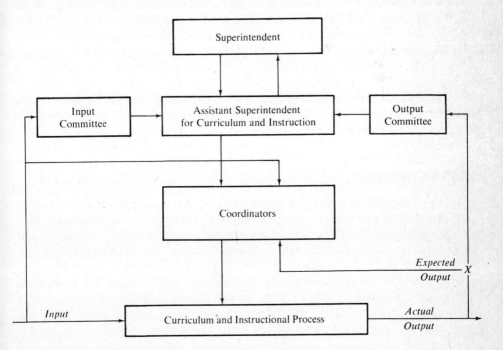

FIGURE 10. Basic System for Centralized Decision Making in Curriculum and Instruction

school, junior high school, and senior high school. Last, there is the principal, who is the manager of a particular school building.

It is to be remembered that, though the organizational formation of figure 10 shows that everyone is responsible to someone, in a systems approach no one in the school system is autonomous. In a systems approach, the school system consists of many components that are mutually dependent and mutually responsible. The following paragraphs explain the process that is symbolized in figure 10.

Input Committee

The role of the input committee (or person) is that of gathering, analyzing, and organizing the information about the environment that is needed by the system for curriculum and instructional improvement. The input committee endeavors to identify any changes in the environment that might influence the equilibrium of the system. Specifically, this committee is especially interested in identifying any changes in the nature of the student clientele and changes in social, political, economic, psychological, technological, or ideological conditions of the environment. The input committee gathers, for example, information to answer such a question as: Are the needs, interests, and abilities of students who are entering the system changing? The following are examples of output by the input committee: projections of increase or decrease in student population, projections of proportions of ethnic groups in the student population, and projections of course demands.

This component of the system may easily be composed of a divergent group of participants—e.g., administrators, teachers, and other members of the professional staff. Parents, other community members, and (at the secondary school level) also students can justifiably serve as a part of the group because these persons would likely supply an indispensable source of information for this component of the system.

In a large school district, the function of gathering the needed information could be performed by one unit; and the function of organizing and analyzing the information, by a separate unit.

Output Committee

The role of the output committee (or person) is that of comparing actual output with expected output and reporting variances to the appropriate person(s)—i.e., the assistant superintendent for curriculum and instruction (in the centralized approach), or the curriculum and instruction council (in the decentralized approach). The output committee monitors the internal state of the system and its output, and in so doing, provides the assistant superintendent, or the curriculum and instruction council, with a picture of the internal function of the system in terms of the condition of the subsystems, the resources that are available within the system, and the comparison between actual and expected outputs or outcomes. The output committee may consist of professional staff and include parents and community members.

Role Variations

The roles of key persons in a school system that follows a centralized approach to curriculum and instructional improvement differ from those of key persons in a school system that follows a decentralized approach. In the immediately following paragraphs, explanation is given of the roles of key persons in a school system that follows a centralized approach. Subsequent paragraphs present an explanation of key persons in a decentralized approach.

Assistant Superintendent for Curriculum and Instruction

The output of both the input and output committees becomes the input of decision for the assistant superintendent for curriculum and instruction (or some other person filling this role), and is used to produce a decision, policy, or instruction that is sent in the form of an order or directive to any one (or all) of the curriculum coordinators. The output, or feedback, of the input and output committees consists, in part, of reports. In part, the feedback of the output committee reports the variance, if any, between actual output and expected output. When there is a variance, the assistant superintendent for curriculum and instruction (or some other person filling this role) must decide whether an existing policy or procedure can be used to eliminate the variance, or whether a new policy or procedure or a revision in policy or procedure is needed to produce the expected output.

The assistant superintendent for curriculum and instruction is responsible for the management of the curriculum and instructional system. He or she can authorize solutions to problems in the curriculum and instructional system, except those that are within the jurisdiction of the superintendent of schools or the school board. The role of the assistant superintendent for curriculum and instruction is to integrate and coordinate the efforts of the curriculum coordinators in the system.

A building principal would be responsible to the assistant superintendent for curriculum and instruction for matters that are related to curriculum and instruction. For all other administrative matters, however, the principal would be responsible to the superintendent of schools.

Curriculum Coordinator

The role of the curriculum coordinator (sometimes called curriculum director) is implementing the rules or instructions of the assistant superintendent for curriculum and instruction. A change in process is basically attributed to the teacher, for it is the teacher who is an integral part of the teaching-learning experience. The teacher is the final decision maker concerning the actual experiences to be provided his or her students; and it is the teacher who decides how each learning experience is presented, guided, and evaluated for the particular students that are involved.

Sometimes a retraining or educating of staff is needed if a change in process is to be effected. In any event, the coordinator keeps the output committee informed of the changes that are implemented in the process.

The role of the coordinator in a subsystem is comparable to the role of the assistant superintendent for curriculum and instruction in the curriculum and instructional system. Curriculum coordinators are responsible for the integration and coordination of the programs in their own subject areas (e.g., mathematics, English) or level (e.g., middle school, junior high school, senior high school). The role of the curriculum coordinator is that of manager of an implementation subsystem of the curriculum and instruction system. The number of curriculum coordinators employed in a particular school system depends on several factors, among which are (1) number of curriculum and instructional problems and (2) size of budget.

Superintendent of Schools

The superintendent of schools (or supervising principal) manages the decision-making process for the total school system. He or she is concerned with broad policies and long-range planning, rather than everyday problems of the school system. The superintendent of schools is responsible for integrating and coordinating the efforts of the various subsystems, such as students and personnel, finance, buildings and grounds, and curriculum and instruction. Each subsystem is, in turn, integrated and coordinated by another administrator. The superintendent of schools is usually too busy to operate, integrate, and coordinate the curriculum and instructional system and, therefore, often delegates these duties to someone who may be titled the assistant superintendent for curriculum and instruction.

In a school system, the superintendent of schools and the staff constitute the problem-solving or decision-making component of the system. The superintendent has the responsibility for assessing the needs of the community and for analyzing its expectations in order to make recommendations to the school board.[2] Subsequently, the school board studies the recommendations. If the board accepts the recommendations, it subsequently develops appropriate policies for the district. It is the responsibility of the superintendent to see that the policies are carried out. The literature that deals with the roles of administrators in curriculum and instruction is, in part, confusing. To this author, it is conceivable that the superintendent can delegate the duties of curriculum and instructional improvement to an assistant administrator—such as the assistant superintendent for curriculum and instruction—but the superintendent retains the responsibility for a quality program.

Principal

The role of the principal has traditionally been that of head or leader of a particular school building. In the system structure that is presented in this section, the role of the principal is that of decision maker in administrative matters, and decision implementer in curriculum and instructional matters. In the centralized systems approach to curriculum and instructional improvement, the principal is expected to be a participant in identifying dysfunctions or problems in the system that should be referred to the pertinent component for solution. He or she is not expected to be the one who actively participates in the improvement of instruction.

Some may object to the principal's being cast in this role. The literature dealing with the role of the principal is confusing. This author conceives the following role as an alternate—if not preferred—role for the principal. It would retain the principal as the instructional leader of the educational program in a school building. The role would place the principal responsible to the assistant superintendent for curriculum and instruction in curriculum and instructional matters. Furthermore, the role would retain the principal as responsible for a quality program in the building. Though the principal could delegate the duties for curriculum and instructional improvement, e.g., to a curriculum coordinator, the principal would retain the responsibility for a quality program.

Teachers

Teacher as Specialist. The role of the teacher is that of specialist in the teaching-learning process. The teacher is freed from producing instructional materials and instructional packages to being the chief decision maker in the adaptation of these materials and packages for use by his or her students. The teacher is further freed for studying the needs, interests, and abilities of the students, and arranging and evaluating learning experiences in light of these needs, interests, and abilities.

The teacher is in a position to observe dysfunctions in the implementation components and to raise questions regarding the curriculum. The teacher calls attention to observations and questions in the form of feedback to systems control (i.e., the curriculum and instruction council—to be discussed later in this chapter —or the assistant superintendent for curriculum and instruction) for correction. Teachers are represented on the curriculum and instruction council. Furthermore, teachers make proposals for the improvement of existent materials and packages and the production of new materials and programs.

Teacher as Manager. The systems approach makes a wide variety of resources and materials available to both the teacher and the students in a carefully planned, sequential process. The teacher manages the flow of programs, materials, and resources to and from students as their needs, interests, and abilities require.

Teachers often view the process "as a manipulative approach that locks them irrevocably into a fixed program, with little chance to exert a creative influence over it."[3] The teacher's role as curriculum designer is greatly reduced in curriculum programs where textbooks, materials, student assignments, and tests come ready packaged for student use. In such cases, the teacher is a "manager" with few decisions to make.

It is suggested that the problem may not be so much with the systems approach itself as with the scale of the operation.[4] In most instances, the systems approach includes an entire school district with all its schools, different content areas, and entire faculty. As a macro system, it fails to take into account the individual teacher in a particular school or class. A micro or subsystem is needed that would be compatible with the larger system, but would be designed for an individual school or classroom and would allow the teacher to exert influence over the instructional program.

It is the teacher who ultimately designs or develops the curriculum in the day-to-day interaction with students. It follows that the teacher should be allowed to select, adapt, or modify goals; choose pertinent content; and design the evaluative measures that will be used.

Experience with programs suggests that teachers do have the talent to design exciting programs that meet the needs, interests, and abilities of their students.[5] The teacher's efforts, however, should be supported by components of the curriculum system that make specialized training, resources, and consultant help available when needed. In this construct, the teacher is more the designer and developer of curriculum and a primary influence on the instructional program, rather than a "manager" of resources.

It is not suggested that there is no place for efficient management skills and an integrated systems approach. Instead, it is suggested that the values of teacher choice and decision making be included. Both have a place, but at different levels, in the curriculum and instructional system.

Additional Roles.   Teachers serve additional roles. If they are aware of the nature of students and community, they can justifiably serve on the input committee for studying the environment and supplying information for use by the system for curriculum and instructional improvement. Furthermore, since they are involved in the teaching-learning process and monitor and evaluate learning, they are equipped to serve on the output committee for determining causal relationships when actual output does not equal expected output.

Supervisors

Variations of Role.   It is also important to examine the role of supervisors in a system for curriculum and instructional improvement. It is generally agreed that the goal of supervision is the improvement of instruction. There is less agreement, however, on what the supervisor should do to bring about, or insure, this improvement. At one end of the continuum is the suggestion that the supervisor should observe the performance of teachers and rate them according to the degree to which they are doing what they are supposed to be doing. At the other end of the continuum is the suggestion that the supervisor should serve as a resource person for teachers, should be involved with individual teachers only on the teacher's own terms, and should never be involved in the rating process. A third suggestion is that all teachers should be trained in supervision, and that, instead of designated supervisors, teachers should serve as supervisors of one another. This third concept is the concept of peer supervision.

This writer believes that neither extreme in position is a satisfactory role for the supervisor. If the supervisor is cast in the role of an "inspector," the teachers will probably spend considerable effort in trying to conceal areas in which they need help. They will not, therefore, tend to request assistance from the supervisor. However, if the supervisor is cast in the role of a resource person—a helping person—teachers do not feel threatened; but, neither do they get the facile input of the supervisor, who is characterized by a system-wide perspective. It appears, therefore, that the role of the supervisor falls somewhere between the two stipulated extremes.

Centralized and Decentralized Roles. It is to be noted that, in a centralized decision-making system, the supervisor assumes a role nearer to the inspector end of the continuum. Hopefully, the supervisor establishes a climate in which teachers feel free to ask for assistance. In a decentralized decision-making system, the supervisor assumes a role closer to the other end of the continuum, establishing such a climate that teachers accept input regarding the system-wide goals and programs. In either case, however, the supervisor is the subject-matter expert, and, as such, has considerable input into the whole system of curriculum and instructional improvement.

Other Professional Personnel

Decision making in the curriculum and instructional system involves all professional personnel—teachers, administrators, coordinators, supervisors, department heads, student activity directors, guidance counselors, librarians, and school nurses. The systems approach to curriculum and instructional improvement gives each professional member an opportunity to participate. As problems arise, and as solutions are sought to these problems, the competencies of the various personnel members are used where they are of benefit.

School Board

The school board is a policy-making body. The question may be asked as to whether America is on the verge of a totally new legal structure for public education. This question is suggested in part by the recent attempts of the United States Office of Education "to apply the systems approach to public education through financing the development of Educational Policy Research Centers . . ." and by the growing relationship between "the Office of Education and big industrial companies which—if the views of some present and former Office of Education officials prevail—may induce business to help run the public schools either under contract with a school board or some other government agency." [6] Studies are already under way for possible modifications of the basic form of the school board, and logical alternatives to the school board, which would relieve school boards of their responsibilities and leave them only in advisory roles.

Students

The role of students in a curriculum and instructional improvement program may be of two types. First, students of appropriate maturity may be included in curriculum and instructional planning, in assessing the nature of the student population for which the curriculum is planned, and in evaluating curriculum and instruction. It is perceived that students may serve on committees for curriculum and instructional planning, curriculum and instructional evaluation, study of curriculum issues, and solution of curriculum problems. Today's school youth, in some instances, have expressed a desire to be involved in decision making. High school students of appropriate maturity and interest could be involved in decision making concerning the basic curriculum plan. It is expected that junior high school students and middle school students, because they are younger and less mature, can rarely make a contribution in a committee setting.

Apart from committee involvement and reaction, students can be contacted in groups or on an individual basis for their views and reactions to curriculum and instructional issues and problems. Herein lies the second type of role that students may play in a curriculum and instructional improvement program. Furthermore, in individual contact, students of senior high schools can be consulted regarding their own personal curriculum. At the junior high school and middle school levels, students can be involved indirectly through parent advisement. Nevertheless, at all levels, teacher polling of students should be useful.

Community

The community consists of the parents of the students of the school and the non-parent members of the community. Some of the community members may very well be alumni of the school.

Justification of Roles. Various obvious reasons exist for providing opportunities for the community to participate in a curriculum and instructional improvement program. Illustratively:

1. Parents hold certain aspirations for their sons and daughters; and in these aspirations, school experiences, offerings, and attainments play a real part.

2. The community looks to a school for contributions in the development of good citizens and, in some instances, for future workers in the businesses, industries, and professions of the community. From experience with the graduates of the school, the community has an opportunity to evaluate these graduates and their apparent strengths and weaknesses.

3. The community looks upon the school as its school. Indeed, it is the taxes of the community that support a school. Certainly the community should have an opportunity for participation in curriculum and instructional improvement, wherever justifiable and possible.

4. Involvement of the community should help to promote lines of communication between the school and the community and, hopefully, engender good public relations.

5. In some instances, the community has been known to make suggestions that school personnel themselves have not realized. Such instances may occur because, at times, individuals may be too close to a situation to be able to see the obvious.

Diversity of Roles. Roles exist for community participation in planning, implementing, and evaluating the curriculum. The following statements are added in specificity.

Community representatives can be set up as an advisory group to the school board to reflect community opinion regarding school goals; educational problems; and particular curriculum areas—such as health education and vocational education. If new community groups are not organized as advisory to the school board, already existent groups, such as the Parent-Teacher Organization or the Alumni Association can be used in an advisory capacity.

Community groups can be used in implementing the curriculum. The following ways serve as illustrations:

1. Staffing the library for after-school hours.

2. Participating in tutorial programs.

3. Participating in, or sponsoring, recreational programs.

4. Serving as teacher aides.

5. As business, industrial, or professional people of the community, hosting school personnel in places of business, industry, or profession, so as to clarify for school personnel the current status of these avenues of work, and the requirements of workers in these avenues.

6. As business, industrial, or professional people, coming to guidance classes to explain the qualifications that are required of permanent and temporary workers.

7. Raising money for school needs.

8. Participating in school plays.

Curriculum evaluation should involve the community. Parents can report, from the parents' point of view, the benefits that students derive from the curriculum. Community employers can reflect on the extent to which they have found the graduates prepared to do their particular jobs. Alumni can react to (1) the courses that they took as secondary school students, and the ones that they found useful after graduation; (2) the courses that they did not find so useful; and (3) the courses that they would have liked the opportunity to have taken. Data from home and community are valuable for evaluating the attainment of educational goals.

As will be explained later in this chapter, community members are represented on the curriculum and instruction council. Problems raised in council—or by some individual or group of persons outside of council—are screened in council for determination of legitimacy, and if termed legitimate are routed to the appropriate component or combination of components in the system or subsystem for solution. They may be routed to a committee of the council for study and investigation. Community members may, in fact, be part of such a committee. In all cases, problems are dealt with in a systematic fashion. In a systems approach, the procedure for problem raising and the machinery for problem solving are the built-in safeguards against having a problem solution pushed on a school. Thus, problem solutions cannot enter the system as input, but can be considered in a search for alternative solutions. Such procedures safeguard the interest of the students, the professional staff, and the community.

Cooperative Roles and Responsibilities

A systems approach is designed to coordinate divergent input by competing groups, and to facilitate integration of ideas and cooperation. Various groups are organized so that they are mutually dependent upon one another. The nature of the cooperative effort that is provided should be one that all those who are involved can view as viable. Each participant should see his or her role as one in an operation that is designed to bring about a quality educational program.

In a system, there is a minimum of compartmentalization of responsibility.[7] In other words, responsibility for dysfunction is not attributed to any particular component or subsystem. In addition, "one individual is not responsible to any other particular individual; but, rather, is globally responsible to everyone in the system including teachers, administrators, parents, and students." [8]

The expertise of individuals is focused on the tasks that they are best qualified to perform. Individuals may be organized in a variety of ways for contributing to curriculum and instructional improvement.

Curriculum and Instruction Council

The curriculum and instruction council (variously termed curriculum and/or instruction council) is a popular organization for coordinating effort for curriculum and instructional improvement. Such a council may be used to coordinate efforts in an individual school, or among the various schools of a school system.

Functions. The council screens all problems that enter what may be considered the systems-design component of the system for curriculum and instructional improvement. The systems-design component devises solutions to particular types of curriculum problems. This component can be conceptualized as a subsystem of the curriculum and instructional system. As a decision-making system, it has input, a process, and output. Its input consists of curriculum problems. The process includes the redesigning of curriculum systems and the designing of new systems. Its output consists of solutions to curriculum problems.

The council, which is the control unit of this systems design, screens, routes, assigns, schedules, coordinates, expedites, and follows up the problem input; and, in so doing, the council integrates and coordinates the decision-making process. In screening, the council decides which problems have system-wide implication. If the problem has system-wide implication, it is given either to a task force, committee, or individual possessing the expertise for proposing a solution to the problem. Proposed solutions are submitted to the council for approval. If approved, they are forwarded to the assistant superintendent for curriculum and instruction for authorization. If not approved, they are either returned to the task force, committee, or individual (from where they came) for further study, or revised by the council and forwarded to the assistant superintendent for curriculum and instruction for authorization.

The following are perceived to be additional functions of a curriculum and instruction council:

1. The council should formulate general policy to act as a guide for curriculum and instructional improvement activities taking place in the system.
2. The council should expedite adequate communication between the various components of the system. The council should be aware—and should keep all of the components of the system aware—of the curriculum and instructional

improvement activities that are taking place in the system, and the results of these activities. In doing so, duplication of effort will be avoided, and the council is in a position to lend guidance and help where needed. At the same time, communication lines should be open so that staff, community, and students can react to problems that are being considered by the council.

3. It is expected that as solutions are sought to problems, meetings will be held so that task forces, committees, or individuals can present progress reports. At such times, the council can give assistance or guidance as needed.

4. In a school system that follows a centralized approach, the council serves as an adviser to the assistant superintendent for curriculum and instruction. All recommendations for curriculum and instructional improvement—and all curriculum guides and publications—are approved by the council and, subsequently, submitted to the assistant superintendent for curriculum and instruction for authorization. The council can make suggestions for needed materials and facilities and the allocations of existent materials and facilities. The assistant superintendent for curriculum and instruction is the curriculum and instructional leader of the school system. The council aids this assistant to fulfill this role by supplying information about the needs of the system, and recommendations for answering the needs. In a school system that follows a decentralized approach, the assistant superintendent acts as the executive officer of the council. The assistant's responsibility is to coordinate the efforts of the council, and to provide leadership in getting the council's work done. The council, in this instance, makes decisions rather than recommendations. This concept will be developed more fully in the next section of this chapter.

This author would assign to the council the added function of involving all who should be involved in the writing or rewriting of the philosophy of the school system, and the formulating or revising of the objectives for the school system and the departmental or content subsystems. It is perceived further that the council should broadly define the content to be included in each subsystem (e.g., mathematics, English); the sequence and duration of the content; the way that content will be organized; and the methodology by which it will be taught. These particular broad statements should become the bases upon which instructional materials are designed.

Representation.   Both the community and the components of the school system are represented on the curriculum and instruction council. Specifically, the members of the council and their roles are as follows.

Teachers should have the greatest representation on the council. Since teachers are an integral part of the teaching-learning experience of the students, they should be regarded as an important source of information regarding the needs, interests, and abilities of the students of the school, and determining the adequacy of a particular curriculum change to answer those student needs, interests, and abilities. The teachers' role consists of imparting views regarding objectives and policies pertinent to the school. Views regarding objectives and policies should also be solicited of other members of the professional staff—e.g., department heads, student activity directors, guidance counselors, librarians, and school nurses.

The actual written statement is prepared by a task force, committee, or individual assigned to this project. Teachers and other professional staff members who are assigned to this project need not be council members.

It is to be noted that, in a systems approach to curriculum and instructional improvement, teachers are concerned with participating in defining objectives and deciding content. It is to be further noted that, in a systems approach to curriculum and instructional improvement, the actual production of such materials as teaching-learning units, resource units, curriculum guides, courses of study, and learning activity packages (LAPs) is accomplished by specialists who are included in the design component of the system; who are expert in producing the specified materials; and who, consequently, are given full time to produce the materials.

Both the administrative and the supervisory staffs should be represented on the council because of the expertise that they can lend to council duties. The role of these staff members is that of working participants, as are the rest of the members of the council.

The school board should also be represented on the council. Authorization of the school board is needed for recommendations that the council makes. The school board is a policy-making body. It is of optimum benefit to interpersonal relationships if policies that are made are a consensus of the board members, the professional staff, and the community, rather than the preferences of any one group. The board should cooperate with the council. Furthermore, it should provide for time and resources, so that the council can fulfill its responsibilities. In illustration, it should provide money for released time, so that the professional staff can work on curriculum and instructional improvement, if released time is needed and requested. It should provide needed materials, clerical help, money for staff development, money for the availability of consultants, and so on. Also, it should be in favor of curriculum and instructional improvement.

The role of parents and other community members consists of participation in the definition of the objectives and the policies of the school, and participation in the evaluation of the curriculum. This is to say that parents and other community members should be allowed to participate in determining the purposes of the school, and the content that will be used to attain these purposes. However, when and how the content is taught should be decided by the educators of the school. To fulfill their role, parents and other community members may be asked to identify school matters that are of concern to parents and the community, to identify those that should be studied and discussed in community groups, and to lead study and discussion in existent community organizations and feed back to the council the views of these groups regarding school objectives, purposes, and curriculum. Students and alumni are also judged to be in a position to feed back such views for curriculum and instructional improvement.

Members of the council are to be regarded as mutually dependent. Each council member is dependent on all other members for the expertise that each lends to the council for the accomplishment of its work as a component of the system for curriculum and instructional improvement.

Committees. Curriculum and instruction councils accomplish much of their work by organizing committees or task forces for performing the work or tasks of the council. The committees or task forces may consist of members of the council and individuals who are not members of the council. Illustrative tasks are: studying some particular curriculum problem and recommending a possible solution, conducting research and experimentation in curriculum, and evaluating existing programs. Curriculum committees—with varying memberships of teachers, parents, alumni, students, school nurses, school counselors, school librarians, school administrators, department heads, activity directors, and community members—are used sometimes separately from, and sometimes jointly with, a curriculum and instruction council to accomplish a variety of purposes.

Role Modifications in Decentralized Decision-Making Systems

In the preceding paragraphs, an explanation has been given of the roles of key persons in a centralized approach to curriculum and instructional improvement. An explanation of the roles of key persons in a decentralized approach will be presented in the following paragraphs. Figure 4, chapter 1, schematizes both the centralized and decentralized approach to decision making for curriculum and instructional improvement.

Assistant Superintendent for Curriculum and Instruction. The role of the assistant superintendent for curriculum and instruction is quite different in a decentralized decision-making system. In a decentralized system, the assistant superintendent provides leadership to, and coordinates the efforts of, the curriculum and instruction council. He or she really acts as the executive officer of this council and, frequently, promotes a collegial relationship, rather than a suprasubordinate relationship. The council makes decisions, and the assistant superintendent directs the implementation of the decisions.

Curriculum Coordinators. Curriculum coordinators help the assistant superintendent in implementing the decisions of the curriculum and instruction council. They also serve as staff consultants to the council and play a major role in providing expert information at all stages of curriculum and instructional improvement and implementation. In addition, they are involved in the supervisory process. Their relationship with the teachers whom they supervise is primarily consultative, rather than evaluative. Curriculum coordinators interpret research in their respective fields for teachers and administrators. Furthermore, they conduct local research, thus providing the output committee with data on overall program effectiveness.

Superintendent of Schools. The description that has been given of the role of the superintendent in a centralized decision-making system applies in a decentralized decision-making system with subtle modifications. Primarily, he or she has the responsibility for continued insistence that all major curriculum and instruction decisions evolve by a group process, rather than from individuals in the hierarchy.

Principal. The role of the principal in the decentralized system is one of strong leadership within the building. The principal is primarily responsible for insuring a curriculum and instructional program of high quality. Also, the principal is expected to use the services of the curriculum personnel (i.e., assistant superintendent for curriculum and instruction, curriculum coordinators, and so forth) and to implement the curriculum and instructional decisions that result from the work of the curriculum and instruction council. Furthermore, he or she is expected to provide consultation to the curriculum and instruction council, and to accept leadership assignments on the council subcommittees.

In general, the principal is the instructional leader of the building, and at the same time, a link between that building and the curriculum and instruction council. The principal is responsible for the supervision and evaluation of the work of the faculty, and the implementation of curriculum and instructional improvement in the building.

Teachers.   Much of what has been said regarding the role of teachers in a centralized system applies to the role of teachers in a decentralized system, also. Whether the decision-making system is centralized or decentralized really refers to action and decisions at the principal or central-office levels. Teachers are expected, however, to participate in the work of the curriculum and instruction council, and to implement program changes and improvements that emanate from the council.

Curriculum and Instruction Council.   The role of this council represents the major departure between centralized and decentralized decision-making systems. The curriculum and instruction council has broad representation (e.g., teachers, curriculum staff, administrators, school board members, students, community members). The assistant superintendent for curriculum and instruction serves as the executive officer of the council. Principals generally chair the subcommittees of the council; however, other professionals (e.g., teachers and curriculum coordinators) are expected to chair appropriate subcommittees, also.

The input committee and the output committee are permanent subcommittees of the council. As the local situation dictates, there may be other permanent committees; however, much of the work of the council is accomplished through the establishment of *ad hoc* committees or task forces. These committees are given charges by the council. Upon the completion of their individual charges, each committee submits a report to the council; and each report is acted upon by the council. Subsequently the committees are discharged.

The output of the council, through its executive officer—the assistant superintendent for curriculum and instruction—is conveyed to the superintendent and, ultimately, to the school board, if required.

In the decentralized decision-making approach, the council, rather than any one person, develops programs and makes decisions and recommendations for curriculum and instructional improvement. Curriculum workers and supervisors are primarily staff persons who provide expert services to the council, teachers, and administrators.

Summary

This chapter explains the roles and the responsibilities of all who should participate in the curriculum and instructional improvement program. Emphasis is given to the senior high school, junior high school, and middle school, rather than the elementary school and pre-elementary school.

If a curriculum and instructional improvement program is to be effective, it must be characterized by cooperative action. This is true at all operational levels— national, interstate, state, and local. Local curriculum and instructional improvement is especially close, important, and relevant to the actual teaching-learning situation. For this reason, this chapter deals primarily with roles and responsibilities at the local level—school district, school, group of teachers, and individual teacher.

There is a wide variation in the degree of centralization in decision making for curriculum and instructional improvement in school systems. This variation is partly a result of system size and resources; however, it is more likely due to tradition, the administrative and leadership styles of top management, and the desires of the local school board. In order to accommodate this variation, this author has discussed the roles and the responsibilities in both a centralized and a decentralized approach to curriculum and instructional improvement.

The chapter proposes a model (for each approach) that represents a basic system for decision making (in curriculum and instruction) in a school. The explanation that accompanies each model identifies and explains the roles and the responsibilities of the following: input committee, output committee, assistant superintendent for curriculum and instruction, curriculum coordinator, superintendent of schools, principal, teachers, supervisors, other professional personnel, school board, students, and community.

The curriculum and instruction council (variously termed curriculum and/or instruction council) is a popular organization for coordinating effort for curriculum and instructional improvement. Such a council may be used to coordinate efforts in an individual school, or among the various schools of a school system. Both the community and the components of the school system should be represented on the curriculum and instruction council. The chapter explains the functions of the council, specifies the various members, and depicts their roles.

Curriculum and instruction councils accomplish much of their work by organizing committees or task forces for performing the work or tasks of the council. The committees or task forces may consist of both members of the council and individuals who are not members of the council. The chapter closes with a listing of the tasks that may be performed by such committees or task forces.

Curriculum and instructional improvement, in this book, is viewed in terms of a systems approach including four major stages. Chapter 4 initiates the first of the four stages. Specifically, chapter 4 assesses program relevance in light of the needs, interests, and abilities of the students, and the needs and demands of the school community.

NOTES

1. Clifford H. Edwards, "Community Involvement in a Systems Approach to Curriculum," *High School Journal* 56 (January 1973): 169. Reprinted by permission.

2. Robert E. Boston, "Management by Objectives," *Educational Technology* 12 (May 1972): 50.

3. Ambrose A. Clegg, Jr., "The Teacher as 'Manager' of the Curriculum," *Educational Leadership* 30 (January 1973): 308. Reprinted by permission.

4. Ibid., pp. 308–9.

5. Alberta P. Sebolt, "The Community as a Learning Laboratory," *Educational Leadership* 29 (February 1972): 410–12.

6. Elaine Exton, "How Will 'Systems Approach' Affect Role of School Boards?" *School Board Journal* 155 (September 1967): 13. Reprinted by permission.

7. Edwards, "Community Involvement," p. 171.

8. Ibid., pp. 171–72.

Related Readings

Boston, Robert E. "Management by Objectives." *Educational Technology* 12 (May 1972): 49–51.

Clegg, Ambrose A., Jr. "The Teacher as 'Manager' of the Curriculum." *Educational Leadership* 30 (January 1973): 307–9.

Edwards, Clifford H. "Community Involvement in a Systems Approach to Curriculum." *High School Journal* 56 (January 1973): 167–73.

Exton, Elaine. "How Will 'Systems Approach' Affect Role of School Boards?" *School Board Journal* 155 (September 1967): 13–15, 27.

Feyereisen, K. V.; Fiorino, A. J.; and Nowak, A. T. *Supervision and Curriculum Renewal: A Systems Approach.* New York: Appleton-Century-Crofts, 1970.

March, James E. "Breaking Tradition Forges School Community Ties." *Phi Delta Kappan* 50 (January 1969): 270–74.

Marks, James R.; Stoops, Emery; and King-Stoops, Joyce. *Handbook of Educational Supervision.* Boston: Allyn and Bacon, 1971.

Saylor, J. Galen, and Alexander, William M. *Planning Curriculum for Schools.* New York: Holt, Rinehart and Winston, 1974.

Sebolt, Alberta P. "The Community as a Learning Laboratory." *Educational Leadership* 29 (February 1972): 410–12.

Work Sheet 3A
Questions for Class Dialogue

Student's Name _____

Date _____

Directions: Study chapter 3 with the following questions in mind. Prepare responses for each question, so that you can intelligently participate in class dialogue. Space is provided with each question, so that you can record any notes that will aid you in the dialogue.

1. Discuss the efforts that are made for curriculum and instructional improvement at the following levels: national, state, and local.

2. Who are the professional personnel at each of the three levels of management in a system for curriculum and instructional improvement?

3. What is the role of the input committee (or person) in a system for curriculum and instructional improvement?

4. What is the role of the output committee (or person) in a system for curriculum and instructional improvement?

5. (a) What is the role of the assistant superintendent for curriculum and instruction in a system for curriculum and instructional improvement?

(b) What is the relevance of the output of both the input committee and the output committee to the assistant superintendent for curriculum and instruction?

6. Discuss the role of each of the following in a system for curriculum and instructional improvement: curriculum coordinator, superintendent of schools, and principal.

7. Discuss the role of the teacher as specialist—and the role of the teacher as manager—in a systems approach to curriculum and instructional improvement.

8. Discuss the role of supervisors in a curriculum and instructional improvement program.

9. Succinctly, give the role of each of the following in a curriculum and instructional improvement program: school board, students, community, and other professional personnel who have not been included in these questions at the end of chapter 3.

10. What place does compartmentalization of responsibility have in a system for curriculum and instructional improvement?

11. (a) What is the function of a curriculum and instruction council?

(b) Who should serve on a curriculum and instruction council?

Work Sheet 3B
Library Search

Student's Name _____

Date _____

Directions:
1. Use library sources to discover federal governmental rulings that have been made over the years regarding curriculum.
2. Note your findings in the space below.

Work Sheet 3C
Examination of State Curriculum Regulations

Student's Name _____

Date _____

Directions:

1. Obtain a copy of the curriculum regulations regarding the middle schools, junior high schools, and senior high schools in your state. These curriculum regulations may be obtained by referring to the school code of your state or by writing to your state department of education.
2. Learn the curriculum regulations regarding the middle schools, junior high schools, and senior high schools in your state.
3. Do the state curriculum regulations permit experimentation and innovation, or do they restrict the curriculum to a traditional nature? Record your explanations in the space that is provided below.

Work Sheet 3D
Interview of School Board Member

Student's Name _____
Date _____

Directions:
1. Identify the rulings of the school board regarding the curriculum of the local middle school, junior high school, and/or senior high school. Obtain the information by interviewing a member of the school board.
2. Record your findings below.

Work Sheet 3E
Related Source

Student's Name _____

Date _____

Directions:

1. Read the following:

> If our assumption is correct that the education of students is the single most important consideration of schools and that the struggle for power competes with quality education, then it seems clear that all parties concerned should begin expending their energies for the good of students and channel their efforts into areas which can best be served by their level of expertise. The nature of the cooperative effort provided for should be one which all those involved can perceive as viable.

2. Refer to:

> Edwards, Clifford H. "Community Involvement in a Systems Approach to Curriculum." *High School Journal* 56 (January 1973): 167–73. (The above-quoted material is taken from this reference.)

3. Expound upon the meaning of the above-quoted material in light of the rest of the article referred to above, and chapter 3 in your text. Record your explanation in the space below.

Work Sheet 3F
Roles in a Systems Approach

Student's Name _____

Date _____

Directions:

1. Interview the curriculum coordinator of some middle school, junior high school, or senior high school where a systems approach is used in curriculum and instructional improvement. Learn the roles of the various individuals and groups that are involved in curriculum and instructional improvement in that school.
2. Record your findings below. Compare the roles with the roles that are discussed in chapter 3 in the text. Make recordings of your comparison in the space provided below.

Work Sheet 3G
Roles in an Approach That Is Not a Systems Approach

Student's Name _____

Date _____

Directions:
1. Interview the curriculum coordinator of some middle school, junior high school, or senior high school where a systems approach is not used in curriculum and instructional improvement. Learn the roles of the various individuals and groups that are involved in curriculum and instructional improvement in that school.
2. Record your findings below. Compare the roles with the roles that you discovered in connection with Work Sheet 3F. Make recordings of your comparison in the space that is provided below.

Work Sheet 3H
Teacher Interviews

Student's Name _____

Date _____

Directions:
1. Interview 6 teachers in a middle school, junior high school, or senior high school. Derive data from the teachers as to whether they see the role of the teacher (in the teaching-learning process) as a specialist or manager. Ask for an explanation. Also, derive data from the teachers as to the role that they perceive for teachers in curriculum and instructional improvement.
2. Record your data below. Record the conclusions that you can draw from the data.

Work Sheet 3I
Meeting Attendance

Student's Name _____
Date _____

Directions:
1. If possible, attend a meeting of a curriculum committee—or curriculum and instruction council—in some middle school, junior high school, or senior high school.
2. Note who constitutes the members of the committee or council, and the roles of the individual members. Compare your findings with your learnings from chapter 3 in the text.
3. Record your findings and learnings in the space below.

Work Sheet 3J
Association Meeting Attendance

Student's Name _____

Date _____

Directions:
1. If possible, attend a curriculum association meeting for the purpose of hearing advocations of roles of individuals and groups who should be involved in curriculum and instructional improvement.
2. Discuss your learnings below.

Work Sheet 3K
Symposium

Student's Name _____

Date _____

Directions:
1. Conduct a symposium on roles in curriculum and instructional improvement. If possible, use representatives of the groups mentioned in chapter 3—e.g., teachers, students, counselors, parents, principals, librarians.
2. In the space provided below, record the learnings that you derived from the symposium.

Work Sheet 3L
Extension of Learning

Student's Name _____

Date _____

Directions:
1. Choose one of the following readings, or one of the readings at the end of chapter 3, to extend the learnings that you have attained from the chapter.
2. Read critically.
3. Synthesize your learnings for class dialogue.
4. Space is provided at the end of this work sheet for notes that you may want to make.

Readings:
1. March, James E. "Breaking Tradition Forges School Community Ties." *Phi Delta Kappan* 50 (January 1969): 270–74.
2. Marks, James R.; Stoops, Emery; and King-Stoops, Joyce. *Handbook of Educational Supervision.* Boston: Allyn and Bacon, 1971.
3. Saylor, J. Galen, and Alexander, William M. *Planning Curriculum for Schools.* New York: Holt, Rinehart and Winston, 1974.

4

Needs Assessment of Youth
and the Community

Curriculum and instructional improvement, in this book, is viewed in terms of a systems approach including four major stages. This view was presented in chapter 2. The first stage assesses program relevance, necessitating an examination of the curriculum and instructional program in light of the needs, interests, and abilities of the students; the needs and demands of the school community; and the school philosophy and objectives. The second stage—i.e., planning program improvements—involves the choosing of program modifications or changes that will satisfy the particular needs. The third stage consists of an implementation of program improvements. The fourth and last stage is an evaluation of program outcomes.

This chapter initiates explication of stage one, listed above. The chapter focuses on input into the curriculum and instructional system—specifically, on the exploration of the needs, interests, and abilities of the students and the needs and demands of the community.

As has already been discussed, figure 7, chapter 1, and figure 8, chapter 2, present a model that symbolizes the above-given stages—components in a system for curriculum and instructional improvement. As noted in chapter 2, students and community are represented as external variables in the model. As external variables, they determine objectives and affect curriculum decisions.

System Intervention

An important consideration revolves about the idea that system-based program improvement is basically an intervention into an on-going system. The orderliness of the systems approach demands operation from a data base, rather than from whims, feelings, panaceas, and the like. Therefore, an important aspect of the intervention is the collection of data. In a system for curriculum and instructional improvement, data must be collected regarding the nature and the needs of youth and the needs and demands of the community. Also, it is critical to collect objective data on current system performance. Once the nature and the needs of youth—and the needs and demands of the community—are understood, an analysis of current system performance can be made in terms of these needs. It will be this analysis that provides direction to system intervention. Once there is guidance with regards to system intervention, action that leads to system correction can be taken.

It is imperative from the point of view of systems that feedback be collected in order to ascertain the effects of the correction. In electro-mechanical systems, there generally is very little lag between system modification and output change. In human systems, there may be considerable time lag. In a system for curriculum and instructional improvement, considerable time may pass before the output reflects the modifications. This does not make the collection of feedback less important. It only makes it more difficult.

This chapter, therefore, discusses the collection of appropriate data, so that directed system intervention can occur. More comments will follow in subsequent chapters regarding the collection of feedback to insure system regulation.

Value of Needs Assessment

Sometimes school districts implement educational programs without clearly stated needs or reasons. When a school program is adopted without a determined reason, the change may not bring any improvement. When, however, the change has a rational base, and objectives are stated clearly with means for achieving them, the change will probably, more often, result in improvement.

Before a program change is initiated, a systematic assessment of the existing curriculum should be taken. Such an assessment should include the demands that the community makes of the school, yet, also, a realization that the needs of the learners should be given first concern. Formal program evaluation, by means of reliable instruments, is regarded to be "an excellent method for assisting in the determination of program relevance." [1]

"Needs assessment procedures seem to be keyed to the concept that relevancy of education must be empirically determined from the outset by a formal procedure, which precedes educational planning, design, and implementations." [2] "Needs assessment," in most forms, "identifies and documents the discrepancies between 'what is' and 'what should be' and provides a valid starting point for education." [3] Stated, in part, another way, educational needs are determined by the distance of students' present behavior from some desired behavior.

Value Questioned

Once the distance between students' present behavior from some desired behavior is established, it is expected that the school's resources can be put "to bear upon reducing or eliminating the distance." [4] It must be noted, however, that this method of determining what a curriculum will be or should be rests upon at least three premises.[5]

The first premise is that the school is a purposeful institution, and the purpose of the school can best be interpreted to be the producing of desired changes in students' behavior. Schools as social institutions have, for a long time, accepted the charge to make over students into individuals who think, feel, and act with appreciation and efficiency. The school, in other words, is regarded as the stimulus that acts upon the student, who responds in some way, and the character of the response indicates the extent to which the school has succeeded. Students, and others, are insisting that it is not up to the school to be the initiating agent in the process of changing people. These persons would assign the role of the initiator to the student. These persons would change the premise to read thus: "Individuals are purposeful by nature and are able in varying degrees to articulate their own lives, so that the school can work *with* them toward making those lives more as the individuals want them to be." [6]

The second premise is that desired behaviors can be determined by educators. However, critics of schools, both inside and outside the establishment, are calling for relevance. Educators are being told that it is not appreciated when they determine where the learner will find himself, in terms of his behavior, after a period of instruction.

The third premise is that when it is determined that desired behaviors are not a part of the student's life, the school can alleviate or eliminate that condition through the formulation of a curriculum and instructional program. The assumption is that educators "have a well-filled and diversely compartmentalized bag of tricks." [7] However, there is "little evidence to support the view that one set of learning opportunities is more effective than another for producing certain outcomes, that one teaching strategy can be clearly demonstrated to be superior to another, that certain environmental factors are more effective in terms of student learning than some others, and, more important, that we can articulate with any clarity the reasons for making selections among the curricular and instructional offerings that *are* available." [8]

The raising of the above issues in relation to needs assessment is not to reject the technique as a whole. It is simply hoped that when educators decide to operate within a needs assessment technique to determine the nature of large segments of a student's life, that they are aware of the boundaries and the methodologies that will limit their moves and, to a large extent, shape the product. It is further hoped that educators give enough deliberation to the choice to use (or not use) a needs assessment technique that they can defend their choice clearly. Such deliberation should help to widen the vision of the educators—and help focus energies in consideration of what school is, and should be.

Process of Needs Assessment

A systems approach to needs assessment suggests, first, specifying the problem in the product. The second step suggests hypothesizing some possible causes in the system that may be producing less than the optimum product. In only rare instances can an educational problem be isolated as resulting from only one cause. To illustrate: The fact that the reading comprehension of a specified group of ninth-graders is "below the national norms of their age or grade level may be caused simultaneously by the . . . [students'] past training at home or school, by their exposure to one teaching method instead of several alternatives, by their being taught in large groups instead of through tutorial methods, by the lack of time . . . [students] spend actually reading, by inadequate curricular materials and equipment, by the lack of funds to hire reading specialists . . ., etc." [9]

"A third step in needs assessment suggested by the systems approach is the establishment of priorities to deal with the hypothesized trouble spots." [10] Interrelations among the elements and operations in the system are dynamic and complex. It is, therefore, impossible to deal with all of the elements at once. Either an assistant superintendent for curriculum and instruction (or some person serving in this capacity) in a centralized system, or the curriculum and instruction council in a decentralized system, would need to establish priorities among the hypothesized trouble spots, so that the most important ones would be checked and corrected first. In the illustration used above, wherein the reading comprehension of ninth-graders falls below national norms, the hiring of a reading specialist might be assigned the highest priority since he or she could attempt to find a solution to several problems at once, and all of the other possible causes would be given their own priorities. It is to be noted that the third step in needs assessment may also be worded to be the establishing of priorities among the hypothesized trouble spots to determine existing needs effectively.

The above-given explanation of the process of needs assessment relates to the explanation of system analysis in chapter 1, wherein it is specified that system analysis is an approach to problem solving that begins with a needs assessment and moves systematically to define the problem and the objective, specify the requirements of a solution, identify alternate solutions, and design a system for meeting the requirements of a solution.

Documentation of Identified Needs and Their Priorities

Needs assessment, in most forms, identifies and documents the variance between "what is" and "what should be." The process for identifying "what is" is explained above. The process for documenting what has been identified is explained, in part, below.

Flow charting is a technique that might be used as a first step toward documentation.[11] A flow chart might be constructed which would assist with the planning, sequencing, and identification of alternatives and decision points. A flow chart provides, furthermore, "a tangible descriptive analysis that may be presented to a variety of people, such as board members, outside consultants, and school staff, to obtain a degree of consensus among these members of the education community" regarding the nature and the priority of the trouble spots.[12] The consensus of opinion among the members of the groups lends more validity to the existence of a specified need than does the observation of a single individual. Quantifiable techniques and correlational analyses can be used "to document the consensus in which the administrator is interested." [13] In illustration, "priorities of needs established in the flow chart may be ranked by different individuals and rank-order correlations may be obtained to yield indices of consensus." [14]

In the illustrative problem given above, the reading comprehension of ninth-graders falls below the national norms. The system components and operations that may have a bearing on student achievement are represented in figure 11. By studying this model, one can systematically hypothesize as to which components in the system may be causing the problem. Once the components are identified, there is a need to establish priorities indicating which should be worked with first. One may, for example, decide to concentrate on sources of achievement information and, specifically, on student motivation.

Documentation of Intensity of the Problem

A variety of measures exist for documenting the degree to which some problem exists in the desired product. These measures are often found in the testing programs of the school district.[15] However, tests that are usually used in school districts do not measure all of the desired characteristics of the product. Furthermore, unfortunately, school testing programs yield normative evaluation, by which an individual student's performance is compared to the performance of a large group. A more desirable evaluation is "a criterion-referenced evaluation which indicates how much of a given trait (information, attitude, motivation, etc.)" any given student demonstrates.[16] Some curriculum materials and teaching methods exist (e.g., IPI) that have built-in tests that are criterion-referenced in nature. The results of both normative and criterion-referenced tests can be used to document the degree to which a problem exists.

In addition to tests, other measures may be used for documenting the degree to which some problem exists in the desired product. One alternative is to use self-evaluations by students and reactions by parents and peers.[17] Questionnaires and/or interviews may be used to gather data from students, their parents, and their peers. Another alternative to gathering data by testing is the use of observation in both school and contrived situations.

Though tests are available for evaluation in the cognitive domain, valid evaluative measures are lacking for determining student characteristics in the affective domain. Presently, the documentation of the intensity of problems that exist in the affective domain lies, by necessity, on data gathered from other sources. An illustration of such a source is the school's record of truancy.

Data gathering, by any technique, may be conducted by the appropriate sub-committee of the curriculum and instruction council, by the assistant superintendent for curriculum and instruction (or a delegated expert), or professional staff member who has the needed expertise to do the job.

Documentation Regarding Operation of the System

It is logical to question the part that the system has played in the variance that exists between the product and the desired product. The flow chart technique

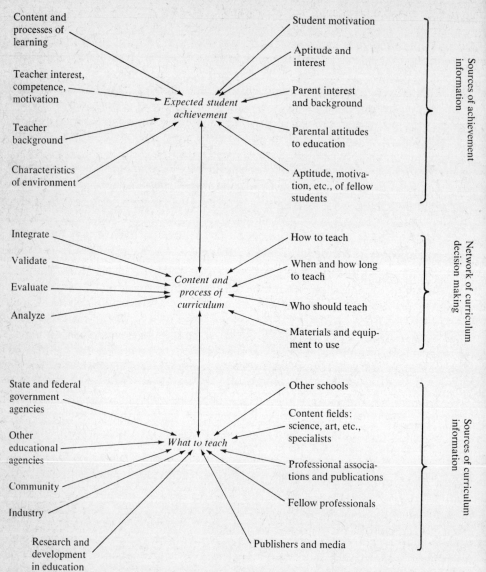

FIGURE 11. Model: Interrelationships of System Components and Operations to Teaching and Learning

SOURCE: B. H. Banathy, "Information Systems for Curriculum Planning," *Educational Technology* 10 (November 1970): 26–27; cited in Lesley H. Browder, Jr., William A. Atkins, Jr., and Esin Kaya, *Developing an Educationally Accountable Program* (Berkeley: McCutchan Publishing, 1973), p. 81. Reprinted by permission of the publisher.

mentioned previously will enable the administrator "to hypothesize some trouble spots in the various components and operations of the system leading to the product." [18]

The identification of trouble spots in the components and operations of the system is aided by periodically obtained data from an ongoing program of evaluation. A formal ongoing program of evaluation will yield additional benefits. It is desirable to use formal evaluation as a means for examining the existing school program. When the evaluation is planned and coordinated properly, the evaluative exercise can serve to increase the justification of program objectives and the promotion of faculty identification with the objectives. The following chapter explores the area of school objectives. An interdisciplinary approach to evaluation (e.g., whereby junior high school teachers help to evaluate the middle school curriculum, or mathematics teachers participate in the evaluation of the science curriculum) builds teachers' interest in subject areas other than those that they teach. Subsequently, when priorities are established for improvement, resistance to change should be at a minimum if the teachers are knowledgeable of the objectives, problems, and needs of each subject area in the school.

A formal program of evaluation can, among other things, serve to appraise the extent to which existing learning experiences relate curricular objectives to student needs. An evaluative instrument, such as the *Evaluative Criteria,* published by the National Study of Secondary School Evaluation, can be of invaluable help in program assessment.[19] Such an instrument is helpful in assessing the quality and quantity of inputs to the school, such as personnel and facilities, and in assessing the relevance of processes and the success of program outputs in relation to the philosophy and the objectives of the school. This type of instrument "lends itself to quick quantification and qualification of data and provides a proven format for the evaluation." [20] Such evaluative instruments pertain, mostly, to secondary schools. Developments have been made for providing evaluative criteria for the schools of the lower levels. The importance and the various means for assessing, measuring, and evaluating the outputs of the system are further explored in chapter 8.

External Appraisal

Upon the completion of a comprehensive assessment of the school's program by the professional staff, parents, and students, a report should be prepared and distributed. Subsequently, it would be desirable to have an external appraisal for the purposes of substantiating, amending, or refuting the findings that resulted from internal appraisal. Any middle school, junior high school, senior high school, or elementary school that desires external appraisal can seek the assistance of the State Department of Education, regional accrediting association, regional professional associations, university specialists, or educators of neighboring schools.[21]

Decisions Relative to Assessed Needs

As a result of the internal and external appraisals, a list of recommendations is made and priorities are established for each recommendation. Those recommendations that are expeditious and should be implemented immediately are so indicated. On the other hand, those recommendations that involve long-range planning, substantial expenditure of money, and so forth, are also singularly designated.

The number of identified needs will warrant the taking of one of four courses of future action: "(1) to leave the program(s) alone; (2) to modify, or, other-

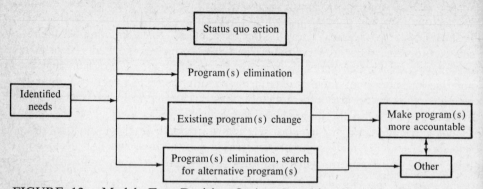

FIGURE 12.   Model: Four Decision Options Resulting from Needs Assessment

SOURCE: Lesley H. Browder, Jr., William A. Atkins, Jr., and Esin Kaya, *Developing an Educationally Accountable Program* (Berkeley: McCutchan Publishing, 1973), p. 102. Reprinted by permission of the publisher.

wise, change the existing program(s); (3) to eliminate it (them); or (4) to eliminate it (them) and replace it (them) with some other alternative program(s)." [22] Figure 12 illustrates these four options. Certainly this level of analysis and decision making does not correspond with the sophisticated analysis of quantifiable tools and techniques, such as management by objectives (MBO), planning-programming-budgeting system (PPBS), program evaluation review technique (PERT), and operations research (OR).

Awareness of Needed Data

If needed data are to be searched and retrieved, an awareness should exist regarding the components of the system and their functional interdependence. Also, an awareness should exist regarding the nature and needs of the students and the needs and demands of the community, and possible sources of data regarding both the students and the community. The following paragraphs are both informative and directional.

Learner Needs

Regardless of the magnitude of societal pressures that influence the curriculum and instructional program, the needs of the learners must be given primary importance if the program is to be relevant to them. The needs of the learners are one of the most basic considerations in curriculum planning. Needs may be regarded in two categories—the needs of learners in general and the needs of the individual learner. Further, needs may be considered in a variety of perspectives—personal, social, academic, and vocational. It is the responsibility of the public school to meet both the common and the specific needs of learners.

Nature of the Learner and Nature of Learning

Psychological Principles.   Certain psychological principles regarding the nature of the learner—and the nature of learning—have implications in curriculum and instructional improvement. Some of these psychological principles, and their implications for curriculum and instructional improvement, are as follows:

1. No two individuals are exactly alike. Each student, therefore, needs different learning experiences if he or she is to derive the greatest possible benefits.

2. Most persons are more alike than different. It is possible—and even necessary—to provide common learning experiences for all students.

3. According to Carl R. Rogers, one becomes self-actualizing by discovering one's true self. Students need a curriculum, therefore, that helps them to become themselves, and to grow in all aspects.

4. According to Edward L. Thorndike, individuals have three types of intelligence—mechanical, abstract, and social. A student may be very competent academically, but not so competent socially or mechanically. Learning activities should not, therefore, be solely academic in nature. However, students should have the opportunity to learn through different kinds of experiences.

5. Jean Piaget hypothesizes that intelligence is an accumulative effect of transfer of training and learning, that transfer of training and learning develops inner structures, and that certain structures are probably better developed and, therefore, more capable of further development than others. Thus, an importance is implied for matching a student's developmental stage with content—and teaching method.

6. Jerome S. Bruner contends that the most fundamental ideas of the disciplines, though not formally stated, should be presented to children at an early age. Bruner's expounding of this concept implies that if ideas are to be taught thoroughly, they should be presented to children early, and should be presented repeatedly as students mature and are capable of elaborating on the concepts in greater breadth and depth. A curriculum that handles concepts in this way is referred to as a spiral curriculum.

7. Motivation promotes learning. Stressing the importance or value of the material to be learned to the learner promotes motivation. A curriculum should relate both to the immediate and the long-range goals of students.

8. Transfer of learning is the act of using in one situation something that has been learned in another situation. Thorndike has advocated that skills, attitudes, and understandings be taught directly as they are wished to be learned. The behaviorist, B. F. Skinner, has proposed that behavior be instilled into a student by a conditioning process. Certain implications exist regarding the theory of transfer of learning for the secondary school curriculum. One implication is that secondary school courses should be designed for transfer of learning by emphasis on generalizations, applications, meaningful learning, and attitudes. Another implication is that the process of learning is more important, for transfer of learning, than mere unrelated facts that may be acquired. Learning by discovery seems to make transfer of learning more likely.

Studies. Many studies about the nature of learners have been conducted during the past fifty years. Learners have been studied from various points of view. Arnold Gesell and others have studied thousands of children at specified ages and have, subsequently, made generalizations about their physical, mental, and behavioral characteristics at these ages. Willard C. Olson has conducted longitudinal studies in which, periodically, he has observed and examined children in their development from childhood to adolescence, and has identified and studied individual patterns of growth and development. Robert Havighurst has constructed lists of developmental tasks from infancy through later life. The findings in the above studies, and others, generally are in agreement. Consequently, certain accepted generalizations emerge about various groups of learners. These generalizations can justifiably serve as partial bases upon which curriculum and instructional improvement is planned. The following paragraphs give insight into the characteristics and needs of middle school students, upon which, in part, a curriculum and instructional program can be based.

Characteristics and Needs of Middle School Students

The following, through study, have been found to be characteristic of individuals of middle school age:

1. Small muscles continue to develop, increasing manipulative skills.
2. Coordination is improving, especially hand-eye.
3. This is the period of prepubescence at which time physical growth slows down. Beginning of pubescence may appear in a very few boys and girls.
4. Overtaxing of heart needs watching.
5. Posture needs watching.
6. Eyes need to be considered. Attention now may prevent more serious trouble later.
7. This is a period of untidiness, overabundance of energy, frequent accidents.
8. Children show increased span in a wide range of activities.
9. This is the gang age, the age of secret clubs.
10. Children are critical of their families.
11. Relationship to group and approval of peers are important.
12. It is the age of collecting—cards, stamps, etc.[23]

The above-listed characteristics suggest that middle school students have the following needs:

1. Opportunities to develop independence.
2. At least ten hours of sleep.
3. Physical equipment (desks, chairs, etc.) carefully adjusted to each individual.
4. Uniformity and fairness in rules and punishment.
5. Real need of regularity, as opposed to schedule changes.
6. Whole body activities.
7. Sympathy and understanding of adults.
8. Help in finding a place in the group.
9. Opportunity to learn to be a good follower as well as a good leader.[24]

Havighurst has defined a developmental task as "a task which arises at or about a certain period in the life of the individual, successful achievement of which leads to his happiness and to success with later tasks, while failure leads to unhappiness in the individual, disapproval by the society, and difficulty with later tasks." [25] He has listed the following developmental tasks of middle childhood, which seems comparable to the age period of middle school students:

1. Learning physical skills necessary for ordinary games.
2. Building wholesome attitudes toward oneself as a growing organism.
3. Learning to get along with age-mates.
4. Learning an appropriate masculine or feminine social role.
5. Developing fundamental skills in reading, writing, and calculating.
6. Developing concepts necessary for everyday living.
7. Developing conscience, morality, and a scale of values.
8. Achieving personal independence.
9. Developing attitudes toward social groups and institutions.[26]

The following paragraphs give insight into the characteristics and needs of junior high school students, upon which, in part, a curriculum and instructional program can be based.

Characteristics and Needs of Junior High School Students

Students in grades 7, 8, and 9 are said to be characterized as follows:

1. Showing gradually emerging heterosexual development.
2. Showing the emergence of a new pattern of religious problems.
3. Seeking security in regard to his approaching adult status, his own peer group or "gang," and himself.
4. Desiring group approval.
5. Being self-conscious and bashful.
6. Feeling a need for independence from parental authority, manifested at times by defiance toward other forms of adult authority.
7. Daydreaming and proneness to emulate other personalities in the process.
8. Feeling more intensified emotions than adults, but for shorter periods of time.
9. Awkwardness.
10. Proneness to save face.
11. Widening his interests.
12. Self-centeredness, as evidenced by carelessness and thoughtlessness, resulting primarily from physical and emotional changes.
13. Tending to be overly aggressive when thwarted.
14. High physical resistance to disease.
15. Showing off, as evidenced by being faddish and boastful.[27]

The above-listed characteristics suggest that junior high school students have the following needs:

1. Varied programs to meet different maturity levels.
2. Organized clubs and group activities based on boys' and girls' needs and interests.
3. Help in understanding physical and emotional changes which are beginning to take place.
4. Warm affection and sense of humor in adults: no nagging, scolding, or talking down.
5. Sense of belonging in the peer group.
6. Opportunities for boys and girls to do things together in group situations.
7. Opportunities for greater independence and for carrying more responsibility without pressure.
8. Special help for those who are maturing much faster or much more slowly than their companions.
9. Personal acceptance of the irregularities of both physical and emotional growth.
10. Acceptance of continued need for some dependence on adults.
11. Help in developing skills which make it possible to take part successfully in group activities.
12. Recognition of individual capacities and abilities, with planning of special programs to meet needs and avoid discouragements.[28]

In 1944 the Educational Policies Commission of the National Education Association set forth a statement known as the Imperative Needs of Youth.[29] The following list was derived by a revision of these Imperative Needs of Youth by a group of junior high school administrators who set forth the following statement as especially applicable to junior high school students:

1. All junior high school youth need to explore their own aptitudes and to have experiences basic to occupational proficiency.
2. All junior high school youth need to develop and maintain abundant physical and mental health.
3. All junior high school youth need to be participating citizens of their school and community, with increasing orientation to adult citizenship.
4. All junior high school youth need experiences and understandings, appropriate to their age and development, which are the foundation of successful home and family life.
5. All junior high school youth need to develop a sense of values of material things and of the rights of ownership.
6. All junior high school youth need to learn about the natural and physical environment and its effect on life, and to have opportunities for using the scientific approach in the solution of problems.
7. All junior high school youth need the enriched living which comes from appreciation of and expression in the arts and from experiencing the beauty and wonder of the world around them.
8. All junior high school youth need to have a variety of socially acceptable and

personally satisfying leisure-time experiences which contribute either to their personal growth or to their development in wholesome group relations, or to both.

9. All junior high school youth need experiences in group living which contribute to personality and character development. They need to develop respect for other persons and their rights to grow in ethical insights.

10. All junior high school youth need to grow in their ability to observe, listen, read, think, speak, and write with purpose and appreciation.[30]

The following paragraphs give insight into the characteristics and needs of senior high school students, upon which, in part, a curriculum and instructional program can be based.

Characteristics and Needs of Senior High School Students

Senior high school students are generally believed to be characterized thus:

1. Mood swings—sometimes defiant and rebellious, sometimes cooperative and responsible.

2. Often searching for ideals and standards, anxious about the future, trying to "find himself."

3. Preoccupied with acceptance by one social group, particularly by members of the opposite sex.

4. Afraid of not being popular, of ridicule, of not being like other adolescents; oversensitive to the opinions of others.

5. Concerned about his own bodily appearance.

6. Desirous of asserting independence from his family, but willing to return to adults for moral support.

7. Sometimes responds better to teachers than to parents; tends to identify with an admired adult.

8. Wants responsibility but is often unstable in judgment.

9. Wants the independence of earning his own money.

10. Sometimes acts as if he "knew it all," but is insecure within himself.

11. Responds well to group responsibility and group participation.

12. Shows intense loyalty to his own group.[31]

The above-listed characteristics suggest that senior high school students have the following needs:

1. Acceptance by peers.

2. Adequate knowledge and understanding of sexual relationships and attitudes.

3. Help in accepting his permanent physical appearance.

4. Opportunities to carry responsibility and make decisions.

5. Opportunities to earn and save money.

6. Provision for recreation with members of the opposite sex.

7. Assistance in learning about and choosing a vocation.

8. Organized group activities, based on group planning and participation.

9. Help in establishing more mature relationships with other members of the family.

10. Guidance which is kind, unobtrusive, and free of threat to one's freedom.

11. Warm, understanding, supportive acceptance by parents.

12. Guidance in physical activities to prevent overdoing.

13. Opportunities to develop his own interests and skills.

14. Help in keeping a balance between group needs and individual needs and interests.

15. Guidance in developing special skills and talents.

16. Help in accepting and understanding those outside one's own group.

17. Help in understanding why people feel and behave as they do.[32]

Havighurst has identified the following developmental tasks that a secondary school student must perform if he or she is to grow from childhood to adulthood:

1. To learn to understand oneself, to live with and compensate for one's inadequacies, and to make the most of one's assets.

2. To learn what it is to be a young man or young woman and to learn to act accordingly.

3. To develop a suitable moral code.

4. To learn how to act one's part in a heterosexual society.

5. To determine, prepare for, and become placed in his vocation.

6. To acquire a suitable philosophy of life.

7. To build a system of values.

8. To establish himself as an independent individual free from his mother's apron strings.

9. To learn how to make reasonable decisions in serious matters on his own responsibility without undue reliance on an older person.

10. To master the social and intellectual skills and knowledges necessary for adult life.

11. To learn the skills of courtship and to establish close friendships with persons of the opposite sex as preparation for finding a suitable mate.

12. To break away from his childhood home.

13. To learn what kind of person he is himself and to learn to live with himself.[33]

It is to be noted that those who have created lists such as those given above regarding middle school, junior high school, and senior high school students have usually warned that such lists are not to be viewed as "models or norms but only as general descriptions or 'age profiles.' "[34] Such lists are useful for obtaining a broad view of expectations that may be held for particular groups of students.

Needed Student Data and Sources of These Data

While the identification of the needs of students or learners in general is an important consideration in the improvement of the curriculum and instructional program, the analysis of the unique needs of learners in a particular community is mandatory. For example, the needs of maturing learners in some suburb in the nation will undoubtedly differ from the needs of maturing learners in some rural section of the country or in one of the cities.

Data are needed about the nature and status of the growth and development of those students to be educated. The preceding section of this chapter adds insight regarding growth and development of learners, with implications for curriculum and instruction. The professional staff of a school already has a broad and/or deep knowledge of many of the factors basic to curriculum and instructional planning through their prior study of psychology, sociology, philosophy, teaching methodology, and so on. Books and periodicals abound in these areas to add to the background of the professional staff.

Additional needed student data are specified as follows. Data are needed about student population and enrollment—e.g., "numbers, trends, births, age distribution; race or ethnic background; projected birth rates and rates of population growth; projected enrollments." [35] Data are needed regarding school progress—e.g., "normal, retarded, or accelerated progress by grade, multiunit, or level." [36] Data are needed regarding dropouts—e.g., "rate, causes, characteristics of the dropouts; school status; postschool status." [37] Also, data are needed regarding career plans— e.g., "extent of continuation in college and other postsecondary institutions; current career choices and plans; career patterns of graduates; mobility among young persons; . . . situations among minority groups in postsecondary schooling and occupational opportunities." [38]

Much of the needed data regarding student population and enrollment should be available in existent records—census data reports, pupil data records, national and state reports of vital statistics, individual school records, system-wide records, follow-up studies, conference records, guidance records, records concerning students before and after leaving school, and so forth. Additional needed statistical data about the student body of the school, characteristics of the students, and follow-up data can be collected by the teachers, counselors, or administrators of the school, or by school research bureaus. Interpretation of the data should be made by all persons who are involved in curriculum and instructional improvement, including parents.[39]

Governmental agencies, study commissions, school survey committees, and other such groups periodically provide research studies, reports, and interpretative studies.[40] Though such writings do not yield data particularly applicable to, and specifically descriptive of, a particular school population, they depict national and/or state situations and project future situations. At the same time, they are useful to a particular school by illustrating methods for collecting data, and helping the school to interpret these data.

Community or Environment

Certain relationships exist between a school and its community. Community, or environment, is explained here in a systems context. "The environment is the context within which a system exists." [41] The community of a school system is the environment within which the school exists. The community not only surrounds the school, but it is also affected by the school.

A system exists "within a given space that is set aside from . . . [its environment] by . . . [its] boundaries." [42] Furthermore:

> The boundaries of a system delimit the system space and set aside from the environment all those entities, their attributes and relationships, that belong to the system.
> The boundaries of the school can be described in physical, economic, psychobiological, psychological, and social terms. The physical boundaries of the school are multiple. One such boundary is the limits of the physical plant. A larger boundary is the geographical area within which the school operates and which it serves.
> Economic boundaries can be defined in terms of resources available to the school. Psychobiological boundaries refer to general student characteristics (such as age or aptitudes). Psychological bounds refer to feelings, attitudes and perceptions about the school.
> The society not only surrounds the school but creates it and is affected by its own creation.[43]

There are breaks in the boundaries of the school system through which it communicates and interacts with its community (and through which the school system receives its input) and sends its output back into the community. The boundaries of a school system are not usually drawn sharply and do not isolate the school system from its community. The less the boundaries are defined and the more breaks there are in them, "the more open the school is and, consequently, the more kinds of input the school has to cope with." [44]

Anything that the school receives from its community is called input. The school receives multiple input from the community. Specifically, the community makes certain expectations, demands, and requirements of the school, and the school seeks to satisfy them. These expectations, demands, and requirements constitute part of the input of the school system. The community, furthermore, makes certain restrictions upon a school system's operations. These restrictions are, also, regarded as constituting input. Finally, the community provides the school's resources— human, financial, and material. These resources are, also, input. The community sends students into the school to be educated. The students constitute the most important input. The students who have been educated and the knowledge that has been produced constitute the main output of the school into the community.

Certain additional relationships exist between the school and its community. The community is the suprasystem of the school, and the school is a subsystem of the community. Other subsystems of the community include government, industry, business, and so forth. In other words, a community is a multisystem; but, so also is the school. A school system may be subdivided into the following subsystems: (1) students and personnel, (2) finance, (3) buildings and grounds, and (4) curriculum and instruction. The school system interacts with, and is influenced by, the other subsystems of the community—government, industry, business, and so forth. The subsystems of a school interact with, and are influenced by, one another. The central subsystem of the school is curriculum and instruction; the other subsystems are built around it.

A school is expected to cope with constant change in the community's demands, expectations, and constraints. However, certain problems exist. Often the demands, expectations, and constraints are not clear—and frequently ambiguous.

And, always, there are great variations in the differences that exist among individual students. Schools meet varying demands, expectations, and constraints. For example, a suburban school is asked (by a community) to fulfill demands, expectations, and constraints that are different from those that an urban school or a rural school is asked to fulfill. Nevertheless, regardless of the location of the school, it is expected to adjust to the demands, expectations, and constraints that are made by its community. The school is expected to make the required adjustments and to produce the output that is specified by its community. By so doing, the school manifests its responsibility towards the community that it serves, and maintains its compatibility with its community.

To the extent that a school lacks accountability by not being able to guarantee educational outcomes, a community becomes increasingly reluctant to answer the school's requests for additional resources. However, if the output of education is constantly assessed and measured, and adjustments are designed that are based on that output, a school can fulfill its expectations, realize desired educational outcomes, and remain compatible with its community. In such a situation, a school can expect its community to accommodate it and to provide the resources that it needs, so that it can function.

Needed Community Data and Sources of These Data

Data are needed about the following aspects of the community: "social, cultural, and economic characteristics of neighborhoods or groups served; the nature of the peer culture, especially at adolescent level; recreational facilities and opportunities for cultural and intellectual activities; incidence of delinquency and crime." [45] Data are needed about family and home conditions, e.g., "socioeconomic status of family; social class; occupations; composition and status of family; aspirations; educational level of parents; cultural and intellectual climate; community activities; personal relations; emotional climate; nature and extent of any disadvantages." [46]

Needed data should be available from census records; home visitations; welfare, court, and police records; survey of recreation facilities, libraries, community centers; conferences with staffs of neighborhood agencies; pupil personnel records; conferences with parents; talks with pupils; and so on. [47]

Occupational and career data are needed regarding "occupational patterns in the community; occupational trends, locally and nationally; opportunities for career education in the community or area." [48] These data should be available from "Department of Labor studies for the United States and local and/or state on occupations, manpower needs, employment trends, occupational outlook." [49]

The following additional data are needed about the culture and social groups of the community. Data are needed about values, e.g., "the mores and traditions of the citizens of the local school district and of subgroups within the community; evidence on pluralism in values; the 'counterculture' movement; diverse points of view on morality; evidence of anomie, despair, lack of commitment or faith in American beliefs; factors in alienation of youth." [50] Data are needed regarding expectations, e.g., "demands made on the schools; views on purposes, functions, and goals of the schools; approval or disapproval of activities, programs, regulations, policies, practices, courses, teachers, and administrators; political views." [51]

Data are needed regarding the political power structure in the community, e.g., "controllers and molders of public opinion; attitudes of citizens on educational and public issues and matters; attitudes of citizens on political activities of teachers." [52] Finally, data are needed about trends, problems, and issues in local community, e.g., "prospects for the future of the community; problems of relations with surrounding and nearby communities; attitudes of citizens on community matters, problems, and conditions." [53]

The needed data regarding the culture and social groups of the community should be available from the following sources: "opinion polls, community surveys; editorials in local news media; selection of news and 'slanting' in local press; city ordinances on liquor, pornography, amusements, etc.; views of political leaders and office holders; activities and views of local civic, patriotic, educational, and political action groups; 'ear-to-the-ground' listening; observations; citizens' advisory groups; PTA plans, programs, and actions; census records; government planning and commissions at state and local levels; student investigations; local authorities; laws enacted." [54]

Summary

Curriculum and instructional improvement, in this book, is viewed in terms of a systems approach including four major stages. This view was presented in chapter 2. The first stage assesses program relevance, necessitating an examination of the curriculum and instructional program in light of the needs, interests, and abilities of the students, the needs and demands of the school community, and the school philosophy and objectives. This chapter initiates explication of stage one.

Before a program change is initiated, a systematic assessment of the existing curriculum should be taken. Such an assessment should include the demands that the community makes of the school, but, at the same time, a realization that the needs of the learners should be given first concern. The chapter explains the process of needs assessment. It is to be noted that the process of needs assessment relates to the explanation of system analysis in chapter 1, wherein it is specified that system analysis is an approach to problem solving that begins with a needs assessment and moves systematically to define the problem and the objective, specify the requirements of a solution, identify alternate solutions, and finally design a system for meeting the requirements of a solution.

Sometimes school districts implement educational programs without clearly stated needs or reasons. When, however, the change has a rational base and objectives are stated clearly, together with means of achieving them, the change will probably result in improvement. Consequently, an argument can be made for the value of needs assessment. Educators who decide to operate within a needs assessment technique to determine the nature of large segments of a student's life are cautioned to be aware of the boundaries and the methodologies that will limit their moves and, to a large extent, shape the product.

Needs assessment, in most forms, not only identifies but also documents the variance between "what is" and "what should be." The process for documenting the variance is also explained.

A variety of measures exists for documenting the degree to which some problem exists in the desired product. These measures are described. Documentation is also needed regarding the part that the system has played in the variance that exists between the product and the desired product. Means for attaining this desired documentation are also presented.

Upon the completion of a comprehensive assessment of the school's program by the professional staff, parents, and students, it is desirable to have an external appraisal. The purposes of the external appraisal should be to substantiate, amend, or refute the findings that resulted from internal appraisal. As a result of the internal and external appraisals, a list of recommendations is made, and priorities are established for each recommendation. Those recommendations that are expeditious and should be implemented immediately are indicated. On the other hand, those recommendations that involve long-range planning, substantial expenditure of money, and so on, are also singularly designated.

If needed data are to be searched and retrieved, an awareness should exist regarding the components of the system and their functional interdependence. Also, an awareness should exist of the nature and needs of the students, the needs and demands of the community, and possible sources of data regarding the students and the community. An explanation is given regarding (1) learner needs, (2) psychological basis to curriculum and instruction, (3) characteristics and needs of middle school students, (4) characteristics and needs of junior high school students, (5) characteristics and needs of senior high school students, (6) needed student data, and sources of these data, (7) community or environment, (8) needed community data, and sources of these data.

As stated at the opening of this summary, in this book, curriculum and instructional improvement is viewed in terms of a systems approach including four major stages. The first stage assesses program relevance, necessitating an examination of the curriculum and instructional program in light of the needs, interests, and abilities of the students, the needs and demands of the school community, and the school philosophy and objectives. Chapter 4 focuses on the assessment of program relevance in light of the needs, interests, and abilities of the students, and the needs and demands of the community. Chapter 5 focuses on the assessment of program relevance in light of the school philosophy and objectives.

NOTES

1. James M. Lipham and James A. Hoeh, *The Principalship: Foundations and Functions* (New York: Harper and Row, 1974), p. 206. Reprinted by permission.

2. Roger A. Kaufman, "Accountability, a System Approach and the Quantitative Improvement of Education—An Attempted Integration," *Educational Technology* 11 (January 1971): 21–26; cited in Lesley H. Browder, Jr., William A. Atkins, Jr., and Esin Kaya, *Developing an Educationally Accountable Program* (Berkeley: McCutchan Publishing, 1973), p. 85.

3. Ibid.

4. Gary A. Griffin, "Needs Assessment as a Concealing Technology," *Educational Leadership* 30 (January 1973): 324. Reprinted by permission.

5. Ibid.

6. Ibid., p. 325.

7. Ibid., p. 326.

8. Ibid.

9. Lesley H. Browder, Jr., William A. Atkins, Jr., and Esin Kaya, *Developing an Educationally Accountable Program* (Berkeley: McCutchan Publishing, 1973), p. 79. Copyright 1973 by McCutchan Publishing Corporation. Reprinted by the permission of the publisher.

10. Ibid.

11. Ibid., p. 85.

12. Ibid.

13. Ibid.

14. Ibid.

15. Ibid., p. 86.

16. Ibid.

17. Ibid., paraphrase, p. 87.

18. Ibid.

19. Address for purchasing copies of the *Evaluative Criteria:* National Study of School Evaluation, 2201 Wilson Boulevard, Arlington, Va. 22201.

20. Lipham and Hoeh, *The Principalship,* p. 213. Reprinted by permission.

21. Ibid., p. 214.

22. Browder, Atkins, and Kaya, *Developing,* pp. 101–2.

23. D. A. Prescott, *The Child in the Educative Process* (New York: McGraw-Hill, 1957); cited in Ronald C. Doll, *Curriculum Improvement: Decision Making and Process* (Boston: Allyn and Bacon, 1974), pp. 28–30. Reprinted by permission.

24. Ibid.

25. Robert J. Havighurst, *Human Development and Education* (New York: Longmans, Green and Co., 1953); cited in Chris A. De Young, *Introduction to American Public Education* (New York: McGraw-Hill, 1955), pp. 409–10. Reprinted by permission.

26. Ibid.

27. J. Minor Gwynn and John B. Chase, Jr., *Curriculum Principles and Social Trends* (New York: Macmillan, 1969), p. 399. Reprinted by permission.

28. Ronald C. Doll, *Curriculum Improvement: Decision Making and Process* (Boston: Allyn and Bacon, 1974), p. 32. Reprinted by permission.

29. *The High School Curriculum,* Third Edition, pp. 54–55, edited by Harl R. Douglass. Copyright © 1964 The Ronald Press Company, New York.

30. California State Department of Education, *Handbook for California Junior High Schools,* Bulletin 18 (Sacramento: California State Department of Education, 1949), pp. 6–11; cited in Harl R. Douglass, ed., *The High School Curriculum,* pp. 55–56. See, also, California State Department of Education, *Handbook for Junior High School Education in California* (Sacramento: California State Department of Education, 1969), pp. 13–31.

31. Doll, *Curriculum Improvement,* pp. 32–33. Reprinted by permission.

32. Ibid., p. 33.

33. Havighurst, *Human Development,* pp. 111–47.

34. Doll, *Curriculum Improvement,* p. 34.

35. J. Galen Saylor and William M. Alexander, *Planning Curriculum for Schools* (New York: Holt, Rinehart and Winston, 1974), p. 105. Reprinted by permission.

36. Ibid.

37. Ibid.

38. Ibid., p. 115.

39. Ibid., p. 104.

40. Ibid., p. 105.

41. From p. 6 of the book, *Developing A Systems View of Education* by Bela H. Banathy. Copyright 1973 by Fearon Publishers, Inc. Reprinted by permission of Fearon Publishers, Inc.

42. Ibid.

43. Ibid., pp. 6, 11.

44. Ibid., p. 12.

45. Saylor and Alexander, *Planning Curriculum*, pp. 112–13. Reprinted by permission.
46. Ibid., p. 112.
47. Ibid., pp. 112–13.
48. Ibid., p. 115.
49. Ibid.
50. Ibid., p. 124.
51. Ibid., p. 125.
52. Ibid.
53. Ibid., pp. 125–26.
54. Ibid., pp. 124–26.

Related Readings

Banathy, Bela H. *Developing a Systems View of Education*. Belmont, Calif.: Fearon Publishers, 1973.

_____. "Information Systems for Curriculum Planning." *Educational Technology* 10 (November 1970): 25–28.

De Young, Chris A., and Wynn, Richard. *American Education*. New York: McGraw-Hill, 1972.

Doll, Ronald C. *Curriculum Improvement: Decision Making and Process*. Boston: Allyn and Bacon, 1974.

Douglass, Harl R., ed. *The High School Curriculum*. New York: Ronald Press, 1964.

Dreeben, Robert. "The Contribution of Schooling to the Learning of Norms." *Harvard Educational Review* 37 (Spring 1967): 211–37.

Estvan, Frank J. "Emerging Priorities for the Young." In *The Curriculum: Retrospect and Prospect, 70th Yearbook of the National Society for the Study of Education, Part I*, edited by Robert M. McClure. Chicago: University of Chicago Press, 1971.

Gagne, R. M., ed. *Psychological Principles in Systems Development*. New York: Holt, Rinehart and Winston, 1966.

Glaser, Robert. "Instructional Technology and the Measurement of Learning Outcomes." *American Psychologist* 18 (August 1963): 519–21.

Gwynn, J. Minor, and Chase, John B., Jr. *Curriculum Principles and Social Trends*. New York: Macmillan, 1969.

Kaufman, Roger A. "Accountability, a System Approach and the Quantitative Improvement of Education—An Attempted Integration." *Educational Technology* 11 (January 1971): 21–26.

Lee, Walter S. "The Assessment, Analysis and Monitoring of Educational Needs." *Educational Technology* 13 (April 1973): 28–32.

Popham, James W. *Criterion Referenced Measurement*. Englewood Cliffs, N.J.: Educational Technology Publications, 1971.

Saylor, J. Galen, and Alexander, William M. *Planning Curriculum for Schools*. New York: Holt, Rinehart and Winston, 1974.

Thoresen, Carl E., ed. *Behavior Modification in Education, 72nd Yearbook of the National Society for the Study of Education, Part I*. Chicago: University of Chicago Press, 1973.

Work Sheet 4A
Questions for Class Dialogue

Student's Name _____

Date _____

Directions: Study chapter 4 with the following questions in mind. Prepare responses for each question, so that you can intelligently participate in class dialogue. Space is provided with each question, so that you can record any notes that will aid you in the dialogue.

1. What is the value of needs assessment procedures?

2. On what basis is the value of needs assessment procedures questioned?

3. Is there a difference between need assessment and needs assessment? Explain.

4. Explain the process of needs assessment.

5. Wherein does the process of needs assessment relate to the explanation of system analysis that is given in chapter 1 of this text?

6. By what process may identified needs be documented?

7. What measures can be used for documenting the degree to which some problem exists in a desired product?

8. Relate the use of external appraisal in the assessment of a school program.

9. Name the four courses of possible action that may be taken once needs have been identified.

10. Discuss the importance of considering learner needs in curriculum planning.

11. List some needs of middle school students.

12. List some needs of junior high school students.

13. List some needs of senior high school students.

14. (a) Specify student data that are needed in curriculum planning.

(b) Specify the sources of these data.

15. (a) What is meant by the community of a school system?

(b) Discuss the relationships that exist between a school and its community.

16. (a) Specify community data that are needed in curriculum planning.

(b) Specify the sources of these data.

Work Sheet 4B
Interpretation of Quoted Material

Student's Name _____

Date _____

Directions:

1. Read the following carefully.

> Paying attention to the emerging needs of the young is not soft, sentimental, or sloppy education. Democracy gives first consideration to the individual, and it is during the early years that the groundwork for self-realization is laid. The questions of youth, moreover, are not inconsequential or antithetical to democratic ideals but do, in fact, reflect their essence. Democracy depends on people who sense "who they are" and, thus, can relate sensitively to others. Democracy depends on people who perceive "what this world is really like" and face it realistically instead of trying to escape. Democracy depends on people who determine "what they should do" on the basis of a consistent framework of democratic values rather than by following the crowd or listening to the loudest voice of the moment. Democracy depends on people who "take effective social action" for the accomplishment of group goals instead of depending on edict or resorting to violence. In a very real sense, therefore, the survival of our democratic way of life depends on the priority that the school gives to the emerging needs of children and youth.

> Estvan, Frank J. "Emerging Priorities for the Young." In *The Curriculum: Retrospect and Prospect, 70th Yearbook of the National Society for the Study of Education, Part I,* edited by Robert M. McClure. Chicago: University of Chicago Press, 1971, p. 259. (The above quotation is taken from this reference.)

2. You will remember from chapter 4 in your text that the third step in needs assessment suggested by the systems approach is the establishment of priorities to deal with hypothesized trouble spots. In light of the quoted material above, what priority do you reason should be given to the emerging needs of students in middle schools, junior high schools, and senior high schools? Explain. What implications do you see for curriculum planning in middle schools, junior high schools, and senior high schools? You may wish to read the chapter from which the above-quoted material is taken. If so, refer to the bibliographical notation that is given above. Record your responses to the above questions in the space that is provided below.

Work Sheet 4C
Teacher and Parent Poll

Student's Name _____
Date _____

Directions:
1. As a sequential step to Work Sheet 4B, poll 6 teachers of a middle school, junior high school, or senior high school. In your poll, learn the priority that they give to the emerging needs of children and youth for preserving the democratic way of life. In addition, in your poll, learn other student needs that the teachers identify, and the priorities that the teachers give to these other needs.
2. Poll 6 parents of the same school in which you have polled teachers. In your poll, learn the priority that they give to the emerging needs of children and youth for preserving the democratic way of life. In addition, in your poll, learn other student needs that the parents identify, and the priorities that the parents give to these other needs.
3. Compare teacher priorities with parent priorities that you have attained. Record your findings below.

Work Sheet 4D
Basic Educational Needs Assessment Model

Student's Name _____

Date _____

Directions:

1. Study the following model. It illustrates the following concept: a basic educational needs assessment model is one that compares what is desired, or should be, with what now exists, or is being accomplished. The discrepancy between these two states of affairs can be considered as the existing educational needs.

```
┌─────────────────────────────────────────────────┐
│ Desired Educational Goals                         │
└─────────────────────────────────────────────────┘

   ┌──────────────────────────────┐
   │ Present Accomplishments       │
   └──────────────────────────────┘

                          Educational Needs
```

2. Refer to:
   Lee, Walter S. "The Assessment, Analysis and Monitoring of Educational Needs." *Educational Technology* 13 (April 1973): 28–32. (The above-given statements and model are taken from this reference.)
3. Obtain pertinent data from a middle school, junior high school, or senior high school, and interpret their meaning in light of the model above. Record your interpretation below.

Work Sheet 4E
Phases of the Needs Assessment Process

Student's Name _____

Date _____

Directions:
1. The following three models represent three phases of the needs assessment process. Refer to:
    Lee, Walter S. "The Assessment, Analysis and Monitoring of Educational Needs." *Educational Technology* 13 (April 1973): 28–32. (The following three models are taken from this reference.)
    Study the models carefully.
2. Read the preceding reference carefully. Below each model, record your understanding of it.

Needs-Assessment Model: Phase I

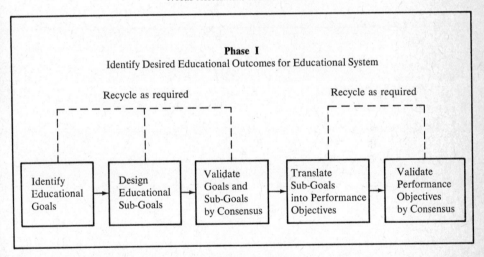

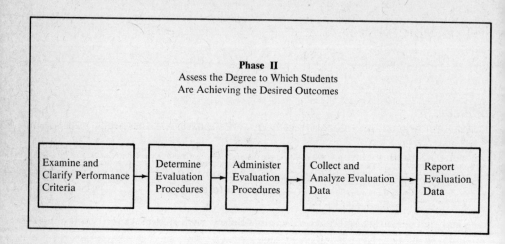

Phase II
Assess the Degree to Which Students
Are Achieving the Desired Outcomes

Examine and Clarify Performance Criteria → Determine Evaluation Procedures → Administer Evaluation Procedures → Collect and Analyze Evaluation Data → Report Evaluation Data

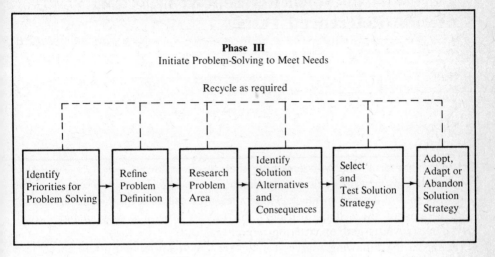

Phase III
Initiate Problem-Solving to Meet Needs

Recycle as required

| Identify Priorities for Problem Solving | Refine Problem Definition | Research Problem Area | Identify Solution Alternatives and Consequences | Select and Test Solution Strategy | Adopt, Adapt or Abandon Solution Strategy |

Work Sheet 4F
Illustrations of Norm-Referenced Tests and Criterion-Referenced Tests

Student's Name _____

Date _____

Directions:
1. From chapter 4, you will remember that:
   A variety of measures exist for documenting the degree to which some problem exists in the desired product. These measures are often found in the testing programs of the school districts. The testing programs may include norm-referenced tests and/or criterion-referenced tests.
2. Refer to the following sources for further discussion of norm-referenced tests and criterion-referenced tests:
   a. Glaser, Robert. "Instructional Technology and the Measurement of Learning Outcomes." *American Psychologist* 18 (August 1963): 519–21.
   b. Popham, James W. *Criterion Referenced Measurement.* Englewood Cliffs, N.J.: Educational Technology Publications, 1971.
3. From the library—or some school—obtain an example of a norm-referenced test and a criterion-referenced test. In the space provided below, record your learnings from an examination of these tests and a study of the sources that are given above.

Work Sheet 4G
Diversity of Adolescents as to Values

Student's Name _____

Date _____

Directions:

1. In the following schema, Robert Havighurst has interestingly represented the diversity of adolescents as to values.

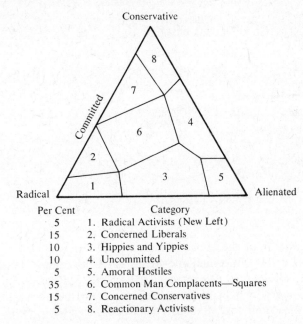

Per Cent	Category
5	1. Radical Activists (New Left)
15	2. Concerned Liberals
10	3. Hippies and Yippies
10	4. Uncommitted
5	5. Amoral Hostiles
35	6. Common Man Complacents—Squares
15	7. Concerned Conservatives
5	8. Reactionary Activists

SOURCE: From *Issues in American Education: Commentary on the Current Scene* edited by Arthur M. Kroll, p. 270. Copyright © 1970 by Oxford University Press, Inc., New York; cited in Chris A. De Young and Richard Wynn, *American Education* (New York: McGraw-Hill, 1972), p. 270. Reprinted by permission.

2. Refer to:

De Young, Chris A., and Wynn, Richard. *American Education.* New York: McGraw-Hill, 1972, pp. 268–71.

3. Draw implications for curriculum planning from the schema and the reference that are given above. Record the implications in the space below.

Work Sheet 4H
Sources of Curriculum Information

Student's Name _____

Date _____

Directions:

1. Study the following model.

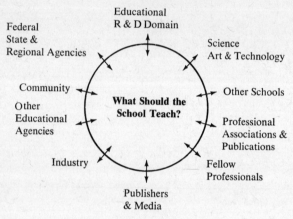

Sources of Curriculum Information

2. Refer to the source of the above model:

    Banathy, B. H. "Information Systems for Curriculum Planning." *Educational Technology* 10 (November 1970): 25–28. Reprinted by permission.

3. Discuss this model in light of your learnings from the above-given reference and chapter 4 in your text. Record your discussion below.

Work Sheet 4I
Sources of Achievement Information

Student's Name _____

Date _____

Directions:

1. Study the following model.

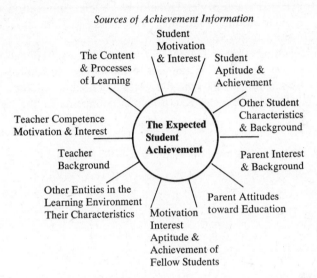

Sources of Achievement Information

2. Refer to the source of the above model:

   Banathy, B. H. "Information Systems for Curriculum Planning." *Educational Technology* 10 (November 1970): 25–28. Reprinted by permission.
3. Discuss the model in light of your learnings from the above-given reference and chapter 4 in your text. Record your discussion below.

Work Sheet 4J
Society and Its Characteristics

Student's Name _____

Date _____

Directions:

1. Refer to:

    Lave, Roy E., Jr., and Kyle, Donald W. "'The Application of Systems Analysis to Educational Planning." *Comparative Education Review* 12 (February 1968): 39–56.

2. A model representing the conceptual structure for the education-planning process is given on page 45 of the above-mentioned periodical. Study the model. What implications can you draw for curriculum planning from the model and the above reference? Record your comments in the space that is provided below.

Work Sheet 4K
Student and Community Data

Student's Name _____

Date _____

Directions:
1. Refer to chapter 4 in the text for student and community data that are needed to plan improvements in the curriculum and instructional program. Refer to chapter 4, also, for the sources of these data.
2. Collect some of the recommended data regarding the students and/or the community of a middle school, junior high school, or senior high school.
3. Draw implications from the data for the curriculum and instructional program. Record your comments in the space provided below.

Work Sheet 4L
Extension of Learning

Student's Name _____

Date _____

Directions:
1. Choose one of the following readings—or one of the readings at the end of chapter 4—to extend the learnings that you have attained from the chapter.
2. Read critically.
3. Synthesize your learnings for class dialogue.
4. Space is provided at the end of this work sheet for notes that you may want to make.

Readings:
1. Dreeben, Robert. "The Contribution of Schooling to the Learning of Norms." *Harvard Educational Review* 37 (Spring 1967): 211–37.
2. Taba, Hilda. *Curriculum Development: Theory and Practice.* New York: Harcourt Brace Jovanovich, 1962.
3. Thoresen, Carl E., ed. *Behavior Modification in Education, 72nd Yearbook of the National Society for the Study of Education, Part I.* Chicago: University of Chicago Press, 1973.

5

Formulation of the
School Philosophy
and Objectives

As stated in the preceding chapter, in this book, curriculum and instructional improvement is viewed in terms of a systems approach including four major stages—the first of which assesses program relevance. The assessment of program relevance necessitates an examination of the curriculum and instructional program in light of the needs, interests, and abilities of the students, the needs and demands of the school community, and the school philosophy and objectives.

The preceding chapter initiates explication of stage one, listed above. The chapter focuses on input into the curriculum and instructional system—specifically, on the exploration of the needs, interests, and abilities of the students, and the needs and demands of the community. The present chapter focuses on the assessment of program relevance in light of the school philosophy and objectives, thus completing discussion of stage one.

Systems are designed to achieve objectives. As noted in the previous chapters, it is important to develop a clear understanding of the needs that the system ought to meet, and some understanding of current system performance. It should follow, logically, that when current system performance is analyzed in terms of the aforementioned needs, system modification will probably be required. System modification occurs within the context of objectives. Goal-seeking is a property of systems, and this chapter offers the reader an exploration of the formulation of system philosophy and objectives. Later chapters will develop the systems concept of goal-seeking in greater detail. As noted earlier, feedback must be collected to insure that the specified objectives have, indeed, been achieved. Subsequent chapters will explore this concept.

Derivation of Objectives

Objectives are here considered in a systems context. In figure 7, chapter 1, and figure 8, chapter 2, a model was presented that symbolizes the components in a system for curriculum and instructional improvement. The model indicates that the philosophy and objectives are derived from the needs, interests, and abilities of the students—and the needs and demands of the community. The preceding chapter expounds pertinent aspects of these sources. A continuous compromise exists between the desired and the possible. In a situation where ultimate achievement is either impossible or improbable, the only possibility is to define the degree of achievement that will be acceptable. A second condition abides. This is to say that the needs, interests, and abilities of the students, and the needs and demands of the community, do not remain constant. As conditions change, the objectives need to be redefined. The best that is hoped for is that a state of equilibrium is maintained between the environment and the system.

The objectives for the curriculum are derived subsequent to the defining of the needs, interests, and abilities of the students and the needs and demands of the community (external variables); and the formulation of the philosophy. At the curriculum and instructional system level, the objectives are stated in general terms. These overall objectives are redefined and made more specific as each succeeding smaller component of the system is designed. It must be cautioned, however, that as the general objectives are redefined and made more specific, each specific objective must be derived from—and must contribute to the accomplishment of—the general objectives.

Certain additional incidents regarding philosophy and objectives are reflected in the model of figures 7 and 8. The following are noted. Philosophy and objectives (internal variables) determine the other internal variables—curriculum design, methods, materials, evaluation—and, in turn, are affected by these internal variables. External variables (such as state curriculum regulations, accreditation requirements, teacher certification requirements, special interest groups, changes in economy, and so forth) also affect the philosophy and objectives. The philosophy and objectives should determine content selection. Learning experiences are intended to achieve objectives; and evaluation, given in terms of goals or objectives, assesses whether the goals or objectives have been attained.

Generality and Specificity of Objectives

The school, as a system, "is established by the society to satisfy a great variety of educational needs." [1] The school, however, is usually not able to address itself to all of the emerging needs because it has limited resources and because it operates under a variety of constraints that are imposed on it by society or the community. Therefore, the school and the community should determine which of the needs are critical, and judge the probability that these particular needs can be satisfied. By this clarification of educational needs, educational requirements of the school are specified. From these educational requirements, school objectives are formulated.

The formulation of school objectives should be directed by certain guidelines. First, the greater the specificity of the objectives, the more accurately they can be measured. Second, objectives that are clear will, among other things, possibly help to create a more favorable view of the school by the community and, consequently, tend to gain support of the school by the community. Furthermore, the clearer the objectives, the more fully will the school envision its responsibility. The clearer the objectives, the easier it is to assess those learning activities that should aid in the attainment of the objectives and those activities that probably would not.

Objectives are viewed from a variety of vantage points—e.g., society, a school system, a school, an individual classroom. As such, they represent a broad spectrum of expectations from the general to the specific. To illustrate, society in the United States would expect school objectives to include the preservation of democracy. A particular school system would incorporate this objective and add specificity to fostering democratic citizenship in the locale of the school district. In turn, a particular school would incorporate the aforementioned objectives, adding the specificity of engendering good citizens in that particular school and its community. Last, students in the classroom would learn the responsibilities of good citizens in a democratic society. Specific expectations in a lesson may be referred to as *behavioral objectives* (to be explained in subsequent paragraphs).

Generality and specificity in objectives may be further explained. The objectives of a school constitute general statements of goals that should be used as guides for the development of the school curriculum. School objectives should be analyzed and, in a traditional setting, allocated among departments. Departmental objectives should be allocated among courses, and course objectives should be allocated among the lessons of that course, as lesson goals or aims. Learning activities should be designed to attain these aims. Figure 13 illustrates the network of objectives that has just been explained.

The aims of the lessons contained in a particular course, when attained and

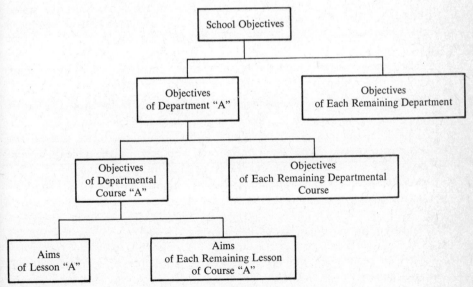

FIGURE 13. Model: Network of Objectives in a School

viewed compositely, signify that the course objectives themselves have been attained; and, ultimately, when the objectives of all courses have been attained, the objectives of the school have been attained. A particular learning activity can be justified only to the extent that it helps in the attainment of a specific aim or objective.

Objectives and Aims

The terms *objectives* and *aims* need to be clarified. Objectives may be defined as goals to be attained, e.g., facts to be learned, understandings or appreciations to be acquired, concepts to be applied, or behaviors, skills, and competencies to be attained. Aims are also defined as goals. Some educators specify aims as short-term goals and objectives as long-term goals. Other educators use the terms in opposite designation. Still other educators make no distinction between aims and objectives.

Some educators subdivide objectives into general objectives and specific objectives. When such a subdivision is made, general objectives are regarded as long-range, and specific objectives as short-range goals.

Behavioral and Humanistic Objectives

Abstract words, such as *appreciation, understanding,* and *knowledge,* were once sanctioned in statements of school objectives, course objectives, and lesson aims. Today, however, such abstract words are no longer sanctioned by some educators for usage in lesson aims and the objectives of the unit of learning embodying the lesson. These particular educators consider behavior to be measurable and advocate that desired accomplishments be stated in terms of changes in student behavior that can be precisely measured. Objectives so precisely written are called behavioral objectives.

A behavioral objective can more succinctly be defined as an objective stated as an activity in which a learner will engage, so that a change will be produced in the learner. Behavioral objectives have these additional aspects:

1. The condition under which the learning takes place (e.g., inquiry method, particular project plan, and so on) may or may not be included.

2. A behavioral verb (not a nonbehavioral verb) should be used. Examples of behavioral verbs are: recite, write, apply, outline, demonstrate, list, compute, classify. Examples of nonbehavioral verbs are: know, learn, master, appreciate, understand. Behavioral verbs are concrete (observable); nonbehavioral verbs are abstract (unobservable or difficult to observe).

3. The level of learning or attainment that is desired should be given—e.g., 70 percent accuracy.

The following are two examples of behavioral objectives:

1. Ability to reduce 20 improper fractions in x-number of minutes with 95 percent accuracy.

2. Ability to type 10 lines of copy in 3 minutes with 93 percent accuracy.

Behavioral objectives are considered difficult, if not impossible, to write in areas that do not deal with the concrete—e.g., appreciation of good literature.

An interest in specific (behavioral) objectives abided about a half-century ago. Then, as now, the approach was the same—an analysis of subject matter into atomistic performance objectives. Then, as now, the movement was against the discipline-centered curriculum. However, there is a difference between the two movements that have occurred a half-century apart. The spirit of the 1920s was reformist in nature. The intention was to appraise the existent curriculum. However, the spirit of the contemporary movement is not one of reappraisal. The current "assumption is that content will not be changed, only divided into minute 'behaviors.' " [2]

Certain cautions must be made. There is no end to the minute pieces into which a curriculum can be broken and, consequently, the multitude of behavioral objectives that can be written. Such a breaking down, however, hampers the student's ability to unify knowledge, synthesize learnings, and draw greater or broader meanings from learning experiences. Furthermore, the more explicitly expressed the objective, the lower the level of the learning process. The writing of behavioral objectives does call for ultraspecificity.

Certain reasons are given for "the very great trouble of developing a full inventory of performance objectives." [3] First, there has been a growing discontent with the traditional ways in which educational goals have been stated. Second, "in using the systems approach in curriculum . . . the goals or objectives for the program must be stated in terms of output specifications." [4] "In education, these performance objectives can often be stated in terms of behaviors." [5] Program revisions and selections of teaching strategies should be based on results assessed by measurable performance or behavioral objectives. Performance or behavioral objectives provide a basis for deciding which program changes or teaching strategies would be most effective.

A third reason for developing performance objectives is that they form a basis for longitudinal validation of the effectiveness of school experiences. If the behavioral attainments of an adolescent leaving school and entering the adult world are not known, there is little basis for relating the person's success in the adult world back to school experiences. Follow-up studies of high school students should be a common practice. Revisions in educational goals should be based on the findings of these follow-up studies.

A fourth reason for developing performance objectives is that they help to make it possible to associate behavior change with program costs. They help, say the advocates of performance objectives, to give more tangible evidence of student learning which should be the major, if not the only, "basis upon which cost-effectiveness analyses should be made in education." [6]

Proponents of performance objectives give the following additional major justification for them. Individualized instructional programs rely on a detailed, sequenced set of performance objectives. A step-by-step sequential measurement of a student's progress in learning must be made if each subsequent learning experience is to be tailored to the student's needs—and tied to what he or she has learned—so that the desired mastery will, hopefully, result.

Humanistic objectives appear to be defined, most frequently, in either of two ways:

1. One definition specifies humanistic objectives as those objectives that are directed to those qualities that make people human—e.g., beliefs, attitudes, and so forth. Humanistic objectives deal with the identification or clarification of values—with the development of a person as an individual, a human being.

2. A second definition identifies humanistic objectives as dealing with individualization of instruction.

Caution is given that behavioral objectives not be emphasized at the expense of humanistic objectives. The author reasons that humanistic objectives and behavioral objectives each have a place in education.

Participants in Goal and Objective Formulation

Teachers, all professional staff members of the school, the school board, students, parents, and community—i.e., everyone who is directly concerned with the process of education—should participate, in some way and at some level, in determining the goals and the objectives of the school.[7]

The formulation of the objectives of the school is a professional responsibility; however, all of the groups included in the list above should be included in the process. A system for curriculum and instructional improvement is proposed and explained in chapter 2. The formulation of objectives is a part of the process for curriculum and instructional improvement. The roles and the responsibilities of all who should participate in the process are presented and explained in chapter 3. The process of curriculum and instructional improvement includes a variety of persons in a variety of ways—e.g., curriculum and instruction council, curriculum committees, individual curriculum workers.

Procedures in curriculum and instructional improvement may span a school system or be concentrated in a particular school, a particular subject area, or other segment of organization. The satisfaction, if not the formulation or revision, of objectives is one of the concerns of these groups in curriculum and instructional improvement. The work of these groups draws on the data presented in the preceding chapter. Specifically, the formulation of objectives, if based on sound curriculum principles, involves needs assessment, and proceeds from an analysis and interpretation of data regarding the needs, interests, and abilities of the students, and the needs and demands of the community.

In the formulation of general objectives and specific objectives, attention should be given to the cognitive, affective, and psychomotor domains. These domains will be discussed later in the chapter. Suffice to say at this point that "domains are categories for classifying major goals; they do not state the purpose of the school but rather the aspects of human development for which goals have been formulated."[8]

The culminating aspect of efforts to formulate objectives for the school should be a critical examination of the goals that are selected. The adoption of objectives for a school system should involve all members of the system staff, and adoption of objectives for a particular school should involve all members of the building staff. Discussions may be held in small subgroups. Representatives of these subgroups would subsequently meet together for final approval.

In a traditional setting, school objectives are divided among the departments of the school; departmental objectives are divided among the courses taught in the particular department; the course objectives are divided among the lessons that constitute the course, or among the objectives of the units that constitute the particular course; and, subsequently, objectives of a unit are divided among the aims of the lessons that constitute the particular unit.

The proponents of behavioral objectives advise that the objectives of the instructional program should be behavioral objectives. Since an instructional program specifies the kinds of learning experiences that the teacher chooses to use with a group of students, or individual students, in attainment of the objectives, the responsibility for the formulation of the behavioral objectives should fall primarily on the teacher who guides the learning experiences. Often in practice, however, staff personnel, or a committee of teachers and staff personnel, prepare instructional guides for a subject area, a particular course, or a unit—each one with pertinent objectives. Lists of behavioral objectives are purchasable commercially. Regardless of who prepares the objectives, they are helpful to teachers only if valid for their particular instructional program.

Validation of Goals and Objectives

In order to conclude that goals and objectives defined for curriculum and instruction are valid, and that the best possible choices of goals and objectives have been made, a professional staff must have as much data as possible about both the young people to be educated and the community to be served because "a curriculum is always planned for students, and about the society that establishes and controls the schools." [9] Once these data are obtained, lists of goals and objectives can be formulated that reflect the best judgment that the "planning group can make on the basis of these data." [10] Based on the data, choices must be made as to goals and objectives to be identified for a particular group of students, or school population. The choices, of necessity, are based on the intelligence, insight, attitudes, and beliefs of those persons whose responsibility it is to make the choices.

The professional personnel who are engaged in the definition of goals and objectives should check the validity of these goals and objectives in light of the data that are available regarding the needs, interests, and abilities of the students, and the needs and demands of the community. An examination and validation of goals and objectives should, furthermore, be based on a broad, continuous program of evaluation of the entire educational program. Evaluation is discussed in chapter 8. In short, a program for curriculum and instructional improvement should consist of an ever-continuing cycle in which, sequentially, data are obtained, a philosophy is formulated, goals and objectives are defined, learning experiences are provided, instructional outcomes are evaluated in terms of the stipulated goals and objectives, data are updated and reexamined, goals and objectives are appraised in light of all factors, learning experiences are redesigned if necessary, instructional outcomes are evaluated in terms of the appraised goals and objectives, and data are updated and reexamined—as the cycle of sequential steps repeats itself.

At times it is necessary "to discard or to include certain goals or objectives because of legal requirements, court decisions, or state or local regulations." [11]

Such a condition does not invalidate the set of goals or objectives that results for a particular school system, particular school, and so on. It is understandable that a school "must operate within a legal structure which in itself is an expression of the values and social expectations of those who control it." [12] If, however, those goals that must be rejected are valid, efforts should be made to have them accepted by those who oppose them.[13] Only those goals that are substantiated by pertinent data should be included in a school program.

Philosophy and Objectives

Every educator has a philosophy of education—a set of beliefs—that guides his or her actions in carrying out responsibilities as teacher, counselor, administrator, librarian, and so forth. Every community member, like every educator, has a philosophy of education that bespeaks the type of education that he or she feels the school should offer if it is to serve the needs, interests, and abilities of the students, and the needs and demands of the community. The students themselves have a philosophy of education that includes, among other things, an enumeration of the school offerings that they consider beneficial to themselves, and those that they do not consider beneficial.

Procedure for Formulation or Revision of the School Philosophy. Prior to the development of a school philosophy, the professional staff should study (1) the qualities that are descriptive of the student body; (2) the definitive needs of the student body, so that its members will become active participants in—and contributors to—community life; (3) the changes that seem to be occurring in the community in regard to economics, nature of society, and so on; and (4) any guiding principle in educational psychology that may be useful. All guides that have ever been offered by educators and/or committees and are known to any member of the professional staff should be kept in mind. Additional ones may be attained by reading professional books and periodicals. Guides that have been offered by various committees and commissions will be discussed later in this chapter.

The resultant school philosophy should reflect the efforts of the professional staff of the school, the school board, the citizens of the community, and the students. These individual groups can develop (their respective philosophy of education) separate from—or in consultation with—each other, or they can work as a single group to produce only one philosophy. If they work as separate groups, differences would need to be reconciled through an exchange of committee members or series of written statements, so that a philosophy would result that would be acceptable to each group. Regardless of the committee structure, the philosophy should not only address itself to the expressed needs and interests of the students, and the needs and demands of the community, but it should also provide ideals toward which efforts can be pointed.

Since each educator has his or her own preconceived ideas regarding education, the members of a professional staff (if they hold ideas that are widely divergent) will encounter difficulty reaching adequate agreement. In such a case, purposefully designed faculty meetings, committee meetings, workshops, or staff development programs can be used to expedite, hopefully, some agreement. On the other hand, in cases where the professional staff is very much one-minded, sessions can be planned for jolting thinking—providing other perspectives. Once the professional staff is thus readied for collaboration of efforts, procedures can be initiated for formulating or revising the school philosophy in reflection of a consensus held by the group.

Given the opportunity to participate in the formulation or revision of a school philosophy, the citizens of the community should represent the social, economic, and intellectual aspects of the community. Also, if possible, the various types of homes from which students come should be represented. Groups such as citizens' committees and advisory committees are helpful only to the extent that they represent adequately the various facets of the community. Citizens should serve on school committees designated for formulating or revising the school philosophy. Regardless of procedure, the resulting philosophy should be acceptable both to the citizens and to the school staff. It is expected, of course, that although the staff is in agreement on a philosophy, it will be flexible enough to incorporate citizen beliefs.

Since it is the students who are most affected by the philosophy of a school, it is justifiable that they be allowed to play a role in the development of that philosophy. Participation can be provided by (1) student placement on subcommittees of school staff committees; (2) placement on a student committee working under the leadership of a teacher, the principal, and so on; (3) membership on citizens' committees; or (4) student government membership.

Ultimately, it is the school board that must accept (or not accept) the philosophy developed by the professional staff, community, and students. Therefore, representatives from the board should also be involved from the beginning. If the board considers the philosophy unacceptable, it should give reasons to support its decision. In such a case, the board might very well evaluate its own philosophy—considering whether it should be revised and brought in closer agreement to that of the staff, community, and students.

Philosophies of Education.   Once the school philosophy has been formulated (or the current philosophy revised), it would broaden the perspective of the professional staff if time would be taken to identify the philosophy of education (and, thus, the purpose of education) that is reflected in the school philosophy.

Philosophies of education vary and conflict. Every philosophy has both proponents and opponents. Some of the major philosophies of education, and the views of proponents and opponents, follow.

1. Existentialists view the purpose of education to be that of enabling the student to discover his or her own morality. The proponents of existentialism feel that schools should not indoctrinate students with commonly accepted moral values, but, rather, should encourage the self-determination of values. However, the opponents of existentialism believe that self-determination of values will, among other things, lead to lawlessness and denial of authority.

2. The proponents of life adjustment say that learning should be related to life—that the curriculum (planned for students who do not plan to go to college) should prepare these students for living useful lives, coping with

everyday problems, and being good American citizens. The opponents of this purpose of education, however, do not consider such a purpose of education to be academically respectable, and view life adjustment school activities as unjustifiable.

3. The proponents of personal psychological development advocate that education should help students to understand, and to accept, themselves. In such a philosophy of education, lessons, exercises, and activities have meaning to the extent that they help the student to find himself or herself—and, through such discovery, to help others in their search of self. Critics of the personal psychological development philosophy say that students should search for themselves. However, once they think that they have found themselves, they should look further, and keep looking to see if they find a different self as they progress through life.

4. The advocates of basic education view the purpose of education to be the teaching of fundamentals. Furthermore, they maintain that real intellectual discipline can be acquired in no other way. Opponents call attention to the emphasis on drill and memorization, and to emphasis on the training of the mind (a concept that has been discredited by educational psychologists).

5. The proponents of a Christian education propose that education should help a student to live a life patterned on the life and teachings of Jesus Christ. They advocate that education should encompass not only the physical, intellectual, and social development of students, but also, if not more importantly, the spiritual. Critics, on the other hand, claim that religious instruction is not the responsibility of the school, but the church.

6. The experimentalists stress learning by doing; they view education as not a preparation for future living, but the process of living. Critics claim that such an education loses sight of subject matter and high standards of achievement.

7. Nationalists view the purpose of education to be the assurance of national survival. Nationalists propose that education must be conducted in such a way as to contribute to the strength of the nation.

It is to be noted that an analysis of the various philosophies shows them to be not as incompatible as they might at first appear to be. Though the emphasis of each philosophy differs, the following are inherent in all: (1) students need an understanding of the history and development of our civilization: of our cultural heritage, and (2) programs based on principles of growth and development should provide for the total growth and development of the individual student.

On the other hand, the basic difference that appears to exist among the philosophies is one wherein society is seen to be best improved by students studying and learning the values, successes, and failures of the past and applying these to present problems and situations—wherein society is seen to be best improved by students studying directly the problems and situations of their own environments.

Some of the controversy in education results from differences in philosophical ideas. Such differences bring about differences in opinion as to what the objectives of a school should be, and the ways in which these objectives should be attained. Two schools of thought emerge when the major differences and consensus among philosophies of education are considered. The two schools of thought are traditionalism (or essentialism) and progressivism. Some of the leaders who are associated with traditionalism are as follows: William C. Bagley, Thomas H. Briggs, Henry C. Morrison, Franklin Bobbitt, Isaac L. Kandel, Arthur Bestor, Robert M. Hutchins, and Hyman G. Rickover. In the minds of most educators, the following are associated with progressivism: John Dewey, Boyd Bode, William H. Kilpatrick, Edward L. Thorndike, Harold Rugg, George Counts, William Van Til, Alice Miel, Lindley J. Stiles, Nelson Bossing, and Harold Alberty.

Differences exist between the tenets of the traditionalists (essentialists) and the tenets of the progressivists. The traditionalists' emphasis in education is on the future—on the preparation of students for adult living. Traditionalists believe that knowledge of one's cultural heritage is a reliable guide for understanding society, its needs, and its problems. However, progressivists insist on education for the present—on preparing students to participate in solving present problems of society.

Traditionalists maintain a superiority for liberal arts subjects; however, progressivists reason that it is not the subject matter, but the way that subject matter is used that makes a difference. Traditionalists would engender varied curriculums, for developing leaders with special talents; but progressivists would engender varied curriculums, so that individual students could grow to their full potential. Traditionalists favor a curriculum that is characterized by imposed discipline, indoctrinated beliefs, and authoritarianism; but progressivists favor a curriculum that is characterized by self-discipline, individual values, creative learning, and practices in democratic living.

It is not to be concluded that traditionalists and progressivists are completely incompatible. For example, likenesses appear in their support of the need for the cultivation of the intellect, the development of critical thinking, and the preparation of students for all aspects of living.

In consideration of the above-listed philosophies of education, most professional staff members would identify their particular school philosophy to be reflective of more than one of the above philosophies. Consequently, they could typify their school philosophy to be eclectic. In further consideration, however, it would be found that, though school philosophies are most often eclectic, the emphasis placed on a particular philosophy differs from school to school.

Formulation or Revision of Objectives. The educational program of a school is built on the school philosophy (formulated or revised as explained in preceding paragraphs), and accepted by the school board. Objectives of the school are an outgrowth of the school philosophy. They specify concretely the purposes of the school, and the beliefs of the framers of the philosophy. The curriculum is intended to carry out these objectives. Methodology, suited to the curriculum, implements the curriculum. The objectives of the school should be used to evaluate the curriculum. To the extent that the objectives have not been attained, there is a need for revision of the curriculum (if, indeed, the objectives are justified), revision of the methods used for the attainment of the objectives, or revision of the objectives themselves if they are inadequate or unrealistic.

The philosophy and objectives of a school bespeak the curriculum, methodology, and organization of that particular school. Furthermore, they indicate the demands that are made of the professional staff for answering the needs, interests, and abilities of the students, and the needs and demands of the community. The philosophy and objectives, also, reflect the understanding of these demands by the professional staff, and the means by which they can best be met. For example, if the philosophy and objectives indicate that the curriculum should provide opportunities for each student to develop to his or her potential, the curriculum, materials, methodology, and organization of the school should be expected to provide individualized opportunities for students to learn and to progress at their own rates. If, on the other hand, a traditional concept is reflected and intended to serve only college-bound students, provisions should be expected to be the traditional classroom, wherein attention is centered on the teacher whose major purpose is seen to be that of dispensing a body of knowledge in a particular subject area.

Formal Statements by Committees, Commissions, and Study Groups

It behooves professional staff members to be aware of the statements of committees, commissions, and study groups (over the years) regarding the objectives of secondary schools. Professional staff members, engaged in curriculum and instructional improvement, should take such statements, study them, and determine whether the objectives as stated, or modified, might reflect the objectives of their particular school. In cases where such statments cannot be adopted, or modified and adopted, a study of them should aid school groups to crystallize their own statements.

It is interesting to note that—over the years—committees, commissions, and study groups have especially addressed themselves to school objectives on memorable happenings in the nation's schools, society, and so on. An enumeration of some of these groups and the objectives that they have recommended follows.

1. In 1918 the Commission on the Reorganization of Secondary Education, appointed by the National Education Association, issued what is perhaps the most historic statement regarding objectives that had been made to that time. The statement (important in the transformation of the American high school from a specialized academic institution into a comprehensive school designed for all American youth) has become known as the Seven Cardinal Principles of Education.[14] Briefly, the principles are (a) health, (b) command of fundamental processes, (c) vocational efficiency, (d) worthy home membership, (e) civic participation, (f) worthy use of leisure time, and (g) ethical character.

2. In 1944 (during World War II), the Educational Policies Commission (which was affiliated with NEA, and is now defunct) published *Education for All American Youth,* in which it presented recommended policies for secondary education. A booklet, entitled *Planning for American Youth,* was prepared from the above-mentioned book. The booklet lists these ten imperative needs

of youth: (a) All youth need to develop salable skills. (b) All youth need to develop and maintain good health and physical fitness. (c) All youth need to understand the rights and duties of the citizens of a democratic society. (d) All youth need to understand the importance of the family for the individual and society. (e) All youth need to know how to purchase and use goods and services intelligently. (f) All youth need to understand the influence of science on human life. (g) All youth need an appreciation of literature, art, music, and nature. (h) All youth need to be able to use their leisure time well and to budget it wisely. (i) All youth need to develop respect for other persons. (j) All youth need to grow in their ability to think rationally.[15]

3. In 1958 (on the heels of the launching of Sputnik by the Russians), the American Association of School Administrators Yearbook Commission cited the following objectives of major importance for secondary schools: (a) maximum development of all the mental, moral, emotional, and physical powers of the individual student and (b) maximum development of the ability and desire of individuals to be good American citizens.[16]

4. In 1962 Vernon Anderson and William Gruhn expressed the functions of the secondary school in terms of the problems of adolescents.[17] Some of the problems are (a) problem of making friends and group contacts, (b) problem of being accepted by and gaining the approval of one's peers, (c) problem of making adjustments to the family, (d) problem of planning for marriage and family responsibilities, (e) problem of formulating values acceptable to one's own group, to parents, and to the culture mores, (f) problem of maintaining a sense of personal achievement, (g) problem of finding something to do with leisure time and places to go with other youth, (h) problem of being accepted by the community, (i) problem of understanding and doing something about world problems, (j) problem of getting along with people, (k) problem of choosing a vocation and getting a job, (l) problem of planning what to do with regard to further education.

5. In 1966 (at a time of great social change in the nation when, for example, people were moving out of cities), the American Association of School Administrators specified these nine imperatives for American education: (a) to make urban life rewarding and satisfying, (b) to prepare people for the world of work, (c) to discover and nurture creative talent, (d) to strengthen the moral fabric of society, (e) to deal constructively with psychological tension, (f) to keep democracy working, (g) to make the best use of leisure time, (h) to make intelligent use of natural resources, (i) to work with other people of the world for human betterment.

6. At a time when the world is undergoing rapid change, the following objectives have been established for promoting quality education in elementary and secondary schools in Pennsylvania:

Quality education should help every child: (a) acquire the greatest possible understanding of himself and an appreciation of his worthiness as a member of society; (b) acquire understanding and appreciation of persons belonging to social, cultural, and ethnic groups different from his own; (c) acquire to the fullest extent possible for him, mastery of the basic skills in the use of words and numbers: (d) acquire a positive attitude toward the learning process; (e) acquire the habits and attitudes associated with responsible citizenship; (f) acquire health habits and an understanding of the conditions necessary for the maintaining of physical and emotional well-being; (g) find opportunity and encouragement to be creative in one or more fields of endeavor; (h) understand the opportunities open to him for preparing himself for a productive life and should enable him to take full advantage of these opportunities; (i) understand and appreciate as much as he can of human achievement in the natural sciences, the social sciences, the humanities, and the arts; (j) prepare for a world of rapid change and unforeseeable demands in which continuing education throughout his adult life should be normal expectation.[18]

Today the objectives of education are no longer viewed (as they once were) to be the transmittal of a body of knowledge for survival. Instead, in this age of knowledge explosion, some educators view the objectives of schools to be the facilitation of self-learning, the process of producing self-learners, who will constantly learn, and change, as it is deemed necessary and justifiable under given circumstances.

At the middle school age (i.e., ages 11 to 14), objectives should be centered about the following areas, and be addressed to the turmoil, uncertainties, and frustrations of students of those particular ages: (1) personal problems associated with self-identification, handicaps, illness, and physical growth; (2) social contacts with peers and adults; (3) family relationships—getting along with parents and siblings; (4) living conditions—dwellings, environment and their effects on the youngster; (5) educational status and plans for the future; (6) work and vocational plans; (7) leisure time and recreational activities.[19]

On the other hand, objectives at the junior high school level are implicit in the following educational functions that are identified for the junior high school:

(1) meeting unique needs and individual differences of early adolescence; (2) developing basic learning skills; (3) preparing to live in a democracy [incorporating] principles of conduct of responsible citizenship, preparation for family living, appreciation of moral and ethical principles, conservation of natural resources, participation in our economic system; (4) providing for personal interests and creative experiences; (5) developing mental and physical fitness; (6) providing for guidance-counseling; (7) developing articulation between school units; (8) providing integration in teaching and learning.[20]

Domains

Developing behavior is based, in part, on the curriculum. The following words express it well:

What the individual is at any time and what he finally becomes can be most accurately described by his behavior. The basic function of the school is to aid the individual in his progress toward maturity and independence, toward becoming a self-sufficient, fully functioning individual. The becoming is never finished, for the progress of the individual does not end with formal schooling but is continuous throughout life. At any time, the level attained will be indicated by his behavior pattern.[21]

A committee of college and university examiners has expressed the view "that educational objectives stated in behavioral form have their counterparts in the behavior of individuals. Such behavior can be observed and described, and these descriptive statements can be classified." [22] Various classifications of educational objectives have been proposed.

Cognitive Domain. Bloom (working with others) has studied cognitive processes for the purpose of assessing learning outcomes, and has classified the cognitive processes in a hierarchial order from simple to complex, thus: (1) knowledge, (2) comprehension, (3) application, (4) analysis, (5) synthesis, (6) evaluation.[23] These cognitive processes constitute the cognitive domain. Domains can be defined as "categories for classifying major goals; they do not state the purposes of the school but rather the aspects of human development for which goals have been formulated." [24]

The above-listed hierarchy is also referred to as a taxonomy; however, as Bloom (together with his coworkers) indicates, it cannot be truly considered such in a scientific way because (1) the determination of the levels has been done somewhat arbitrarily and (2) the approach that has been used is just one of several approaches that could have been used for identifying cognitive categories.

It is to be noted that although the taxonomy lists cognitive processes in a hierarchial order, there is doubt that the processes actually follow in this order in all learning situations. Nevertheless, the taxonomy should be suggestive to teachers for formulating learning situations of a wider variety of activities. Though it is a frequent occurrence for learning activities to place at the lower levels of cognitive learning, this need not always be so.

Affective Domain. Bloom (with coworkers) has also developed a system for classifying affective processes of learning. These affective processes—e.g., attitudes, beliefs, appreciations, interests, values—constitute the affective domain. Some educators view cognitive and affective processes as two separate domains. Other educators view them as inseparable. Bloom and his fellow workers see a very complex relationship between the cognitive and affective domains, maintaining that each cognitive learning situation has an affective counterpart, and each affective situation, a cognitive counterpart.

One must guard against the questionable assumption that a student learns only the particular thing that may have been set up for him or her. A student acquires certain unanticipated collateral learnings, also. For example, a student may attain such collateral learnings as attitudes toward what it is that he or she has learned, and attitudes toward learning itself. Herein lies a caution against programmed instruction and narrowly specified behavioral objectives: because of their specificity, they will lessen the possibility for collateral learning.

Psychomotor Domain. Bloom has given study, also, to psychomotor processes. The psychomotor domain is concerned with muscular activities—i.e., the movements of the body, limbs, or other parts of the body (fingers) that are necessary for a given action.

Psychomotor processes may be categorized as to lower level psychomotor processes and higher level psychomotor processes. The lower level psychomotor processes of reflex movements and basic fundamental movements (of locomotor, nonlocomotor, or manipulative nature) are thought to develop naturally under normal conditions. The higher processes refer to perceptual abilities, physical abilities, adaptive skill movements, and expressive or interpretative movement, and can be built upon to develop complex skills in such areas as physical education, vocational education, and business education. The lower level processes operate independently of the cognitive and affective processes, but the higher level processes do not operate independently of the cognitive and affective processes.

A distinction is made between skills and abilities, as used here. Abilities may be regarded as general traits of the individual. Abilities develop at different rates, and they are mostly the result of learning. Abilities are important to the individual as they are available in the learning of new tasks. Skill, however, pertains to the level of proficiency that is attained in a task.

A Modified Set. A set of three categories, slightly modified from the set proposed by Bloom—with some illustrations under each category—appears below.

1. Knowledges and understandings.
   a. America was discovered by Columbus in 1492.
   b. A foot is equal to twelve inches.
   c. Carbon dioxide is commonly used in fire extinguishers.
   d. Water is made of two parts hydrogen and one part oxygen.
   e. London is the capital of England.
   f. The square of a binomial is the sum of the squares of the two terms of the binomial plus or minus twice their product, the sign of the cross-product term being that of the second term of the binomial.
   g. The understanding of the meaning of democracy, the concept of evolution, orientation in a new community or school, the meaning of cartels, the significance of endocrine glands for physiological processes.

2. Attitudes, ideals, and appreciations.
   a. The ideal of being courteous, the ideal of being honest, the desire to be well thought of, the desire to be like a certain person, the desire to be respected as a good worker, the desire to be of service to one's fellow men.
   b. Interest in national public affairs, interest in flowers, interest in airplanes, interest in skillful speech, interest in improving one's social graces, interest in the advancement of the field of medicine.
   c. Liking for good literature, dislike for ostentatious dress, liking for exercise, liking for company of intelligent people, dislike for cheap literature and low-grade movies.
   d. Open-mindedness in matters of religion, appreciation of the good qualities of the Chinese, fair opinion of people of low economic status, favorable opinion of democracy, and unfavorable opinion of unfair practices.

3. Skills, habits, and behavior patterns.
   a. Ability to add, subtract, multiply, etc., ability to think logically, ability to outline or abstract printed materials, ability to translate French.
   b. Riding a bicycle, dancing, operating a machine, skating.
   c. Various habits of courtesy, various habits of neatness, various habits of healthful and sanitary living, various habits of thought (such as withholding

judgment until all, or practically all, pertinent data have been considered), various habits of personal appearance.

d. Self-control, effective communication, efficient work habits, competence in manipulation of quantities.

e. Competent family membership, general sociability, fairness and consideration in dealings.

f. Efficiency in recreational and vocational pursuits, responsibility in economic affairs.

g. Intelligence and helpfulness in civic participation, responsibility in supporting community decisions.[25]

The above list holds certain implications for curriculum and instruction. For one thing, it is illustrative of the types of expectations that a teacher should hold for his or her students. Second, it is to be noted that behavior is made up of the three general categories. It appears that "possessions in the first and second determine the competence with which the individual will be able to perform the third, that is, behavioral goals such as those listed in the third category may be achieved only through the psychological possession of the goals listed in categories one and two. The curriculum is the instrument by which the school stimulates the individual experiences necessary for the . . . [student] to gain such a possession of the contributory goals that he will, in fact, achieve the behavioral goals." [26]

Moral Dimension. Professional literature (more recent than literature regarding the cognitive, affective, and psychomotor domains) has, also, focused on a moral dimension. This moral education tends away from preaching with a hope of instilling moral virtues in children and youth. But, rather, it focuses on justice and equity—on equality of opportunity, equality of human rights, and the dignity of human beings. It focuses, furthermore, on (1) equipping the rising generation with the power to identify and to attack social inequalities and social iniquities, and (2) the developing of a rising generation to bring about a better society and social order.

Summary

Curriculum and instructional improvement, in this book, is viewed in terms of a systems approach including four major stages. The preceding chapter initiates explication of stage one and, in so doing, focuses attention on the exploration of the needs, interests, and abilities of the students, and the needs and demands of the community. The present chapter focuses on the school philosophy and objectives, thus completing discussion of stage one.

The objectives for the curriculum are derived subsequent to defining the needs, interests, and abilities of the students; the needs and demands of the community; and the formulation of the philosophy. At the curriculum and instructional system level, the objectives are stated in general terms. These overall objectives are redefined and made more specific as each succeeding smaller component of the system is designed.

Objectives may be defined as goals to be attained—e.g., facts to be learned; understandings or appreciations to be acquired; concepts to be applied; or behaviors, skills, and competencies to be attained. Behavioral objectives are defined as objectives stated as activities in which a learner will engage, so that a change(s) will be produced in the learner. Humanistic objectives are directed to those qualities that make people human—e.g., beliefs, attitudes, and so on. A second definition identifies humanistic objectives as dealing with individualization of instruction. Certain cautions are made regarding behavioral objectives. Writing behavioral objectives calls for ultraspecificity. However, the more explicitly expressed the objectives, the lower the level of the learning process.

The formulation of the objectives of the school is a professional responsibility. However, the school board, students, parents, community—everyone who is directly concerned with the process of education—should participate, in some way and at some level, in determining the goals and the objectives of the school.

The proponents of behavioral objectives advise that the objectives of the instructional program should be behavioral. Since an instructional program specifies the kinds of learning experiences that the teacher chooses to use with a group of students, or individual students, in attaining the objectives, the responsibility for the formulation of the behavioral objectives should fall primarily on the teacher who guides the learning experiences.

The professional personnel who are engaged in the definition of goals and objectives should check the validity of these goals and objectives in light of the data that are available regarding the needs, interests, and abilities of the students, and the needs and demands of the community. Furthermore, an examination and validation of goals and objectives should be based on a broad, continuous program of evaluation of the entire educational program.

The school philosophy should reflect the efforts of the professional staff of the school, the school board, the citizens of the community, and the students. The school philosophy should be examined to identify the philosophy of education (thus, the purpose of education) that is reflected in the school philosophy. The chapter presents and explains some of the major philosophies of education.

The philosophy and objectives of a school bespeak the curriculum, methodology, and organization of that particular school. Furthermore, they indicate the demands that are made of the professional staff for answering the needs, interests, and abilities of the students, and the needs and demands of the community.

Over the years committees, commissions, and study groups have addressed themselves to stating objectives on memorable happenings in the nation's schools, society, and so forth. The chapter elaborates on some of these committees, commissions, and study groups, and the objectives that they have recommended for secondary schools.

In the formulation of general objectives and specific objectives, attention should be given to the cognitive, affective, and psychomotor domains. Bloom (working with others) has studied cognitive processes for the purpose of assessing learning outcomes, and has classified the cognitive processes in a hierarchial order from simple to complex: (1) knowledge, (2) comprehension, (3) application, (4) analysis, (5) synthesis, and (6) evaluation. Bloom (with coworkers) has also developed a system for classifying affective processes of learning. These processes —e.g., attitudes, beliefs, appreciations, interests, and values—constitute the affective domain. Bloom has given study, also, to psychomotor processes, which constitute the psychomotor domain. This domain is concerned with muscular activities

—with the movements of the body, limbs, or other parts of the body (fingers) that are necessary for a given action.

Professional literature (more recent than literature regarding the cognitive, affective, and psychomotor domains) has, also, presented a moral dimension. It focuses on justice and equity.

NOTES

1. Bela H. Banathy, *Developing a Systems View of Education* (Belmont, Calif.: Fearon Publishers, 1973), p. 26. Reprinted by permission.

2. Daniel Tanner and Laurel N. Tanner, *Curriculum Development: Theory into Practice* (New York: Macmillan Co., 1975), p. 292. Reprinted by permission.

3. David S. Bushnell, "A Systems Approach to Curriculum Change in Secondary Education," *Educational Technology* 10 (May 1970): 47. Reprinted by permission.

4. Ibid.

5. Ibid.

6. Ibid.

7. J. Galen Saylor and William M. Alexander, *Planning Curriculum for Schools* (New York: Holt, Rinehart and Winston, 1974), p. 149. Reprinted by permission.

8. Ibid., p. 148.

9. Ibid., p. 161.

10. Ibid.

11. Ibid.

12. Ibid.

13. Ibid.

14. From the book, *The Educator's Encyclopedia,* pp. 35–36, by Edward W. Smith, Stanley W. Krouse, Jr., and Mark Atkinson. Copyright © 1961 by Prentice-Hall, Inc. Published by Prentice-Hall, Inc., Englewood Cliffs, New Jersey.

15. National Association of Secondary School Principals, *Planning for American Youth* (Reston, Va.: National Association of Secondary School Principals, 1944), p. 10.

16. Vernon E. Anderson and William T. Gruhn—*Principles and Practices of Secondary Education,* Second Edition, pp. 96–100. Copyright © 1962 The Ronald Press Company, New York.

17. Vernon E. Anderson and William T. Gruhn, *Principles and Practices of Secondary Education,* 2nd ed. (New York: Ronald Press, 1962), pp. 96–100. Reprinted by permission.

18. "Ten Goals of Quality Education," *Pennsylvania Education* 119 (September-October 1970): 19. Reprinted by permission.

19. Joseph C. DeVita, Philip Pumerantz, and Leighton B. Wilklow, *The Effective Middle School* (West Nyack: Parker Publishing Co., 1970), p. 91.

20. Alvin W. Howard and George C. Stoumbis, *The Junior High and Middle School: Issues and Practices* (Scranton, Pa.: Intext Educational Publishers, 1970), pp. 23–24. Reprinted by permission.

21. *The High School Curriculum,* Third Edition, pp. 30–31, edited by Harl R. Douglass. Copyright © 1964 The Ronald Press Company, New York.

22. Benjamin S. Bloom, ed., *Taxonomy of Educational Objectives* (New York: Longmans, Green and Co., 1956), p. 5; cited in Douglass, *The High School Curriculum,* p. 31. Reprinted by permission.

23. Benjamin S. Bloom, J. Thomas Hastings, and George F. Madaus, *Handbook on Formative and Summative Evaluation of Student Learning* (New York: McGraw-Hill, 1971), pp. 271–73. Reprinted by permission.

24. Saylor and Alexander, *Planning Curriculum,* p. 148. Reprinted by permission.

25. Douglass, *The High School Curriculum,* pp. 31–32. Reprinted by permission.

26. Ibid., p. 32.

Related Readings

Banathy, Bela H. *Developing a Systems View of Education.* Belmont, Calif.: Fearon Publishers, 1973.

Bloom, Benjamin S., ed. *Taxonomy of Educational Objectives.* New York: Longmans, Green and Co., 1956.

Bloom, Benjamin S.; Hastings, J. Thomas; and Madaus, George F. *Handbook on Formative and Summative Evaluation of Student Learning.* New York: McGraw-Hill, 1971.

Bushnell, David S. "A Suggested Guide for Developing a Systems Approach to Curriculum Improvement." *Education* 90 (April 1970): 351–62.

_____. "A Systems Approach to Curriculum Change in Secondary Education." *Educational Technology* 10 (May 1970): 46–48.

Butler, Donald J. *Four Philosophies and Their Practice in Education and Religion.* New York: Harper and Row, 1968.

DeVita, Joseph C.; Pumerantz, Philip; and Wilklow, Leighton B. *The Effective Middle School.* West Nyack: Parker Publishing Co., 1970.

Ellis, D. O., and Ludwig, F. J. *Systems Philosophy: An Introduction.* Englewood Cliffs, N.J.: Prentice-Hall, 1962.

Feyereisen, K. V.; Fiorino, A. J.; and Nowak, A. T. *Supervision and Curriculum Renewal: A Systems Approach.* New York: Appleton-Century-Crofts, 1970.

Harrow, Anita J. *A Taxonomy of the Psychomotor Domain.* New York: David McKay Co., 1972.

Howard, Alvin W., and Stoumbis, George C. *The Junior High and Middle School: Issues and Practices.* Scranton, Pa.: Intext Educational Publishers, 1970.

Kapfer, Miriam B., ed. *Behavioral Objectives in Curriculum Development.* Englewood Cliffs, N.J.: Educational Technology Publications, 1971.

Mager, Robert F. *Preparing Instructional Objectives.* Palo Alto, Calif.: Fearon Publishers, 1962.

McAshan, H. H. *Writing Behavioral Objectives.* New York: Harper and Row, 1970.

Plowman, Paul D. *Behavioral Objectives.* Chicago: Science Research Associates, 1971.

Rich, John M. *Humanistic Foundations of Education.* Worthington, Ohio: Charles A. Jones, 1971.

Saylor, J. Galen, and Alexander, William M. *Planning Curriculum for Schools.* New York: Holt, Rinehart and Winston, 1974.

Vargas, Julie S. *Writing Worthwhile Behavioral Objectives.* New York: Harper and Row, 1972.

Work Sheet 5A
Questions for Class Dialogue

Student's Name _____

Date _____

Directions: Study chapter 5 with the following questions in mind. Prepare responses for each question, so that you can intelligently participate in class dialogue. Space is provided with each question, so that you can record any notes that will aid you in the dialogue.

1. Explain the derivation of objectives, but do it in a systems context.

2. Explain the relationship of general objectives and specific objectives in a curriculum and instructional program.

3. Distinguish between objectives and aims.

4. (a) What are behavioral objectives?

   (b) Give two examples of behavioral objectives.

(c) Discuss the precautions against the ultraspecificity of behavioral objectives.

5. What are humanistic objectives?

6. Who should participate in the formulation of school goals and objectives?

7. Discuss the process of validating goals and objectives.

8. Discuss the procedure for formulating or revising the school philosophy.

9. (a) Explain the importance of well-written school objectives.

   (b) Discuss the procedure for formulating or revising the school objectives.

10. (a) Why does it behoove professional staff members to be aware of the statements of committees, commissions, and study groups (over the years) regarding the objectives of secondary schools?

(b) Give some such statements of objectives that have been made from time to time.

11. (a) What is the definition of domains as given in chapter 5 of the text?

(b) What is meant by the cognitive domain?

(c) What is meant by the affective domain?

(d) What is meant by the psychomotor domain?

(e) What implications do the cognitive domain, affective domain, and psychomotor domain have in the teaching-learning process?

Work Sheet 5B
Derivation of Objectives

Student's Name _____

Date _____

Directions:
1. Obtain the objectives of a middle school, junior high school, or senior high school.
2. Read and understand the objectives.
3. Visit the particular school to learn the procedure by which the objectives were derived. Compare your findings with the explanation in chapter 5 regarding the derivation of objectives. Record all of your comments below.

Work Sheet 5C
Characteristics of Well-Stated Objectives

Student's Name _____

Date _____

Directions:
1. List and discuss the characteristics of well-stated objectives. Use the space below to record your work.
2. Refer to:
    a. Bushnell, David S. "A Suggested Guide for Developing a Systems Approach to Curriculum Improvement." *Education* 90 (April 1970): 351–62.
    b. Mager, Robert F. *Preparing Instructional Objectives.* Palo Alto, Calif.: Fearon Publishers, 1962.

Work Sheet 5D
Comparison of Objectives

Student's Name _____

Date _____

Directions:
1. Obtain the objectives of a junior high school and senior high school in some school district. Examine the two sets of objectives to see whether you can conclude that the objectives of the senior high school logically follow those of the junior high school.
2. Visit the two schools to see whether you can learn the nature and the amount of dialogue or communication that transpired between the two schools before the two sets of objectives were formulated.
3. Record your findings below.
4. If you wish, you may conduct a similar activity with a middle school and secondary school in some school district, rather than a junior high school and senior high school.

Work Sheet 5E
Bases of Objectives

Student's Name _____

Date _____

Directions:
1. Obtain the objectives of two middle schools, two junior high schools, or two senior high schools.
2. Examine the two sets of objectives for similarities and differences.
3. Visit the pertinent schools to learn the student and community data upon which the objectives are based.
4. Record your findings and comments below.

Work Sheet 5F
Behavioral and Humanistic Objectives

Student's Name _____

Date _____

Directions:

1. Obtain a set of behavioral objectives or humanistic objectives from some middle school, junior high school, or senior high school.
2. For class, be prepared to explain where the objectives apply in the curriculum, and how they were formulated.
3. Use the space below to make notes that will aid you in class discussion.

Work Sheet 5G
Objectives Committee

Student's Name _____

Date _____

Directions:
1. Assemble an objectives committee with 4 of your classmates.
2. Write a set of 6 behavioral objectives.
3. Refer to any of the following for help in your writing:
   a. Mager, Robert F. *Preparing Instructional Objectives.* Palo Alto, Calif.: Fearon Publishers, 1962.
   b. McAshan, H. H. *Writing Behavioral Objectives.* New York: Harper and Row, 1970.
   c. Plowman, Paul D. *Behavioral Objectives.* Chicago: Science Research Associates, 1971.
   d. Vargas, Julie S. *Writing Worthwhile Behavioral Objectives.* New York: Harper and Row, 1972.
4. List your objectives below. In class, be prepared to defend that your objectives are well stated.

Work Sheet 5H
School Committee Meeting

Student's Name _____

Date _____

Directions:
1. If possible, attend the meeting of a school committee that is writing a school philosophy—or, school objectives, departmental objectives, or course objectives.
2. Report the attainments of the committee during the meeting, and the procedures of work that were followed. Use the space below for your report.

Work Sheet 5I
School Philosophy

Student's Name _____

Date _____

Directions:
1. Obtain the school philosophy of a middle school, junior high school, or senior high school.
2. Read it carefully.
3. Identify the philosophy of education (thus, the purpose of education) that is reflected in the school philosophy. Recall your learnings from chapter 5 in the text to aid you with this activity.
4. Record your response below. Be prepared to explain it.

Work Sheet 5J
School Philosophy and Objectives

Student's Name _____

Date _____

Directions:
1. Consider:
   It has been said that a school philosophy gives the purpose of the school, and the objectives state how the school is going to attain its purpose.
2. Obtain the school philosophy and objectives of some middle school, junior high school, or senior high school.
3. Read the philosophy and the objectives carefully. Do the objectives specify how the school is going to attain the purpose that is given in the philosophy? Explain. Be definitive.
4. Make notes below that will aid you in class discussion regarding the information that you have obtained.

Work Sheet 5K
Philosophy and Objectives Writing

Student's Name _____

Date _____

Directions:
1. Together with 4 of your classmates, form a philosophy and objectives committee.
2. As a committee, write the philosophy and objectives of some middle school, junior high school, or senior high school. Be prepared to explain the derivation of the objectives and the bases for the philosophy that the committee has written.
3. Use the space below for your writing.

Work Sheet 5L
Extension of Learning

Student's Name _____

Date _____

Directions:
1. Choose one of the following readings, or one of the readings at the end of chapter 5, to extend the learnings that you have attained from the chapter.
2. Read critically.
3. Synthesize your learnings for class dialogue.
4. Space is provided at the end of this work sheet for notes that you may want to make.

Readings:
1. Butler, Donald J. *Four Philosophies and Their Practice in Education and Religion.* New York: Harper and Row, 1968.
2. Kapfer, Miriam B., ed. *Behavioral Objectives in Curriculum Development.* Englewood Cliffs, N. J.: Educational Technology Publications, 1971.
3. Rich, John M. *Humanistic Foundations of Education.* Worthington, Ohio: Charles A. Jones, 1971.

6

Selection and Organization
of Curriculum Content for Middle
and Secondary Schools

Stage two in curriculum and instructional improvement involves choosing program modifications or changes that will satisfy the needs that have been identified and validated, and promoting the attainment of the objectives that have been formulated and validated in stage one. Chapters 4 and 5 have dealt with stage one. This chapter deals with stage two.

Background

Over the years, changes have taken place in the curriculum of the school—e.g., new subject matter has been introduced, subject matter has emerged correlated with other subject matter, and so forth. Methods and materials for implementing the curriculum have changed and, in some cases, improved. However, over the years, the process of curriculum design has not changed radically. Curriculum design is the pattern or framework of learning activities.[1] Various curriculum designs will be described in this chapter.

The process of curriculum design has remained "basically an additive one in which newly developed items are added to the existing framework."[2] Currently, students graduate (or leave school) and enter a world that is complex and changing rapidly. Preparations for that world cannot be met by a curriculum that is designed to equip students for a rather stable and uncomplicated world. Thus, a process for curriculum design is needed that will "tap the rising reservoir of new knowledge and generate new curriculum structures capable of preparing students for the future." [3]

Curriculum design is related to curriculum theory. At the core of every curriculum theory is the recommendation of an appropriate design. As presented in chapter 2, curriculum has been viewed in a variety of ways—(1) a body of subjects or subject matters that is to be covered by the teachers and the students, (2) all of the experiences that a learner has under the guidance of the school, (3) objectives to be attained, and so on. As such, subjects or subject matters, experiences, and objectives, respectively, serve as the bases for curriculum design. When subjects or subject matters are the bases of design, curriculum is reflected as an accumulated body of knowledge to be transmitted. When experiences are the bases of design, curriculum is reflected as a process. In the use of objectives as the bases of design, curriculum revolves around ends, rather than means to ends.

Systems analysis, discussed in earlier chapters, provides a new rationale for designing curriculum, using given resources to achieve specified objectives, and using feedback for system regulation. As suggested in chapter 2, the definitions of *curriculum* and *system* are practically synonymous. In the view presented in this book, curriculum as a system moves from objectives formulated in the cognitive, affective, and/or psychomotor domains to planning curriculum improvements, implementing curriculum improvements, and evaluating the outcomes. The following explanations should be helpful.

Holism in Curriculum

Writings contain identification and explanations of the areas that curriculum should seek to develop, and explanations of interrelationships among those areas. The areas are as follows: (1) formalized perceptions, by human beings, of realities that have become known as the academic disciplines; (2) human processes—i.e., those attributes and abilities that set human beings apart from the animal world; and (3) attitudes and values expounded in society.[4] These areas are symbolized in the model that is presented in figure 14.

The above-mentioned areas usually compete for time and financial support in a curriculum. Conflict in curriculum regarding these areas should not exist if the theory of curriculum design is holistic. Recent trends in education emphasize the holism and interactive nature of the educational-living process. The following paragraphs explain a theory of curriculum design that is holistic. The explanation begins with a reference to the areas that are represented in figure 14.

Perceptions of Reality. Perceptions of reality constitute one of the three areas symbolized in the model. The statements that follow give meaning to this particular area of concern in curriculum.

The traditional subject matter of curriculum has consisted of study in the natural sciences (biology, physics, chemistry, and their related disciplines); mathematics-arithmetic; grammar; history, geography, and the other social sciences; and finally, the aesthetics of music, art, physical education, drama, and the industrial arts. These areas represent man's attempt to catalog, systematize, and record his perceptions and knowledge of reality. Although there is a great deal of commonality

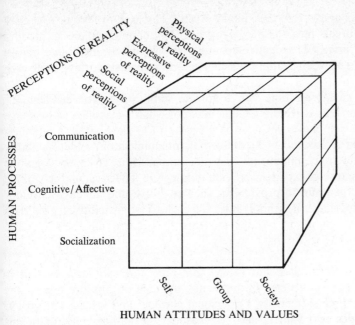

PERCEPTIONS OF REALITY

Social perceptions of reality
Expressive perceptions of reality
Physical perceptions of reality

HUMAN PROCESSES

Communication

Cognitive/Affective

Socialization

Self   *Group*   *Society*

HUMAN ATTITUDES AND VALUES

FIGURE 14.   Three-Dimensional Curriculum Model

SOURCE: Paul A. Nelson, "Curriculum Management by Design," *Educational Leadership* 30 (January 1973): 314. Reprinted with permission of the Association for Supervision and Curriculum Development and Paul A. Nelson. Copyright © 1973 by the Association for Supervision and Curriculum Development.

where specific phenomena have been defined and agreed upon, and while we can agree on most principles in each of the areas cited, there are differences and no two individuals perceive everything exactly alike.

Perceptions of reality can be classified into three broad areas: (a) physical reality or the natural sciences; (b) expressions of reality or the aesthetics; and (c) social reality or the social sciences. [These categories are shown in figure 14.] [5]

Attention is called to both the unique and generic principles inherent in the diverse perceptions of reality.

. . . Any model of curriculum must seek to include both these realms of specific and general beliefs within the learning sequence.

The general reality perceptions of the physical sciences are often seen as giving us the "scientific method," the "discovery method," and/or the "inquiry method." Actually, these methods have flexibility across all of the perceptions of reality. [6]

In curriculum, of the three categories into which perceptions of reality have been divided, least attention is probably given to expressive perceptions of reality. It is logical that students should be given increased opportunity to express their perceptions. It is conceivable that opportunities and learning experiences in the expression of perception will sharpen a student's perception of reality.

Human Processes. Human processes constitute another area that is symbolized in figure 14. Human processes, here, refer to those attributes and abilities that set human beings apart from the animal world.[7] The area of human processes seems primarily to break into these categories: (1) communication, a broader field than language arts; (2) affective-cognitive development, integrated rather than separated; and (3) socialization, which is more than just working well with others.[8]

These particular categories hold the following implications for curriculum.[9] First, communication skills currently include much of what is classified as language arts; however, heavier emphasis needs to be placed on (1) the speaker's intention as well as the listener's reception, (2) nonverbal communication, and (3) ability to use various media to communicate. Second, emphasis is given to cognitive development; but, learning experiences should integrate affective and cognitive development, rather than aim to provide for such cognitive and affective development separately. Third and last, schools have the added responsibility of providing students with a curriculum that equips students to become members of, and function in, an increasingly pluralistic society.[10]

Attitudes and Values. Attitudes and values constitute still another area that is symbolized in figure 14. As depicted in the model, the area of attitudes and values subdivides into these three segments: (1) personal attitudes and values; (2) group, or subculture, attitudes and values; and (3) societal, or national, attitudes and values.[11]

Tension, violence, vandalism, and unrest throughout the nation bespeak the lack of development of worthy attitudes and values on the part of individuals. Since students are under a continuous, long-term influence of the school and the curriculum, the school is held responsible, in part, by some for the attitudes and values that students hold. Development of curriculum concerned with attitudes and values should incorporate all segments of this area, such as those relating to self, group, and society.

Potential Curriculum Designs. A variety of curriculum designs are possible, relative to the areas symbolized in figure 14. A curriculum can be designed within any one of the three areas—perceptions of reality, human processes, attitudes and values. Also, it can be designed incorporating any two or all three areas.

Another approach consists of analyzing the categories within a particular area and designing a curriculum that unifies curriculum ideas from those categories. For example, a curriculum relative to perceptions of reality can focus on physical perceptions of reality, or any one of the other two categories in the area of perceptions of reality. Or, a curriculum could represent a unity of curriculum ideas from any two or all three of the categories contained in the area of perceptions of reality.

Additionally, a higher degree of sophistication of curriculum design can be advanced. At this higher point, curriculum is designed for any three-dimensional combination that is identified. An example of such a three-dimensional combination consists of the following: expressive perceptions of reality, personal attitudes and values, cognitive-affective development. Of course, there are specific outcomes that can be listed for each area, but the greatest concern is "the degree of mix" that can be perceived and achieved, so that student learning and development may be optimum.[12]

Benefits of Holism in Curriculum. Today, attention is being called to the interactive nature of, and the interrelationships that exist among, the areas of curriculum—namely, "the organized disciplines of knowledge, the human processes, and the unique attitudes and values an individual acquires toward and about himself, his reference groups, and his society." [13] Usually, although these areas are found in most curriculums, they are unnecessarily separated and compete for emphasis. At the same time, however, when learning activities are planned in one of the areas, involvement of one or more of the other areas is included, though the inclusion is not consciously planned. For example, it is impossible to teach perceptions of reality (one of the areas with which curriculum is concerned) without involving communication, cognition, or socialization (i.e., the subdivisions of human processes, a second area with which curriculum is concerned). In other words, by necessity, human processes are involved in the teaching of perceptions of reality. The tendency is to teach one, and to assume that the other will occur.[14] On the contrary, both types of experiences should be carefully and conscientiously planned.

The interaction and interrelationship of curriculum goes one step further. Students who engage in reality or become human in process also confront and shape their beliefs, attitudes, and values.[15] A more effective curriculum cognizant of all aspects of modern human education will result to the extent that an awareness exists of all factors—their interactions and interrelations—and that they are provided for in the curriculum. The areas should be interwoven "just as life is a series of interwoven fibers and strands." [16] As such encounters and experiences are provided, the curriculum begins to become more lifelike.

Usefulness of Model. Figure 14 facilitates insight regarding the areas that curriculum should seek to develop, and the interrelationship of these areas. The model can be used to examine a specific sector in isolation (e.g., communication), an individual set (e.g., human processes), or, more appropriately, various three-dimensional combinations that can be developed for specific curriculum outcomes (e.g., societal attitudes and values, communication, and expressive perceptions of reality). The model suggests that, no matter which side is attended, the other areas are also affected. The model does not, however, indicate or suggest the specific outcomes that should be placed in any of the categories. In each school, they can be individually assigned. In short, the model provides a framework for examining the curriculum in light of what it does—with suggestions for a richer, fuller development.

Curriculum Design Emphasizing Objectives or Competencies

In an objective-based or competency-based curriculum design, a direct relationship is assumed among objective, learning activity, and performance. All curriculum designs anticipate some type of eventual performance on the part of the learner; but they assume less of a relationship among these components. Furthermore, they anticipate that "the learner's ultimate behavior will be the outgrowth of many learning experiences." [17]

In a curriculum design that is based on objectives or competencies, "the desired performances are stipulated as behavioral or performance objectives or competencies, learning activities are planned to achieve each objective, and the learner's performance is checked as a basis for his moving from one objective to another." [18] For example, "in social studies he learns how to read a map and demonstrates this competency before he learns about and demonstrates his knowledge of particular geographic locations and relations." [19]

Once objectives are identified and stated as behavioral or performance objectives or competencies, these steps follow: "(1) ordering the objectives and sub-objectives and placing them in a time frame; and (2) selecting instructional activities to promote the attainment of the objectives within the time period. Preassessment, instruction . . ., and evaluation follow." [20] It is recommended that criterion-referenced tests (designed exclusively to measure objectives taught) be used for evaluation.[21]

In short, "a design based on specific objectives or competencies is characterized by specific, sequential, and demonstrable learnings of the tasks, activities, or skills which constitute the acts to be learned and performed by students." [22]

Of all the curriculum designs discussed in this chapter, the one based on behavioral or performance objectives or competencies might seem to be the most suited to a systems approach to curriculum improvement. However, the selection of a single curriculum design is an oversimplification. Other curriculum designs should be incorporated as pertinent. The design should be determined by the objectives. For example, "if the synthesis of knowledge and skills is an objective . . ., then the organization of content should promote synthesis." [23] If the objective is to promote social consciousness, then the curriculum design should promote social consciousness. In other words, the curriculum that is designed should be the most appropriate to the objectives that are being considered.

Other Types of Curriculum Design

Designs that Emphasize Organized Knowledge. As was noted in chapter 2 and earlier in this chapter, curriculum is viewed, by some, as a body of subjects or subject matters that are to be covered by the teachers and the students. Correspondingly, one curriculum design is characterized by subjects, usually, but not necessarily, derived from the major disciplines of knowledge. This design is referred to as the *subject curriculum design*. The curriculum plan is divided into subjects, which themselves are often subdivided into such divisions as grades and marking, or reporting, periods. The emphasis is on the learning of subject matter from books and other written and printed materials.

The *subject-discipline curriculum design* emerged in the 1950s. Unlike the subject curriculum design, this particular design does not emphasize the memorization of facts, but "the perception of the structure of the subject field—its concepts, modes of inquiry, and organization of knowledge." [24] The subject-discipline design "was prompted by the impossible load of . . . growing subject matter, the desire to give students a mode of inquiry that would permit them to study the subject on their own initiative after mastering its structure. . . ." [25] The structure of a discipline is "the set of fundamental generalizations that bind a field of knowledge into a unity, organize this body of knowledge into a cohesive whole, fix the limits of investigation and inclusion of knowledge for the discipline itself, and provide the basis for discovering what else exists within the field." [26]

Confusion sometimes exists as to subject, and the structure of a subject.[27] Traditional school subjects, such as chemistry, mathematics, and so on, are well-ordered disciplines; and each has its own distinct structure. When incorporated into the curriculum, the decision to be made consists of what part of the structure to include, and when and how. Though established disciplines and the subjects derived from them have an inherent order or structure, many so-called subjects do not have an inherent order. In the latter cases, these subjects may be so varied, and their structure of such diverse quality, that the total order or structure is confused. Such is the case with consumer economics, general mathematics, and so forth, as school offerings for which special scope and sequence plans have been created. The situation of confused structure is repeated in the case where two or more disciplines have been incorporated as one—e.g., the incorporation of history, sociology, geography, anthropology, and so on, as social studies.

Designs that Emphasize Society. Curriculum designs that emphasize society are characterized by a central element of focus "on social activities and/or problems, and these define the scope of the curriculum or a major portion of it." [28] These social activities and/or problems may be the centers about which the curriculum is organized, or "they may serve primarily as criteria for the selection of content within the subject or other organizational unit." [29]

Three possible design theories are at the core of curriculums that emphasize society. The theories are:

(1) the social functions or areas of social living or persistent life situation approaches that are based on the belief that the curriculum design should follow the persistent functions, areas, or life situations in man's existence as a social being; (2) the theory that the curriculum should be organized around aspects or problems of community life—the community school concept; and (3) the social action or reconstruction theories that hold the improvement of society through direct involvement of the schools and their students to be a major goal or even the primary goal of the curriculum.[30]

Designs that Emphasize the Learner. Curriculums of this design have been known as student-centered or experience-centered. This design falls in the realm of progressive education, and more recently, open, alternative, or humanistic education. An application of this curriculum design is the *open classroom,* which combines practices of earlier progressive education with the English "informal" schools and modern technology.[31]

The characteristics of this particular curriculum design are as follows:

1. The curriculum plan is based on a knowledge of learners' needs and interests in general and involves diagnosis of the specific needs and interests of the population served by the plans.
2. The curriculum plan is highly flexible, with built-in provisions for development and modification to conform to the needs and interests of particular learners and with many options available to the learners. In fact, the learner may develop

his own curriculum plan in some designs, but with guidance in selecting options and in planning.

3. The learner is consulted and instructed individually at appropriate points in the curriculum and instructional process.[32]

Certain approaches are possible in striving to meet the needs and interests of learners. The following are included among these approaches: curriculum tracks in high schools; ability grouping in middle schools, junior high schools, or senior high schools; elective systems in secondary schools; and programs for special groups, such as the academically talented, underachievers, potential dropouts, and so on. Though these curriculum plans focus on the needs and interests of learners within the categories, they do not have individual suitability of needs and interests. Individualization is maximized when provisions exist for options by individual students.[33] Such opportunities exist in some middle schools and junior high schools through special interest activities, exploratory courses, and other opportunities that provide for students to explore and deepen their interests. At the senior high school level, attempts to meet individual needs and interests are made by means of a system of elective courses and mini courses, and a wide range of cocurricular activities.

As previously stated, this particular curriculum design is based on the needs and interests of the learner. Actually, it is the needs and interests principle— rather than a particular design—that has most importance, influence, and applicability. In each of the curriculum designs discussed in this chapter, there are occasions when decisions regarding curriculum must be made regarding each student's program and progress, at which time the needs and interests principle is applied.

Emergent Curriculum Designs

There are always concerns in society and education that are expressed as curriculum demands and proposals. As such, they may eventually emerge as curriculum designs. Furthermore, American society is plagued by many problems—e.g., vandalism, violence, environmental pollution, inflation, poverty, and so forth. "For each of these, there are formulas as to what the schools should do to solve or alleviate the problem. Any of these 'formulas' may become a 'subject' in the curriculum—indeed, some already have—or, a new and pervasive emphasis that becomes, in time, a curriculum design." [34]

Interrelationship of Content with Objectives

In order to expedite understanding of the explanations that follow relative to the interrelationship of content with objectives (in a systems analysis context), a discussion of the subsystem hierarchy of the total instructional system is necessary. The discussion proceeds thus.[35]

The total instructional system is referred to as the curriculum. The curriculum includes all of the learning experiences (formal and informal) that are provided for the students, and it consists of vertical and horizontal subsystems. In the traditional curriculum, the vertical subsystems are referred to as *grade levels,* and the horizontal subsystems consist of the *content areas*—music, mathematics, English, and so on. Other characteristics may be used to identify the vertical subsystems and the horizontal subsystems.

Bisystems constitute the next lower level of the system. Bisystems have both a level and a content dimension. The location of a bisystem is the point where a vertical and a horizontal subsystem intersect. In a traditional curriculum, examples of a bisystem would be tenth-grade music, eleventh-grade mathematics, and so forth. Each bisystem is subdivided into units of study or instructional packages, and each unit or instructional package contains certain objectives, and a set of procedures designed to achieve the objectives. A procedure consists of a set of activities that are structured to achieve a specific objective(s). Examples of activities are as follows: writing a book report, viewing a filmstrip, making a chart, or interviewing a community resource person. To summarize, the instructional system or curriculum is composed of subsystems, bisystems, instructional packages or units of study, procedures, and activities.

Preconditions. In a systems approach to curriculum design, the first step is the formulation of objectives. The objectives describe the desired end product of the system. At this level, the objectives should be precise, but not specific. Statements that are similar in degree of precision to the Ten Imperative Needs of Youth or the Ten Goals of Quality Education in Pennsylvania, as given in chapter 5, would be satisfactory here.

Once these objectives have been formulated, systems analysis requires that they be analyzed, so that preconditions can be determined to produce the desired results. The preconditions are a restatement of the objectives, as objectives, stated in more specific terms. The objectives that result from the preconditions that are derived from the overall objectives become the objectives of the subsystems.

Objectives and Content at the Subsystem Level. The objectives of the subsystems serve as a guide for determining the types of content and curriculum designs that will be needed to achieve the overall objectives of the instructional system or curriculum. Examples of the types of content are communication skills, physical perceptions of reality, and so on. These particular types of content can be defined in general terms, such as oral communication skills, written expression skills, physics, mathematics, and so forth. The curriculum designs may take the forms already described in this chapter—e.g., subject design, discipline design, social design. The types of curriculum design are determined by the objectives.

The objectives of the subsystems are studied to determine the preconditions that are necessary if these objectives are to be achieved. These preconditions, stated as objectives, are conceived to be the objectives of the bisystems, to be discussed next.

Objectives and Content at the Bisystem Level. At the bisystem level, the preconditions are determined that will be needed to achieve the subsystem objectives. As the preconditions are determined—as the tasks are identified that students must be able to perform to satisfy the subsystem objectives—they are stated in behavioral terms as the objectives of the bisystem. The content decisions of the subsystem level are also refined at the bisystem level, so that, at least, a general scope and sequence dimension can be ascribed to the content. Scope refers to the depth and detail to which content will be studied. Sequence refers to the order in which content is presented and the point in the curriculum at which it is introduced. Care is needed that the objectives and content are ascribed to the appropriate horizontal and vertical subsystems.

Objectives and Content of Units of Study or Instructional Packages.   The objectives and content that are defined at the bisystem level are, in turn, analyzed to determine the preconditions that are necessary for their accomplishment. The determined preconditions are defined as objectives, and become the objectives of the units of study or the instructional packages. The number and size of units or packages should not be decided by the time available, but, rather, by the objectives that are to be achieved. Those concepts, values, and facts that are given greater emphasis in the objectives will receive greater emphasis in the units of study or instructional packages. Those that are given less emphasis in the objectives will receive less in the units or packages. The extent of time given to content is referred to as *duration*.

A critical—perhaps the most critical—component of any approach to curriculum and instructional improvement comes into operation when the design of the curriculum and instructional system has been completed. It is imperative that the administrative procedures within the school are *at least* compatible with the design. The ideal, of course, is that administrative procedures actually evolve *from* the design.

All too often, the curriculum and instructional practices and procedures—indeed the whole culture of the school—seem to be determined by existing administrative arrangements. Therefore, it is suggested that continuous attention needs to be directed to administrative practices and possible alternative procedures. If this suggestion is followed, principals and other administrators need to be involved, and need to have a vested interest in the new approach.

Procedures.   The procedure is the lowest-level subsystem of the curriculum. An instructional package or unit is not complete until its procedures have been identified and designed. A procedure consists of at least one objective, content, activity (i.e., methods and materials), and a means of evaluation.

The designing of procedures advances thus. The objectives of instructional packages or units are analyzed, and the preconditions that are necessary to achieve the objectives are determined. The objectives of a procedure are derived from the preconditions that are determined. Furthermore, the preconditions will determine the number of procedures that are needed to accomplish the objectives of the instructional package or unit. Each procedure will have at least one objective. The selection of content, as well as methods and materials, is based on learner characteristics and needs and the objective(s) to be attained.

In designing procedures, the last step is the design of some means of evaluation to determine the effectiveness of the procedure in achieving its objective(s). Evaluative means may be of various kinds—e.g., performance activity, written test, constructed project. The objectives will help to determine the most appropriate type of evaluation. Methods and materials will be given greater discussion in chapter 7, and evaluation, in chapter 8.

Design Process. The process of systems analysis that is discussed above concentrates on analyzing successively smaller components of the curriculum, with a statement of objectives resulting for each instructional subsystem level from subsystem through bisystem, unit or package, and procedure.[36] When the procedures have been planned, the process changes direction and starts back up through the system. Procedures are assembled into units or packages, and evaluative instruments are designed to determine the accomplishments of students in terms of the objectives of the unit or package. Units or packages are grouped into bisystems, and evaluative instruments are designed to determine the accomplishments of students in terms of the objectives of each bisystem. Evaluation beyond this point is optional.

Aspects Peculiar to Middle School Curriculum Design

Essentially, the middle school is an alternative to the traditional junior high school. The middle school is a transitional school between the elementary and secondary school levels. The emergence of the middle school dates to the 1960s.

Little consistency appears to exist in grade grouping in the middle school. In some school systems, the middle school includes grades 6 through 8; in some, grades 5 through 8; in some, grades 5 through 9; and, in others, grades 6 and 7 only. Most middle schools do not incorporate grade 9. This, therefore, places the ninth grade back into the senior high school, where it had been during the early 1900s prior to the emergence of the junior high school. Placement of the ninth grade in the senior high school carries implications for this grade as an integral part of the curriculum at the senior high school level. This placement puts apparent constraints on the curriculum of the ninth grade.

The middle school is an attempt to overcome the weakness of the junior high school which, instead of being a distinct institution adapted to the particular needs of preadolescents, is often merely a junior imitation of the senior high school. The middle school better allocates students of particular development. Today, children are maturing earlier. Sixth-graders are increasingly out of place in the elementary school. Accordingly, some middle schools include grade 6. Ninth-graders are more nearly like senior high school students, rather than students of those grades preceding the ninth. Accordingly, some middle schools do not incorporate ninth-grade students.

Proponents of the middle school note that it is designed to provide students with a far wider range of learning experiences than would be possible in the self-contained elementary school classroom, without, at the same time, incorporating the departmentalized structure of the senior high school. The middle school is intended to accommodate the special needs, interests, and abilities of students during the years between childhood and adolescence. The middle school is further intended to facilitate a program that introduces the students gradually to specialization and encourages group activities, all with provision for individual differences.

The curriculums that are proposed for the middle school bear certain similarities.

All of the proposed curriculums include the standard academic subjects—language arts, social studies, science, and mathematics. The characteristics and needs of students of middle school age suggest that the curriculum of the middle school should provide for "a planned sequence of concepts in the general education areas, a major emphasis on interests and skills for continued learning, a balanced program of exploratory experiences and other activities and services for personal development, and appropriate attention to the development of values." [37] Independent study and exploratory options can provide opportunity for student self-direction and responsibility. Use can be made of team teaching, flexible scheduling, and special offerings, such as industrial arts, homemaking, typewriting, library work, and so on.

Existent middle school curriculums vary. Some come very close to the curriculum that is recommended. Some are in accordance, in part, with the curriculum that is recommended. However, other curriculums are very similar to the elementary or junior high school curriculum.

It is to be noted that interest and desire to improve the education of preadolescents and early adolescents has resulted in initiating middle school curriculums that are noticeably different from the traditional junior high school curriculum. There is little or no evidence, however, that these curriculums are any better.

Aspects Peculiar to Junior High School Curriculum Design

With ascribed grades of 7 through 9, the junior high school places between the elementary school and the senior high school. Established in 1910, the junior high school was intended to be an educational level for providing "instruction and training suitable to the varied and changing physical, mental, and social natures and needs of immature, maturing, and mature" students.[38] The organization and the curriculum of the junior high school were intended to provide for the following: (1) articulation between school levels; (2) exploration; (3) general education—i.e., emphasis upon the most important subjects; (4) differentiation, with earlier specialization; (5) departmentalization; (6) opportunity for use of specialists in subject-matter areas; (7) better preparation for college; (8) economy of time in education, acceleration, and earlier graduation.[39]

During the decades of its development and expansion, the junior high school made attempts to institute a curriculum that would answer the needs, interests, and other characteristics of junior high school students. For example, during the 1930s, 1940s, and 1950s, the junior high school made "notable efforts . . . to develop block-time and core classes for general education." [40]

Block time is a scheduling procedure that places one teacher with the same group of students for two or more consecutive classes. There are two basic types of block-time classes. The first is one in which the teacher teaches each subject separately. The teacher may or may not correlate the two subjects. In the second type of block time, classes are unified around units, themes, or problems that are drawn from one of the subjects in the block-time class. Two examples of subjects that are found in block-time classes are English and history, and science and mathematics.

There is lack of agreement regarding the definition of core curriculum. A list of some of the characteristics of the "true core" follows:

1. The core must be the same for and required of all pupils.

2. The core takes a large block of time, usually one-third to one-half of the school day.

3. The core is guidance-oriented.

4. The true core is problem-oriented.

5. The core recognizes no subject matter lines since it considers all knowledge to be its province.

6. Pupil-teacher planning is a basic part of core.

7. Subject matter and skills are taught as the need arises rather than in any predetermined sequence.

8. Considerable teacher preparation, more than in a traditional situation, is essential.

9. In the core, individual differences are recognized by method rather than by curricular structure.[41]

With the passage of time, the junior high school has been increasingly attacked. Together with the senior high school, it has been criticized as being authoritarian, repressive of students, and slow to change to meet the changing nature and needs of its student population. Furthermore, the junior high school curriculum has been caught in philosophical controversy. Educational results of Sputnik for higher academic standards have increased the pressure of moving senior high school courses and curriculum patterns down into the junior high school grades. To illustrate, foreign languages have been introduced in grade 7 and biology has moved into grade 9. The extension of senior high school practices downward into the junior high school is also reflected in the elective system, multiple-track curriculum, and so on. On the other hand, certain practices have extended upward from the elementary school. Among these practices are: emphasis on general education; attention to skill building; and block-time and core programs that integrate subject matter and instruction around units, themes, or problems and are reflective of the self-contained classroom of the elementary school.

Confusion exists regarding the junior high school. It is observed, however, that the needs, interests, and other characteristics of junior high school students differ from those of elementary school and senior high school students. Therefore, the junior high school should not be viewed as a miniature senior high school or an extension of the elementary school.

The current status of the junior high school curriculum may be described thus. The "true core" curriculum is found in only a small percentage of schools. Block-time classes seem to be increasing in number. Because of a trend toward academic excellence, an increasing amount of knowledge, and a demand for qualified teachers, departmentalization is common in junior high schools. However, the junior high school curriculum feels the continued effect of the middle school movement. In too many cases, the junior high school curriculum mirrors the senior high school curriculum.

Aspects Peculiar to Senior High School Curriculum Design

Generally, the senior high school is a subject-centered, departmentalized, graded organization. One interesting innovation in secondary school organization is the rise of the "school within a school" concept. This idea is manifested by "a number of partially self-contained units, each housing a few hundred students. . . ." [42] Each unit exists as a satellite "near but apart from a central service unit, which includes such common facilities as administrative offices, auditorium, cafeteria, library, and gymnasium." [43] The organization is also referred to as the little school or the house plan. The organization "is designed to recapture the intimacy and individual attention of the small school, while retaining the greater efficiency and more extensive facilities of the large school." [44]

The comprehensive high school is a unitary, multipurpose school that is designed to provide "(1) a general education for all youth as citizens of a democratic society, (2) specialized programs for vocational proficiency for those youngsters planning to enter the world of work after high school, (3) a specialized program of academic preparation for college, and (4) exploratory and enrichment studies and experiences to meet the individual interests of all adolescents." [45]

Alternatives have arisen upon the failure of the urban comprehensive high school to meet the needs of ghetto youth. They are known variously as "street academies," "continuation schools," "second-chance schools," "adapted high schools," and so on.[46] These schools accept students, who are usually public school dropouts, at their own level. The curriculum of these schools is extremely flexible and is intended to serve the individual needs and interests of the students. The school is sometimes housed in an abandoned store. Some of the schools are financed by grants from private foundations or industries. These schools have been especially successful when they emphasize work-study programs with a real opportunity for employment.

"Schools without walls" are another result of the failure of conventional high schools to reach ghetto youth. The earliest of the "schools without walls" was the Parkway School in Philadelphia.[47] The campus of the Parkway School is the community.

Other concepts of secondary education are being experimented with in a variety of cities. Though they vary somewhat in operation, they are similarly based as to informality and freedom to follow individual needs and interests.

The concern of the 1970s and late 1960s for equal educational opportunity for minority groups was preceded in the early 1960s by a growing concern for maximum intellectual development of gifted students. Attempts have been made, in curriculum and instruction, to answer these concerns. Concerns continue regarding all groups of students.

Another significant trend in the curriculum of the comprehensive high school is "the concept that many of the subjects on this level . . . should be primarily communication arts subjects. This concept, briefly defined, is that much of the work by students on this level should be devoted to learning how to use the various subjects as tools or instruments for further learning and study." [48]

Furthermore, the curriculum of the comprehensive high school is being broadened to include many new courses. Greater emphasis is being placed on values, ideals, and attitudes.

The diversity of the student population in the comprehensive high school requires a diversified curriculum. However, the curriculum should also provide a common ground wherein all of the students can examine the problems that are shared by all of society. The curriculum should endeavor to produce "independently thinking and socially responsible members of a free society." [49]

Summary

Stage two in curriculum and instructional improvement involves the choosing of program modifications or changes that will satisfy the needs that have been identified and validated, and promoting the attainment of the objectives that have been formulated and validated in stage one. This chapter explains stage two.

Writings contain identification and explanations of the areas that curriculum should seek to develop, and explanations of interrelationships among the areas. The areas are as follows: (1) formalized perceptions by human beings, of realities that have become known as the academic disciplines; (2) human processes—i.e., those attributes and abilities that set human beings apart from the animal world; and (3) attitudes and values expounded in society.

The above-mentioned areas usually compete for time and financial support in a curriculum. Conflict in curriculum regarding these areas should not exist if the theory of curriculum design is holistic. The chapter explains a theory of curriculum design that is holistic. Explanation is made with reference to a model that is presented in the chapter.

Over the years, the process of curriculum design has not changed radically. Curriculum design is a pattern or framework of learning activities. Various curriculum designs are described in the chapter. Certain observations are made regarding emerging designs.

Systems analysis, discussed in earlier chapters, provides a new rationale for designing curriculum—for using given resources to achieve specified objectives. As suggested in chapter 2, the definitions of *curriculum* and *system* are practically synonymous. In the view presented in this book, curriculum as a system moves from objectives formulated in the cognitive, affective, and/or psychomotor domains, to planning curriculum improvements, to implementing curriculum improvements, to evaluating the outcomes. The chapter provides explanation for planning curriculum improvements by which objectives are refined and content decisions are made. Objectives are analyzed to determine the preconditions that must be met to achieve them, and the preconditions that will contribute to the achievement of the preconditions, and so forth. The process proceeds with a consideration of each instructional subsystem level from subsystem through bisystem, unit of study or instructional package, and procedure.

The chapter closes with a discussion of the aspects peculiar to curriculum design in the middle school, junior high school, and senior high school, respectively.

NOTES

1. J. Galen Saylor and William M. Alexander, *Planning Curriculum for Schools* (New York: Holt, Rinehart and Winston, 1974), p. 189. Reprinted by permission.

2. K. V. Feyereisen, A. J. Fiorino, and A. T. Nowak, *Supervision and Curriculum Renewal: A Systems Approach* (New York: Appleton-Century-Crofts, 1970), p. 130. Reprinted by permission.

3. Ibid.

4. Paul A. Nelson, "Curriculum Management by Design," *Educational Leadership* 30 (January 1973): 313. Reprinted with permission of the Association for Supervision and Curriculum Development and the author. Copyright © 1973 by the Association for Supervision and Curriculum Development.

5. Ibid., p. 314.

6. Ibid.

7. Ibid.

8. Ibid., p. 315.

9. Ibid.

10. Ibid.

11. Ibid., p. 316.

12. Ibid., p. 317.

13. Ibid., p. 313.

14. Ibid., p. 315.

15. Ibid., p. 316.

16. Ibid., p. 317.

17. Saylor and Alexander, *Planning Curriculum*, p. 198. Reprinted by permission.

18. Ibid.

19. Ibid.

20. Ibid., p. 202.

21. W. James Popham and Eva I. Baker, *Systematic Instruction* (Englewood Cliffs, N.J.: Prentice-Hall, 1970), pp. 130–31. Reprinted by permission.

22. Saylor and Alexander, *Planning Curriculum*, pp. 198–99. Reprinted by permission.

23. Feyereisen, Fiorino, and Nowak, *Supervision and Curriculum Renewal*, p. 141. Reprinted by permission.

24. Chris A. De Young and Richard Wynn, *American Education* (New York: McGraw-Hill, 1972), p. 364. Reprinted by permission.

25. Ibid.

26. Saylor and Alexander, *Planning Curriculum*, pp. 206–7. Reprinted by permission.

27. Ibid., p. 207.

28. Ibid., p. 217.

29. Ibid.

30. Ibid., pp. 214–15.

31. Ibid., p. 239.

32. Ibid., p. 231.

33. Ibid., p. 236.

34. Ibid., p. 241.

35. Feyereisen, Fiorino, and Nowak, *Supervision and Curriculum Renewal*, p. 145. Reprinted by permission.

36. Ibid.

37. William M. Alexander et al., *The Emergent Middle School* (New York: Holt, Rinehart and Winston, 1969), p. 19.

38. Chris A. De Young, *Introduction to American Public Education* (New York: McGraw-Hill, 1955), pp. 175, 190. Reprinted by permission.

39. J. Minor Gwynn and John B. Chase, Jr., *Curriculum Principles and Social Trends* (New York: Macmillan Co., 1969), pp. 400–401. Reprinted by permission.

40. Daniel Tanner and Laurel N. Tanner, *Curriculum Development: Theory into Practice* (New York: Macmillan, 1975), p. 460. Reprinted by permission.

41. Leonard H. Clark, Raymond L. Klein, and John B. Burks, *The American Secondary School Curriculum* (New York: Macmillan, 1966), pp. 144–47. Reprinted by permission.

42. De Young and Wynn, *American Education,* p. 202. Reprinted by permission.

43. Ibid.

44. Mauritz Johnson, "Research and Secondary Education," *Educational Forum* 31 (March 1967): 297; cited in De Young and Wynn, *American Education,* p. 202. Copyright by Kappa Delta Pi, an Honor Society in Education. Reprinted by permission.

45. Tanner and Tanner, *Curriculum Development,* p. 458. Reprinted by permission.

46. De Young and Wynn, *American Education,* p. 200. Reprinted by permission.

47. Ibid., p. 192.

48. Gwynn and Chase, *Curriculum Principles,* p. 388. Reprinted by permission.

49. Tanner and Tanner, *Curriculum Development,* p. 457. Reprinted by permission.

Related Readings

Alexander, William M. et al. *The Emergent Middle School*. New York: Holt, Rinehart and Winston, 1969.

Burns, Richard W., and Brooks, Gary D., eds. *Curriculum Design in a Changing Society*. Englewood Cliffs, N.J.: Educational Technology Publications, 1972.

Clark, Leonard H.; Klein, Raymond L.; and Burks, John B. *The American Secondary School Curriculum*. New York: Macmillan, 1966.

De Young, Chris A., and Wynn, Richard. *American Education*. New York: McGraw-Hill, 1972.

Feyereisen, K. V.; Fiorino, A. J.; and Nowak, A. T. *Supervision and Curriculum Renewal: A Systems Approach*. New York: Appleton-Century-Crofts, 1970.

Goodlad, John I. et al. *The Changing School Curriculum*. New York: The Fund for the Advancement of Education, 1966.

Gwynn, J. Minor, and Chase, John B., Jr. *Curriculum Principles and Social Trends*. New York: Macmillan, 1969.

Krug, Mark M. *What Will Be Taught—The Next Decade*. Itasca, Ill.: F. E. Peacock Publishers, 1972.

Nelson, Paul A. "Curriculum Management by Design." *Educational Leadership* 30 (January 1973): 313–17.

Popham, W. James, and Baker, Eva I. *Systematic Instruction*. Englewood Cliffs, N.J.: Prentice-Hall, 1970.

Saylor, J. Galen, and Alexander, William M. *Planning Curriculum for Schools*. New York: Holt, Rinehart and Winston, 1974.

Tanner, Daniel, and Tanner, Laurel N. *Curriculum Development: Theory into Practice*. New York: Macmillan, 1975.

Work Sheet 6A
Questions for Class Dialogue

Student's Name _____

Date _____

Directions: Study chapter 6 with the following questions in mind. Prepare responses for each question, so that you can intelligently participate in class dialogue. Space is provided with each question, so that you can record any notes that will aid you in the dialogue.

1. What is meant by curriculum design?

2. Clarify the proposal that systems analysis provides a new rationale for designing curriculum.

3. Explain the theory of holism in curriculum design.

4. What are the benefits of holism in curriculum?

5. Be able to discuss the constructs of two curriculum designs.

6. How do society and education concerns emerge as curriculum designs?

7. Explain the interrelationship of content with objectives (in a systems analysis context).

8. Present some aspects that are peculiar to middle school curriculum design.

9. Present some aspects that are peculiar to junior high school curriculum design.

10. Present some aspects that are peculiar to senior high school curriculum design.

Work Sheet 6B
Interpretation of Models

Student's Name _____

Date _____

Directions:
1. Observe the following models.

Isolated Areas of the Human
Processes Dimension

Intersection and Unity of Instructional Areas

2. The models are taken from the following reference:
> Nelson, Paul A. "Curriculum Management by Design." *Educational Leadership* 30 (January 1973): 313–17.

Additional concepts from this reference are included in chapter 6 in your text.
3. Read Nelson's article, and review the concepts that are included in chapter 6 in your text.
4. Explain the meaning of the models that are given above. Write your explanation below.

Work Sheet 6C
Examination of Curriculum Materials

Student's Name _____

Date _____

Directions:
1. From a senior high school, obtain a sample course of study and a curriculum guide. In some schools, a curriculum guide is known as a course selection guide.
2. Examine the materials that you have obtained.
3. Distinguish between the materials as to their content and the use that is made of them in the school. Record your conclusions below.

Work Sheet 6D
Examination of Programs of Studies

Student's Name _____

Date _____

Directions:
1. Obtain a program of studies for a junior high and a senior high school of some school district, or a middle and a secondary school of some school district.
2. Derive the meaning of horizontal articulation and vertical articulation from:
   > Good, Carter V., ed. *Dictionary of Education*. New York: McGraw-Hill, 1959.
3. Examine the programs of studies that you have obtained to see whether you can identify provisions for horizontal and vertical articulation.
4. Record the results of your examination below.

Work Sheet 6E
Topical Curriculum and Objective-Based or Competency-Based Curriculum

Student's Name _____
Date _____

Directions:
1. Obtain a topical curriculum and an objective-based or competency-based curriculum from a middle school, junior high school, or senior high school.
2. Compare the two curriculums to discover wherein they are similar and wherein they are not.
3. In the space provided below, record the results of your comparison.

Work Sheet 6F
Core Curriculum

Student's Name _____

Date _____

Directions:
1. Consider:
   There are those who regard the core curriculum as the curriculum design with the greatest potential for meeting the needs, interests, and abilities of students.
2. Obtain the core curriculum of a middle school, junior high school, or senior high school. If this is not possible, obtain a sample core curriculum from some professional education book or educational periodical.
3. Explain the constructs of the curriculum. Write your explanation below.

Work Sheet 6G
Return to Basics Curriculum

Student's Name _____

Date _____

Directions:
1. Consider:
    The return to basics curriculum is coming into vogue.
2. Obtain such a curriculum from some middle school, junior high school, or senior high school. If this is not possible, obtain such a sample curriculum from a professional education book or educational periodical.
3. Explain the constructs of this curriculum. Write your explanation in the space provided below.

Work Sheet 6H
School Visit

Student's Name _____

Date _____

Directions:

1. Spend a day, or a half day, at a middle school, junior high school, or senior high school to become familiar with its academic offerings. Obtain a copy of the program of studies, so as to learn the academic offerings of the school. Visit classes during your stay to get some feeling for the atmosphere of the academic life of the school.

2. Write an account of your learnings and your experiences. Record your account below.

Work Sheet 6I
Cocurricular Activity Programs

Student's Name _____

Date _____

Directions:
1. Learn of the cocurricular activity program of a middle school, junior high school, and senior high school.
2. Compare the programs of the three schools.
3. In the space that is provided below, make a written record of the conclusions that you draw from the comparison.

Work Sheet 6J
School Experiences

Student's Name _____

Date _____

Directions:

1. Visit an alternative school. Or, visit a school with open-space education or a house plan. During your visit, learn the aspects that characterize the curriculum of the school.

2. Make a written record of the curriculum learnings that you have gained from your experiences at the school. Use the space below for your writing.

Work Sheet 6K
Writing a Curriculum

Student's Name _____

Date _____

Directions:
1. Read pertinent professional education books and/or educational periodicals to learn the curriculum advocations for a subject area of your choice relative to the middle school, junior high school, or senior high school.
2. Using your learnings as a basis, write a curriculum for the subject area of your choice for a middle school, junior high school, or senior high school. Give justifications for the components of the curriculum that you write.
3. Do your writing in the space provided below.

Work Sheet 6L
Extension of Learning

Student's Name _____
Date _____

Directions:
1. Choose one of the following readings, or one of the readings at the end of chapter 6, to extend the learnings that you have attained from the chapter.
2. Read critically.
3. Synthesize your learnings for class dialogue.
4. Space is provided at the end of this work sheet for notes that you may want to make.

Readings:
1. Burns, Richard W., and Brooks, Gary D., eds. *Curriculum Design in a Changing Society*. Englewood Cliffs, N.J.: Educational Technology Publications, 1972.
2. Goodlad, John I. et al. *The Changing School Curriculum*. New York: The Fund for the Advancement of Education, 1966.
3. Krug, Mark M. *What Will Be Taught—The Next Decade*. Itasca, Ill.: F. E. Peacock Publishers, 1972.

7

Selection of Teaching Methods and Materials for Middle, Junior High, and Senior High Schools

The preceding chapter explains the second of four stages in curriculum and instructional improvement viewed in terms of a systems approach. This chapter continues the explanation by discussing stage three. Stage three involves the implementation of the curriculum improvements that were planned in stage two.

The chapter explains the place of methods and materials in a systems analysis approach to curriculum and instructional improvement. The explanation includes specification of methods and materials pertinent to middle schools, junior high schools, and senior high schools, respectively.

Methods and Materials in a Systems Analysis Approach

The statements of the following paragraph repeat, in part, concepts that were conveyed in the preceding chapter. They are repeated so that the sequential order of the concepts of this chapter to those of the preceding chapter are emphasized.

Curriculum refers to the total instructional system.[1] It is composed of subsystems, bisystems, units or packages, and procedures. The curriculum includes all of the learning experiences that are provided for the students. It also consists of vertical and horizontal subsystems. In the traditional curriculum, the vertical subsystems are referred to as grade levels, and the horizontal subsystems consist of the content areas—e.g., music, mathematics, English. Bisystems constitute the next lower level of the system. Bisystems have both a level and content dimension. The location of a bisystem is the point where a vertical and a horizontal subsystem intersect. In a traditional curriculum, examples of a bisystem would be tenth-grade music, eleventh-grade mathematics, and so on. Each bisystem is subdivided into units of study or instructional packages, and each of these contains a set of procedures designed to achieve the objectives of the unit or the package. A procedure consists of a set of activities that are structured to achieve a specific objective(s). Examples of activities are as follows: writing a book report, viewing a filmstrip, making a chart. To state it another way, each procedure consists of at least one objective, content, and activity—i.e., methods and materials.

Educational Effectiveness

A systems approach to curriculum and instructional improvement is "a rational, problem-solving method of analyzing the educational process and making it more effective." [2] The system is this process taken as a whole, and incorporating all of its parts—students, teachers, content, methods, materials, physical environment, and the evaluation of the instructional objectives.

"Educational effectiveness is defined in terms of desired changes in student behavior and tested accordingly." [3] Systems analysis attempts to increase educational effectiveness by specifying educational objectives with precision and, subsequently, redesigning the entire educational process to insure student attainment of the objectives.

The model presented in figure 15 presents a design for increasing educational effectiveness. An explanation of the model proceeds thus.

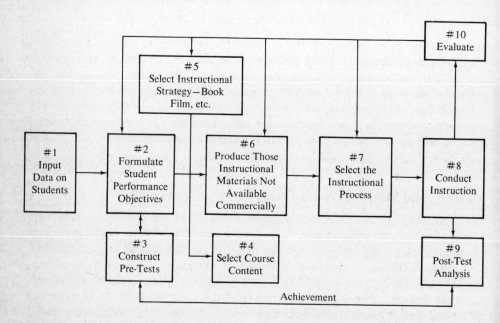

FIGURE 15.   Model: Design for Increasing Educational Effectiveness

SOURCE: Thomas E. Cyrs, Jr., and Rita Lowenthal, "A Model for Curriculum Design Using a Systems Approach," *Audiovisual Instruction* 15 (January 1970): 17. Reprinted by permission.

1. Input data on students involve whatever is known about the student population for whom the instruction is intended. Tests and school records help to establish the level of skill development, knowledge, and attitudes that each student brings into the classroom.

2. All course, unit, and lesson objectives are stated in terms of student performance. The students know exactly what is expected of them, and how they will be evaluated.

3. Each student is pretested, so that the degree to which he has already mastered the unit objectives can be determined. The results of each pretest enable the teacher to diagnose the learning that is required, and the learning packet that should be prescribed.

4. The selection of course content is based on the contribution that it will make in helping the student to attain the formulated objectives.

5. Once the content is chosen, those teaching materials (or media) are selected that are judged most suitable for presenting the content. Examples of such teaching materials are: filmloops, films, printed materials, and other audio-visual media.

6. Instructional materials are produced that are not available commercially. The establishment of a materials production and duplication center is necessary—if one does not exist—to help develop the materials that are needed.

7. Once the objectives have been formulated, and the content and materials have been selected, the instructional process that is deemed most effective should be chosen. The instructional process might be large-group instruction, small-group interaction, independent study, individualized instruction, and so forth. Opinion differs as to whether teaching methods (i.e., instructional process) and materials decisions should be made at the same time, or one set of decisions made subsequent to the other. The teaching experience of the author supports the view that decisions made regarding teaching method should be made at the same time as those regarding materials.

8. The role of the teacher is not one of dispensing information, but, rather, diagnosing learning problems, prescribing learning sequences, conducting small-group discussions, and helping students individually.

9. The student is tested after he or she completes the instructional units and has consulted with the teacher. If there is a significant gain between the pretest and posttest scores, the student goes to the next learning sequence.

10. Every phase of the educational process is evaluated constantly. The constant evaluation provides the data needed to increase educational effectiveness.[4]

Systems Approach to Course Development

As explained earlier in this chapter and the preceding chapter, a course can be considered a subsystem of the instructional system. "The input is the learners' initial knowledge, and the output is the learners' final knowledge. The purpose of course development is to design validated instruction that is guaranteed to convert any input meeting the input specifications to an output that meets the . . . [subsystem's] output specifications."[5]

The suggestion is advanced that a course should be divided into parts, and course development proceed from there.[6] Viewed thus, a course may be referred to as a *system,* and its parts as *subsystems.* This particular terminology will be used in the explanation that follows.

Certain advantages can be given for dividing the system into several subsystems. Some of the advantages are as follows:

1. Development of the latter parts of the course usually requires students who can perform competently in the earlier part of the course. These students will not normally be available unless the earlier parts of the course have already been developed to criterion effectiveness.

2. Directing semiproficient students into the middle of a course is much easier if the course contains several subsystems, each with its own pretest and posttest.

3. If some very slow students do not finish the course, they can go through it again without having to enter subsystems whose content they have already mastered.

4. Decisions about media and teaching techniques can be made at the subsystem level. This greatly increases the flexibility of the system and leads to a more efficient allocation of personnel and resources.[7]

Course development is a time-consuming process. The process is symbolized in figure 16, and proceeds thus.[8]

It is unlikely that the prototype will meet the output criteria. However, information from its performance is used to revise the system and design a second one that works better. Several versions may have to be designed before one results that meets the specifications. The following are required for the development process: (1) a comprehensive test of the system's output, so that the efficiency of the system can be assessed and (2) sufficient data from the testing of the system, so that deficiencies can be pinpointed and revisions made to increase efficiency.

The system may be divided into several subsystems, each with its own defined input and output, and content, methods, and materials specifications. Each subsystem is revised until it meets the desired specifications. Subsequently, the validated subsystems are combined and the total system is tested. If further revisions are needed, they are made until the total system finally reaches the required effectiveness. It is to be noted in figure 16 that

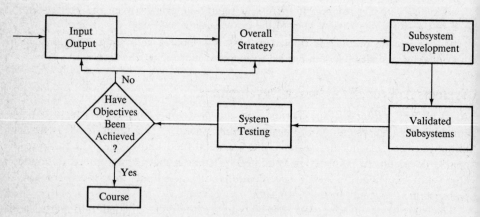

FIGURE 16.   Model: Course Development

SOURCE: Michael R. Eraut, "An Instructional Systems Approach to Course Development," *AV Communication Review* 15 (Spring 1967): 94. Reprinted by permission.

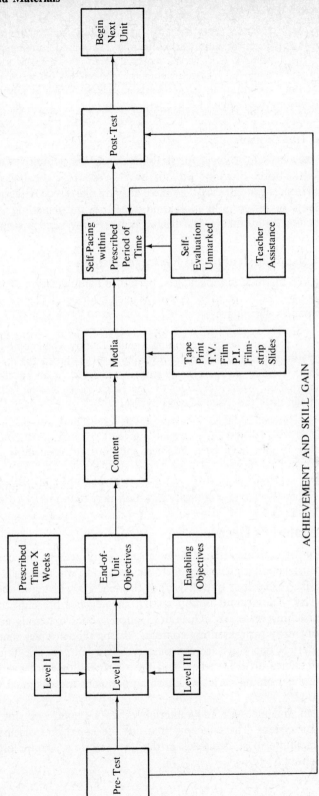

FIGURE 17. Model: Individualized Learning Packet Design

SOURCE: Thomas E. Cyrs, Jr., and Rita Lowenthal, "A Model for Curriculum Design Using a Systems Approach," *Audiovisual Instruction* 15 (January 1970): 18. Reprinted by permission.

one "feedback" arrow returns from System Testing to Input-Output and one to Overall Strategy. Either input-output specifications need modifying, perhaps because students take too long to achieve the required performance level, or the overall strategy must be changed by resequencing the subsystems or, more probably, by raising the output specifications of a subsystem whose output is inadequate as input for the following subsystem.[9]

Individualized Instruction

Three methods may be said to exist for individualizing instruction.[10] One method has been discussed above. Students do not have to start at the beginning of a course, or may omit any content that they have already mastered. A second method is to allow students to progress at individual paces. A third method is tracking. One group of students may take a fast track; another may need a slow one.

Learning Packets, or Instructional Package, Design

Learning packets, or instructional packages, permit individualization of instruction. Figure 17 symbolizes individualized learning packet design. The following explanation accompanies the figure.

1. Each student is pretested before beginning a unit of study. Depending on his or her score, one of three packets of varying difficulty level is chosen for the student. The individualized learning packet tells the student exactly what is expected within a designated time period. Also, it provides the learning sequence to be followed, so that the student can meet the specified objective(s).

2. The learning sequence includes a series of self-tests. Upon completion of the learning sequence, with self-tests, the student is given a posttest to determine if the specified objective(s) has/have been attained and thus the student is ready to progress to the next packet.

3. The teacher is available at all times to choose alternate learning sequences and help individual students with any difficulty that they may have.[11]

Methods and Materials Decisions

The determination of activities that will most effectively present the content of a unit of study or instructional package constitutes methods and materials decisions. Three options exist.[12] The first option is that the teacher will guide the students through the activity. The second option is that the teacher presents the content with the aid of teaching materials. The third option is that materials are selected as the most effective way for presenting content. Among the variables that influence methods and materials decisions are the nature of the learner, the nature of the content, the competence of the teacher, and the resources that are available. The objectives are the determining variable. Learning activities are designed to achieve objectives.

It is to be noted that methods and materials decisions enter only into the procedure level of the system. The concepts that are presented and discussed below are intended to facilitate these decisions in the middle school, junior high school, or senior high school.

Methods and Materials for Middle School Students

The nature of middle school students requires that academic experiences of varied kinds should be provided, so that the students can explore and experiment. Also, the experiences should be such that students will learn to work together as well as individually. The experiences should be appropriate to the stage of growth and development of the students. There appears to be no magic in the selection process of experiences.[13] Suggestions spring from teacher training, staff development, imitation, and intuition. Though there appears to be no magic in the selection process, there should be a willingness to be flexible in the experiences that could be used. The reason for this is that students, teachers, and conditions continually change, so that methods and materials that are effective with a particular group at a particular time may not be so effective at another time with another group, or even the same group. Evaluation of effective teaching and learning includes an assessment of student behaviors in learning, and the performance of students at a level commensurate with their abilities.[14]

A distinction cannot be made as to effectiveness between traditional and innovative teaching methods in the middle school.[15] In a given situation, a traditional method (e.g., lecture, discussion, recitation, lecture-discussion, lecture-demonstration, lecture-laboratory) may be as effective as individualized instruction, team teaching, and so forth.

It is to be noted that some educators make distinctions between the terms *methods, techniques* and *strategies.* A popular distinction specifies methods as a teaching mode that differs from techniques in that methods run for a longer period of time than techniques. As such, techniques are considered of such short duration that several varied techniques can be used in a particular class period. These educators consider methods to be of a longer duration, running a whole class period or an entire academic year. Examples of techniques, so defined, are as follows: using the compass, conducting an experiment, asking a question, and recording a dialogue. Examples of methods, so defined, are these: the lecture method, the socialized recitation method, and the dramatic method. Strategies, by some, are used to relate to the teaching of some particular skill or area of knowledge, e.g., teaching strategies in map making, teaching strategies in biology, and so on. Some educators do not regard team teaching as a method but, rather, a means of organizing students. The same is true of individualized instruction. Also, there are educators who make no distinction as to methods, techniques, or strategies. The following comments are made with relevance to the middle school.[16]

Lecture.   The lecture method appears effective in the middle school if it is used for a short period of time to give specific information and key questions to stimulate student discussion. This method in the middle school should be geared to the nature of middle school students. This involves entertaining questions during the lecture, thus, involving students in discussion.

Discussion.   Students of middle school age are often interested in sharing their ideas and experiences with the teacher and the other students. This built-in motivating factor suggests a high potential of involvement on the part of these students. "The most successful type of class discussion is one that tries to solve problems." [17] Middle school students are capable of problem solving, group planning, and responsibility.

Role Playing. Role playing helps middle school students to see relevance in situations as a result of their being a part of a role-playing experience. This benefit is especially true if the simulated situation deals with individuals of the same age as middle school students. The simulated situation experience can stimulate fruitful discussion. An explanation of the attunement of middle school students to discussion has already been presented in the preceding paragraph.

Programmed Instruction. The middle school student appears to profit from programmed instruction. This type of instruction, of course, allows the student to proceed individually and, thereby, assume responsibility for learning.

Team Teaching. Small-group instruction permits problem solving. The capability of middle school students for problem solving has already been discussed. Certain drawbacks are apparent in large-group instruction. For example, it is difficult to give attention to individual abilities because the group is acted upon as a whole, with no provision for involvement or interaction on the part of individual students.

Individualized Instruction. Independent study should not be the only experience of middle school students. Furthermore, the level of maturity and ability of students of this age should be kept in mind. Many differences exist. Some students of this age may be ready for independent work, and some may not.

Transitional Features. If the middle school is to serve as a transition from the self-contained elementary school to the more flexible organization of the senior high school, students should ease into more liberal settings in the lower part of the middle school, and gradually assume more independence in the upper level. Such transitional opportunities suggest a value for "team teaching, small- and large-group instruction, independent study, and self-contained centers." [18] The school facilities should contain space accommodations to assist these transitional settings.

Learning Centers. Middle school students are "well-informed, discriminating, aware of the world around . . . [them], and geared to the various forms of communication media." [19] This situation suggests the need of a facility, as an integral part of instruction, that would include "books, periodicals, films, filmstrips, maps, pictures, recordings, electronic tapes, transparencies, video tapes, single concept films, microfilm, ..." [20]

Methods and Materials for Junior High School Students

If there is one feature that characterizes the traditional organization of instruction in the junior high school, it is routine sameness. Every class meets at the same time of the day, the same days of the week, every week of the academic year, for the same number of periods as every other class period, or very close to it. The presumption is that every academic subject, especially in the departmentalized junior high school, requires the same period of time to be taught and learned.

There are some exceptions. For example, music and art may be taught for only half of a year, and on a rotating basis. However, the schedule is customarily a regular and tightly constructed one.

Currently, certain approaches are being used to improve instruction in the junior high schools. These approaches appear to hold promise for improving instruction for junior high school students. The approaches are discussed below.

Team Teaching.　Dissatisfaction with the traditional school system, and mounting criticism of American education after World War II, brought about the Staff Utilization Studies in the 1950s. These studies culminated in the Trump and Baynham report of 1961.[21] The report recommended several sweeping changes, including: variability of size in student grouping, increased use of technological aids, independent study for students, and teaching teams. The teams are intended to include a team leader, master teachers, assistant teachers, teacher aides, and clerical assistants. It is further intended that teacher interest and specialization be used to a maximum.

At first, junior high schools did not move into team teaching as rapidly as elementary or senior high schools. Recently, however, there has been a move of junior high schools toward team teaching.

Teachers have, traditionally, been assigned to a classroom and to one or more groups of students. Little attention has been given to individual differences in teaching interests. In addition, not enough attention has been given to the individual differences of students. Traditionally, a class has been treated as though it consisted of students with identical abilities and interests. Thus, team teaching and its related concepts constitute a major change in the way that students are taught. Team teaching can be designed to fit the particular needs of a student population.

Flexible Scheduling.　The opportunities for providing for individualized instruction, diversified student programs, and the unique needs of junior high school students are numerous. Flexible scheduling is an aid in implementing such provisions. In regard to team teaching, large- and small-group instruction, and independent study, for example, flexible scheduling is not necessarily involved, but it permits these processes and others.

Flexible scheduling means that there are variations in the daily instructional organization. Such schedules vary in form. In simplest form, class periods may be of equal length, but the opportunity exists for them to be varied in length or time of the day in which they occur. Flexible schedules are not necessarily modular schedules. A truly flexible modular schedule operates with a unit of time —i.e., ten minutes, fifteen minutes, or any number of minutes that are selected— with a certain number of modules allotted to each subject for one day, but a different number of modules allotted the next day.

The use of a flexible schedule, modular or not, makes it possible to develop a better junior high school program, and a broad exploratory program, which is one of the basic purposes of the junior high school. More courses can be offered. Thus, students are able to explore a greater number of subject areas. The opportunity for a greater number of course offerings can be provided in either of the following ways. There are others, also.

In order to fit in an extra subject, courses can be scheduled to meet only four times a week. In an alternate plan, an eight-period day within a six-period day is planned. In this plan, classes that may be expected to need more time regularly—perhaps industrial arts or homemaking—may be allotted sixty minutes for every class while other classes have only forty-five minutes per class period. A student who takes only the shorter classes may carry five, six, seven, or eight classes.

Ungrading. The concept of ungrading, most popular in elementary schools, is becoming more common in junior high schools. In the application of this concept, grade levels are eliminated. There is no such thing as seventh-, eighth-, or ninth-grade history, English, mathematics, and so forth. Instead, a number of steps or phases in each subject are offered, and students are placed in whichever step or phase that they are ready to work. Students move from one step or phase whenever they are ready. It appears that those who have worked with an ungraded system at the junior high school level have judged the approach highly satisfactory.

Independent Study. Individuals differ, and these differences are pronounced at the junior high school age. However, most junior high schools are based on group-paced learning in which the teacher bases her instruction upon the middle student. Such practices are not suited to the characteristics of junior high school students, nor the functions of the junior high school. Individualized programs, self-directed study, self-responsibility, critical thinking, and problem solving are among the necessary procedures of a junior high school. Independent study is a procedure that puts a heavy emphasis on these procedures.

Most independent study programs have been instituted at the senior high school level, but there have been successful efforts with junior high school students. Most independent study programs involve the more able students, but there is reason to believe that the majority of junior high school students can profit from such a program.

Programmed Instruction. Extensive use can be made of programmed instruction in junior high schools—e.g., in traditional programs, in team teaching, in ungraded schools, in independent study. Programmed instruction gives students individual attention, permits students to progress at their own pace, and affords opportunities for students to explore topics and materials that are not presented in class. All of these benefits are desirable for junior high school students. There are those critics, however, who say that programmed instruction dehumanizes learning experiences.

Libraries. Current trends in instruction in junior high schools dictate an expanded role for junior high school libraries. The library is called by such titles as curriculum center, learning-materials center, or instructional-materials center. Whatever the title, the library is currently responsible for more than printed materials. It is responsible for a variety of audio-visual devices and materials, and the facilities for the production of instructional materials.

Methods and Materials for Senior High School Students

Methods and materials at the senior high school level are being modified to provide greater opportunity for independent study, work in small groups, work-study programs, educational technology, and community-centered learning. The following paragraphs are added in specification of this statement.

Methods. Learning activities in a senior high school can appropriately be carried on by a variety of methods which may be categorized as follows: (1) lecture and verbal presentation; (2) discussion and questioning; (3) practice and drill; (4) viewing, listening, and answering; (5) problem-solving, heuristic, and discovery; (6) laboratory and inquiry; (7) creativity-oriented; (8) role playing, simulation, and games; (9) play, handling, manipulating, acting; (10) telling; (11) independent learning and self-instructional; and (12) community-based.[22] Most of the methods included in the list are known enough not to warrant further explanation. The especial potential and relative newness of the problem-solving, heuristic, discovery, and creativity-oriented methods suggest justification of explanation.

Problem-solving, heuristic, and discovery methods have been widely recommended in recent years. Heuristic teaching involves a general set of student-interactive processes.

Heuristic teaching refers to styles of teaching which emphasize the development of self-initiated and self-directed pupil learning; which stress the pupil's discovery rather than absorbing knowledge; which place the student in the role of the inquirer; which aim at heightening the relevance of school to the pupil's life; which are concerned with the emotional and social development of the pupil as well as with his cognitive growth.[23]

Although various teaching methods may contribute to the development of creativity, such development, in these instances, is incidental, and not the principal end that is sought in the learning experience. Methods designed primarily to develop creative talents are characterized by

creation of things, such as sculpture, visual arts, music, motion pictures, telecasts, photographs, drama, dance form, fashion design, literature, a machine, plans for material objects (buildings, parks, and so on) or an important project or undertaking (conservation of energy sources) that constitute original work by the student; preparing solutions other than those listed or taught in class for a mathematical problem or social issue of some complexity; devising a better way of performing a complex operation or process.[24]

Student activity consists of engagement in creative activities. Teacher activity is quite limited. It consists of "encouraging, stimulating, advising, counseling, supervising, suggesting, explaining, demonstrating; proposing projects for interested students; evaluating product; continuously endeavoring to identify students with potentialities for creative work; judging a student's work or activity." [25]

Materials. Revolutionary changes have occurred in instructional materials and technology since the 1950s.[26] These changes have given the teacher new tools and new materials. Technological aids include video tape recorders and recordings, educational television, television cassettes, teaching machines, microfiche, and the computer in computer-based instruction. The instructional materials center has become a standard component of the senior high school.

The systems approach of viewing a problem as a set of interrelated, interdependent parts which "work together for the overall objectives of the whole" is also being applied to the utilization of teaching materials to meet the objectives that have been defined for a given student(s) in a given subject.[27] The systems approach is also being applied to the planning and erection of school buildings. "The systems approach, when applied to building problems, results in a process whereby resources and needs can be related effectively to performance, cost, and time. . . ."[28]

Summary

Stage three of curriculum and instructional improvement involves the implementation of program improvements. This chapter explains stage three.

Curriculum refers to the total instructional system. The curriculum is composed of subsystems, bisystems, units or packages, and procedures. Methods and materials decisions enter only into the procedure level of the system. The chapter explains methods and materials in a systems analysis context.

A systems approach to curriculum and instructional improvement is "a rational, problem-solving method of analyzing the educational process and making it more effective."[29] The system is this process taken as a whole and incorporating all of its parts—namely, students, teachers, content, methods, materials, physical environment, and the evaluation of the instructional objectives.

"Educational effectiveness is defined in terms of desired changes in student behavior and tested accordingly."[30] Systems analysis attempts to increase educational effectiveness by specifying educational objectives with precision and, subsequently, redesigning the entire educational process to insure student attainment of the objectives. The chapter presents and explains a design for increasing educational effectiveness. The explanation relates to a model that is included.

Course development is a time-consuming process. The process is symbolized in a model that is presented in the chapter. The process, in reference to the model, is explained.

Three models exist for individualizing instruction. In one method, students either do not have to start at the beginning of a course, or may omit any content that they have already mastered. A second method allows students to progress at their own individual paces. In the third method, tracking is provided. One group of students takes a fast track; another needs a slow one.

Learning packets—or instructional packages—permit individualization of instruction. A model in the chapter symbolizes individualized learning packet design, and an explanation accompanies the model.

The chapter concludes with a discussion of methods and materials especially pertinent to the middle school, junior high school, and senior high school, respectively.

NOTES

1. K. V. Feyereisen, A. J. Fiorino, and A. T. Nowak, *Supervision and Curriculum Renewal: A Systems Approach* (New York: Appleton-Century-Crofts, 1970), p. 145. Reprinted by permission.

2. Thomas E. Cyrs, Jr., and Rita Lowenthal, "A Model for Curriculum Design Using a Systems Approach," *Audiovisual Instruction* 15 (January 1970): 16. Reprinted by permission.

3. Ibid.

4. Ibid., pp. 17–18.

5. Michael R. Eraut, "An Instructional Systems Approach to Course Development," *AV Communication Review* 15 (Spring 1967): 93. Reprinted by permission.

6. Ibid., p. 97.

7. Ibid., p. 98.

8. Ibid., pp. 92–100.

9. Ibid., pp. 93–94.

10. Ibid., p. 100.

11. Cyrs and Lowenthal, "Model for Curriculum Design," p. 18.

12. Feyereisen, Fiorino, and Nowak, *Supervision and Curriculum Renewal*, p. 149.

13. Joseph C. DeVita, Philip Pumerantz, and Leighton B. Wilklow, *The Effective Middle School* (West Nyack: Parker Publishing Co., 1970), p. 172. Reprinted by permission.

14. Ibid., p. 173.

15. Ibid.

16. Ibid., pp. 174–89.

17. Ibid., p. 176.

18. Ibid., p. 201.

19. Ibid., p. 208.

20. Ibid., p. 209.

21. J. Lloyd Trump and Dorsey Baynham, *Focus on Change, Guide to Better Schools* (Chicago: Rand McNally, 1961).

22. J. Galen Saylor and William M. Alexander, *Planning Curriculum for Schools* (New York: Holt, Rinehart and Winston, 1974), pp. 252–68. Reprinted by permission.

23. Richard E. Snow, ed., "A Symposium on Heuristic Teaching: A Report of Addresses at a Conference," ERIC Document No. 046893 (December 1970); cited in Saylor and Alexander, *Planning Curriculum*, pp. 257–58. Reprinted by permission.

24. Saylor and Alexander, *Planning Curriculum*, p. 261.

25. Ibid.

26. Harl R. Douglass, ed., *The High School Curriculum* (New York: Ronald Press, 1970), p. 183. Reprinted by permission.

27. Ezra D. Ehrenkrantz, "The System to Systems," *Council of Educational Facility Planners Journal* 8 (November-December 1970): 4–5. Reprinted by permission.

28. Ibid.

29. Cyrs and Lowenthal, "Model for Curriculum Design," p. 16.

30. Ibid.

Related Readings

Bosco, J. et al. "Management Systems for Individualized Instruction." *Education* 96 (Spring 1976): 251–64.

Cyrs, Thomas E., Jr., and Lowenthal, Rita. "A Model for Curriculum Design Using a Systems Approach." *Audiovisual Instruction* 15 (January 1970): 16–18.

DeVita, Joseph C.; Pumerantz, Philip; and Wilklow, Leighton B. *The Effective Middle School.* West Nyack: Parker Publishing, 1970.

Douglass, Harl R., ed. *The High School Curriculum.* New York: Ronald Press, 1964.

Drumheller, Sidney J. *Handbook of Curriculum Design for Individualized Instruction.* Englewood Cliffs, N.J.: Educational Technology Publications, 1971.

Eraut, Michael R. "An Instructional Systems Approach to Course Development." *AV Communication Review* 15 (Spring 1967): 92–101.

Feyereisen, K. V.; Fiorino, A. J.; and Nowak, A. T. *Supervision and Curriculum Renewal: A Systems Approach.* New York: Appleton-Century-Crofts, 1970.

Goodlad, John I., and Klein, M. Frances. *Behind the Classroom Door.* Worthington, Ohio: Charles A. Jones, 1970.

Hoye, Robert E. "Application of the Systems Approach to the Selection of Relevant Teaching Methods and Media." *Education* 15 (April 1970): 363–65.

Popham, W. James, and Baker, Eva I. *Systematic Instruction.* Englewood Cliffs, N.J.: Prentice-Hall, 1970.

Saylor, J. Galen, and Alexander, William M. *Planning Curriculum for Schools.* New York: Holt, Rinehart and Winston, 1974.

Stowe, R. "What Is Instructional Development?" *Audiovisual Instruction* 16 (February 1971): 88.

Trump, J. Lloyd, and Baynham, Dorsey. *Focus on Change, Guide to Better Schools.* Chicago: Rand McNally, 1961.

Wong, Martin R., and Wong, Joyce M. "The Classroom as a System." *Educational Technology* 12 (May 1972): 56–57.

Work Sheet 7A
Questions for Class Dialogue

Student's Name _____

Date _____

Directions: Study chapter 7 with the following questions in mind. Prepare responses for each question, so that you can intelligently participate in class dialogue. Space is provided with each question, so that you can record any notes that will aid you in the dialogue.

1. (a) Define educational effectiveness.

   (b) By what means does systems analysis attempt to increase educational effectiveness?

   (c) Give the components of a model that would symbolize a design for increasing educational effectiveness.

2. Succinctly, explain a systems approach to course development.

3. What are three methods for individualizing instruction?

4. Give the components of a model that would symbolize individualized learning packet design.

5. Give the three options that exist in methods and materials decisions.

6. (a) Specify methods and materials that appear effective for middle school students.

(b) Can a distinction be made as to effectiveness in the middle school between traditional and innovative teaching methods? Explain.

7. Discuss the approaches that are being used currently to improve instruction in the junior high schools.

8. (a) Which methods appear effective for senior high school students?

(b) What does heuristic teaching involve?

(c) Depict the methods that are designed primarily to develop creative talents.

9. Discuss the nature of teaching materials currently available and apparently applicable for teaching senior high school students.

Work Sheet 7B
Systems-Oriented Teacher

Student's Name _____

Date _____

Directions:
1. Consider the following question:

    What specifically would a teacher, oriented toward the systems approach, do in planning for learning that would be different from what his or her nonsystems-oriented counterpart would do?
2. Refer to:

    Wong, Martin R., and Wong, Joyce M. "The Classroom as a System." *Educational Technology* 12 (May 1972): 56–57.
3. Answer the question that appears above. Write your answer below.

Work Sheet 7C
Individualized Instruction Investigation

Student's Name _____

Date _____

Directions:
1. Go to the library to investigate each of the following plans for individualizing instruction:
   a. Individually Prescribed Instruction (IPI), developed at the University of Pittsburgh.
   b. Program for Learning in Accordance with Needs (Project PLAN), created by Westinghouse Learning Corporation and American Institutes for Research.
   c. NOVA Plan, developed at Nova High School, Fort Lauderdale, Florida.
2. Record your learnings in the space provided below.

Work Sheet 7D
Selection of Teaching Methods and Media

Student's Name _____

Date _____

Directions:
1. Refer to:
   Hoye, Robert E. "Application of the Systems Approach to the Selection of Relevant Teaching Methods and Media." *Education* 90 (April 1970): 363–65.
2. Report the suggestions that Hoye makes, in the above-listed article, for the application of the systems approach to the selection of relevant teaching methods and media. Make a written record of your report in the space below.

Work Sheet 7E
Extended Reading

Student's Name _____

Date _____

Directions:
1. Read the following article:
    Bosco, J. et al. "Management Systems for Individualized Instruction."
    Education 96 (Spring 1976): 251–64.
2. Be prepared to discuss your learnings in class dialogue. Use the space below to make notes to aid you in the discussion.

Work Sheet 7F
Classroom Visit

Student's Name _____

Date _____

Directions:
1. Visit a classroom in a middle school, junior high school, or senior high school where individualized instruction is used.
2. Make note of the materials that are used and the procedure in which they are used. Confirm the correctness of your observations with the teacher who is in charge of the classroom where you observe.
3. Record your learnings below.

Work Sheet 7G
Materials Fair

Student's Name _____

Date _____

Directions:
1. Organize a committee for presenting a Materials Fair.
2. In the fair, display hardware and software—individualized and nonindividualized materials—for use in a middle school, junior high school, or senior high school. If possible, make provision that the sales representatives of the companies that market the materials attend the fair.
3. Use the space below for recording the design of your plans for the fair.

Work Sheet 7H
Representative Visit

Student's Name _____
Date _____

Directions:
1. Invite a company representative to the class to demonstrate and explain the use of a computer terminal.
2. Make sure that the explanation includes the applicability of the terminal in classroom instruction.
3. Use the space below to make notes for the preparation of the visit.

Work Sheet 7I
Selecting and Integrating Instructional Packages

Student's Name _____

Date _____

Directions:
1. Study the following model. It represents a systems approach to selecting and integrating instructional packages.

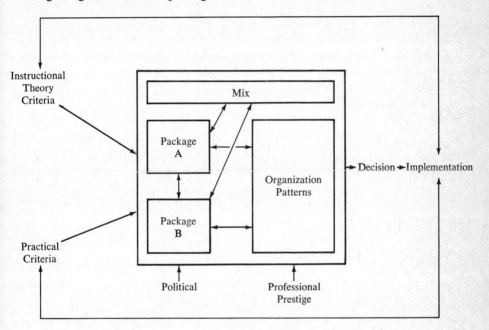

2. Refer to:

> Gordon, Ira J. et al. "A Model for Curriculum Development Decision Making." In *Criteria for Theories of Instruction,* edited by Ira J. Gordon. Washington, D. C.: Association for Supervision and Curriculum Development, 1968, pp. 40–44. (The model above is taken from this reference.)

3. Discuss the concept that is represented in the model given above. Use the space below.

Work Sheet 7J
Decision-Making Process

Student's Name _____

Date _____

Directions:
1. Consider the following statement:
   A . . . way of looking at instructional development is as a process of decision making.
2. Refer to:
   Stowe, R. "What Is Instructional Development?" *Audiovisual Instruction* 16 (February 1971): 88. (The above-given statement is taken from this reference.)
3. Expound upon the statement after reading the above-listed article. Write your explanation below.

Work Sheet 7K
Slides

Student's Name _____
Date _____

Directions:
1. Visit a class in a middle school, junior high school, or senior high school. Note the methods and materials that are used during the course of the class. If possible, make slides of the methods and materials as they are used. Conclude if the teacher is systems oriented or nonsystems oriented. Be able to explain.
2. At the end of the class visit:
   a. Ask the teacher any questions that you may have about the methods and materials.
   b. Confirm with the teacher whether he or she is systems oriented or nonsystems oriented.
3. Show your slides to your curriculum class. Give all pertinent explanation. Use the space below to record any notes that may aid you in your presentation.

Work Sheet 7L
Extension of Learning

Student's Name _____

Date _____

Directions:
1. Choose one of the following readings, or one of the readings at the end of chapter 7, to extend the learnings that you have attained from the chapter.
2. Read critically.
3. Synthesize your learnings for class dialogue.
4. Space is provided at the end of this work sheet for notes that you may want to make.

Readings:
1. Drumheller, Sidney J. *Handbook of Curriculum Design for Individualized Instruction.* Englewood Cliffs, N.J.: Educational Technology Publications, 1971.
2. Goodlad, John I., and Klein, M. Frances. *Behind the Classroom Door.* Worthington, Ohio: Charles A. Jones, 1970.
3. Popham, W. James, and Baker, Eva I. *Systematic Instruction,* Englewood Cliffs, N.J.: Prentice-Hall, 1970.

8

Evaluation of Curriculum and Instructional Programs

Curriculum and instructional improvement, viewed in terms of a systems approach, includes four stages. The fourth and last stage is an evaluation of program outcomes. The preceding chapters have sequentially explained the first three stages, and this chapter explains stage four.

Evaluation Defined

Evaluation is defined in a variety of ways in educational literature. Evaluation will be preliminarily defined in the next few paragraphs. As the chapter develops, additional connotations will be introduced, so that the reader's perspective may be broadened to aid him or her in selecting a definition that seems most logical and, therefore, most serviceable.

Evaluation Distinguished from Measurement. Evaluation is sometimes used as though it were synonymous with measurement. It is not.

> Educational measurement is normally considered to be a process which attempts to quantify the degree to which a particular trait has been acquired by a student. The most common instrument used in measurement is the paper-and-pencil test, which may be a quiz prepared by a teacher, a departmental examination, or a standardized test.[1]

Measurement may be said to involve the collection and analysis of data by means of, for example, an achievement test.

Evaluation uses the data that are derived from both measurement and non-measurement procedures, and arrives at a value judgment. In other words, "the total process of making a value judgment based on evidence derived from both measurement and nonmeasurement procedures is evaluation." [2] Examples of non-measurement procedures are observations, anecdotal records, and interviews. Evaluation may be defined, by another set of words, "as a systematic process for judging the adequacy of the achievement of the objectives of the system." [3]

It is to be noted that evaluation is characterized by both quantitative and qualitative dimensions plus a value judgment as to the extent to which the objectives have been attained. Measurement, however, does not include qualitative descriptions and does not involve value judgments. Measurement is quantitative.

Formative Evaluation Distinguished from Summative Evaluation. Curriculum evaluation may be discussed in terms of the timing of the evaluation and the purpose for which the results are used. As such, a distinction is made between formative evaluation and summative evaluation.[4]

Formative evaluation is concerned with the merits of the curriculum and instructional program. The purpose of formative evaluation is to contribute to the improvement or development of the educational program. Most formative evaluation provides short-term feedback. In formative evaluation, the curriculum and instructional program is subjected to critical scrutiny and appraisal. The evidence or data that are gathered are used subsequently for making decisions as to how the curriculum and instructional program may be further improved or developed. The results of formative evaluation are intended primarily for those who are working on the development of the program.

The purpose of summative evaluation is to assess the overall effectiveness of a program. While formative evaluation is concerned with the plan itself, summative evaluation is concerned with the learners as a result of instruction. Summative evaluations may vary considerably in scope, complexity, and cost. Since summative evaluation is the assessment of an already developed program, the results are intended primarily for those who set policy at various levels—e.g., a school board that will consider the use of a program with the students in a school system. The data that are gathered consist of test scores of all sorts, student reactions to instruction and the program, employer reactions, parent reactions, level of college success, and so forth. It is to be noted that a nebulous line of distinction exists between formative and summative evaluation. The difference lies more with the purpose for which the evaluation is made, rather than the methodology or analytical techniques that are used.

Evaluation and Decision Making. It is to be noted that decision making is not a part of the evaluative process itself. Evaluation provides the knowledge that is needed for decision making. However, decision making involves the making of choices from among alternatives. Figure 18 presents the steps in evaluation for providing data for decision making. It is observed that the three major steps are: (1) delineating information needs, (2) obtaining information, and (3) providing information. A summarization of the steps to be taken in the process of evaluation

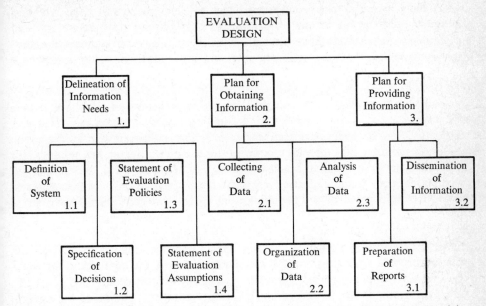

FIGURE 18.   Model: Steps in Evaluation for Providing Data for Decision
             Making

SOURCE: Phi Delta Kappa National Study Committee on Evaluation, Daniel Stufflebeam,
          chm., *Educational Evaluation and Decision Making* (Itasca, Ill.: F. E. Peacock
          Publishers, 1971), p. 156; cited in J. Galen Saylor and William M. Alexander,
          Planning Curriculum for Schools (New York: Holt, Rinehart and Winston, 1974),
          p. 303. Reprinted by permission.

are these: (1) determination of what is to be evaluated, and kinds of decisions
for which evaluative data are needed; (2) kinds of data that are needed for making
the decisions; (3) collection of the needed data; (4) defining of criteria for
determining the quality of the matter that is being evaluated; (5) analysis of the
data in terms of these criteria; and (6) providing information for the decision
makers.[5]

Evaluation Based on Relationship between Input and Output

It should be recalled that the input of a school system is an uneducated individual,
and the output is an educated individual. Most schools restrict their evaluation
program to a measurement of the output of the system.[6] For example, some schools
give standardized achievement tests. The scores attained on the tests are used to
indicate the quality of the output, which is used to indicate the quality of the
program. However, if a view of the evaluative process is to be complete, it must
include the following considerations.

Quality as a Base.   Implication of the quality of a program based singly on the
quality of the output of the program appears to be questionable and misleading.
This statement is explained, illustratively, as follows.[7] A particular school that
receives academically talented students, by the very fact that the students are

academically talented, will produce graduates of high quality. In a second illustration, schools that are located in communities where entering students are poor academically will not graduate students who score higher on standardized tests than graduates of, for example, a school where the students are elite in academic talent.

Effectiveness as a Base. "A measure of the effectiveness of a school system appears to provide a sounder basis for evaluating a school system than measures of 'quality.' " [8] To evaluate effectiveness, a school system needs to design an evaluation program that measures both the input and output of the system. This means that the input needs to be measured as it enters the system; and the output, as it leaves the system. Illustratively, different forms of an achievement test would be administered at the beginning and the end of each school year, or as students begin and end a particular course. The difference between the input scores and output scores will constitute the measure of effectiveness.

It is reasonable to conclude that the most reflective evaluation of a school system is probably a measurement and evaluation of both the quality and the effectiveness of a school's program, rather than quality or effectiveness alone.

Benefits result from the measurement of the input and output of the system. All information that is provided should feed back into the system, and thus enable the staff to take action for improvement. In other words, an evaluation system that is rightly designed to measure effectiveness could lead to improvements in the instructional system. For example, if a pretest is given at the beginning of an academic year, and a posttest at the end of the academic year, an indication is given of the effectiveness of the instruction that was provided—and the needs for improvement. Such indications can also be drawn from a pretest that is given at the beginning of a course and a posttest that is given at the end of the course. A pretest-posttest procedure not only yields implications regarding a program, or course, but also regarding the growth of a group of students or an individual student.

Purposes of Pretesting. A pretest may have either one of two purposes. First, it may be given to see whether students have the prerequisite learnings needed for a particular course. Second, a pretest may be given to determine how much students already know of content intended for a particular course. If students do not have the prerequisite learnings for a particular course, remedial work can be prescribed or intended content can be modified. If students already are familiar with content intended for a particular course, that content can be deleted and other content added. Other modifications also may be deemed prudent.

Comprehensive Curriculum Evaluation

A survey of the literature reveals that interest favors a broad type of evaluation of curriculum and instruction. Several models are available as approaches to the evaluation. A variety of instruments that can be used for evaluation are also available. Basically, a number of points of view regarding evaluation are currently being advanced.

The author sanctions a broad type of evaluation of curriculum and instruction.

The explanation that ensues—incorporating models, instruments, and principles of evaluation—reflects the evaluation approach that the author recommends.

Three Evaluation Models

The McIntyre Model. Evaluation is defined in a variety of ways in educational literature. One definition has already been given and discussed in this chapter. Other connotations include grading, rating, scoring, finding the value of, and so on. In Robert McIntyre's model, evaluation of program and materials is considered to involve "precise specifications, determination of amount, and finding worth in terms of comparable items." [9] It is maintained that the "fact finding should be specific and answer the 'does it work' type of question." [10] It is further maintained that "evaluation is the basis for decision making, and as such, includes both description and judgment, and collection of pertinent data on which to base judgments." [11]

This model is concerned with applications of a systems approach to the evaluation of instructional materials and programs. The explanation proceeds thus.[12] At the heart of the system is the student, singly or in group, who interacts in some way with some type of instructional material and an instructor. The instructor might be a paraprofessional or even another student. The administration system, communication system, performance evaluation system, and so on, surround the interaction of the student(s) with instructional material and instructor. Evaluation is one of a set of interacting systems. It does not function alone.

A general evaluation system model that is used will usually have three or four components. One component of the evaluation system consists of input variables.

> Input variables may include the teacher's reaction to change, the central office, and "these types of kids," the parents' reaction to the school, the program, and the teacher, as well as the type of children involved and the general context of the program.[13]

The second component of this system is referred to as event variables. This second component consists of the events or interactions that occur which facilitate or hinder progress toward the desired outcomes.

The third component consists of the outcomes of the events or transactions. Currently, it appears that favor exists for behaviorally stated objectives and observed behavioral outcomes. A concern for actions and capabilities of individual students gives need to a concern for behavioral objectives. A curriculum that is devised for all students assumes that prescribed learning is not ultimately affected by individual differences. The reminder is given that "some educationally relevant objectives cannot be reduced to behavioral terms and that . . . [students] are not plastic to be molded at will by experience." [14]

The fourth component is sometimes omitted in evaluation. It refers to results as input. When a student or teacher does something in an educational event or interaction, something happens as a consequence. There is an effect, and whether the student or teacher repeats or modifies the behavior depends on the result obtained. The partaker in the educational event or interaction has more and different input.[15]

A choice of approaches exists for the evaluation of materials. The selection of the approach depends on the needs, purposes, and resources of the group or the individual doing the evaluation. One approach is the use of professional judgment of experts or teachers. Another approach is empirical validation of the materials. In the latter approach, "time effort studies and cost benefit analyses would both be appropriate models. . . ." [16] It is to be noted that limitations exist in either approach. Nevertheless, there is potential for something more than an annual examination and yearly revision of courses of study. The data that are gathered are used to modify the system, make decisions, and make the instructional system self-correcting. Justification exists for empirical and judgment evaluations of instructional materials and programs that provide for feedback and improvement that are continual, rather than not.

The Stake Congruence-Contingency Model.   The second evaluation model is that of Robert Stake.[17] The model is symbolized in figures 19 and 20. It is to be noted

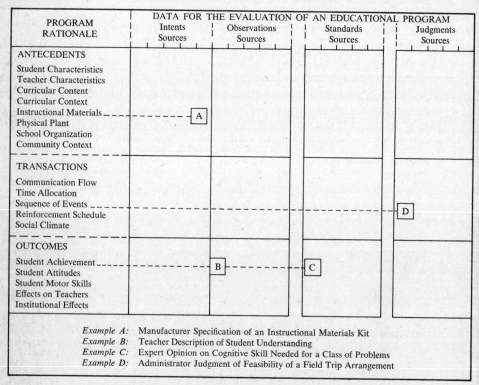

PROGRAM RATIONALE	DATA FOR THE EVALUATION OF AN EDUCATIONAL PROGRAM			
	Intents Sources	Observations Sources	Standards Sources	Judgments Sources
ANTECEDENTS Student Characteristics Teacher Characteristics Curricular Content Curricular Context Instructional Materials Physical Plant School Organization Community Context	A			
TRANSACTIONS Communication Flow Time Allocation Sequence of Events Reinforcement Schedule Social Climate				D
OUTCOMES Student Achievement Student Attitudes Student Motor Skills Effects on Teachers Institutional Effects		B	C	

Example A: Manufacturer Specification of an Instructional Materials Kit
Example B: Teacher Description of Student Understanding
Example C: Expert Opinion on Cognitive Skill Needed for a Class of Problems
Example D: Administrator Judgment of Feasibility of a Field Trip Arrangement

FIGURE 19.   Congruence-Contingency Model for Educational Evaluation: Illustration of Data Possibly Representative of the Contents of Four Cells of the Matrices for a Given Educational Program

SOURCE: Robert E. Stake, "Language, Rationality, and Assessment," in *Improving Educational Assessment and an Inventory of Measures of Affective Behavior,* ed. Walcott H. Beatty (Washington, D.C.: Association for Supervision and Curriculum Development, 1969), p. 16; cited in J. Galen Saylor and William M. Alexander, *Planning Curriculum for Schools* (New York: Holt, Rinehart and Winston, 1974), p. 305. Reprinted by permission.

initially that, according to Stake, both description and judgment are essential in evaluation. An explanation of the model symbolized in the two figures follows.[18]

Figure 19 is addressed to the collection of data. The rows of the first column list the categories of data that the evaluator will need to gather—antecedents, "any condition existing prior to teaching and learning which may relate to outcomes"; transactions, "the countless encounters of students with teacher, student with student, author with reader, parent with counselor—the succession of engagements which comprise the process of education"; and outcomes, "abilities, achievements, attitudes, and aspirations of students resulting from an educational experience." [19]

Data are entered in each of the twelve cells for whichever item is being considered under antecedents, transactions, and outcomes. *Intents* refer to goals or objectives. *Observations* are the descriptive data that may have been derived from any number of sources—e.g., observations, checklists, school records, test results. *Standards* reflect what various individuals—e.g., administrators, teachers, noted

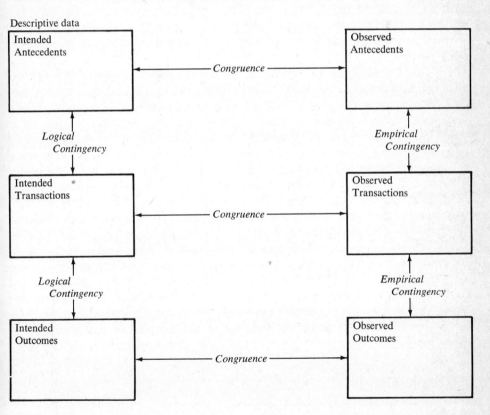

FIGURE 20.   Congruence-Contingency Model for Educational Evaluation: A Representation of the Processing of Descriptive Data

SOURCE: Robert E. Stake, "Language, Rationality, and Assessment," in *Improving Educational Assessment and an Inventory of Measures of Affective Behavior,* ed. Walcott H. Beatty (Washington, D.C.: Association for Supervision and Curriculum Development, 1969), p. 20; cited in J. Galen Saylor and William M. Alexander, *Planning Curriculum for Schools* (New York: Holt, Rinehart and Winston, 1974), p. 306. Reprinted by permission.

educators—say should be the case in each instance. *Judgments* reflect how such persons as parents, students, teachers, feel about the aspects that are being evaluated.

Figure 20 illustrates the method of handling descriptive data collected in figure 19. Specifically, it illustrates the method of handling descriptive data collected for the first and second columns in figure 19. Congruence is identical match between what is intended and what is observed—i.e., intended antecedents and observed antecedents, intended transactions and observed transactions, intended outcomes and observed outcomes. Evaluations usually examine only the congruence between intended and observed outcomes. It is to be noted that here evaluation also includes an examination of the congruence between intended and observed antecedents, and an examination of the congruence between intended and observed transactions.

Contingencies relate to relationships among the variables—antecedents, transactions, and outcomes. An examination of contingencies seeks to determine the antecedents and the transactions that have caused particular outcomes—in other words, the causes of the outcomes that have resulted. The data discussed above are used in making decisions for curriculum and instructional improvement.

The UCLA Model. In the evaluation model developed at the Center for the Study of Evaluation at the University of California at Los Angeles, a clear distinction is made between process evaluation and outcome evaluation.[20] Process evaluation directs attention to analyzing the success with which a program is being implemented. It is also concerned with appraising the value of the new program in terms of measurable gains in student performance. If process evaluation indicates a need for program modification, the appropriate adjustments are made. Unfortunately, too little systematic attention is given to process evaluation. Instead, attention has tended to be focused on summative or outcome evaluation.

After a program change has been made in a school and a process evaluation has been performed, decisions must be made regarding the overall worth of the program. This latter procedure is known as outcome evaluation. Outcome evaluation establishes a basis for any one of the following decisions: (1) continuation of the program with or without modifications, (2) expansion of the program, or (3) termination of the program. Determination of the improvement of student behavior or performance is central to outcome evaluation. Of course, the improvement of student behavior or performance is the purpose of any instructional program.

Aggregate Models

Most efforts to improve curriculum and instruction have been based, over the years, on a segmental curriculum model. Innovations have been adopted, in most cases, without consideration for implications to the rest of the programs. As a result, segmental and unarticulated innovations and programs have not lived up to the promises upon which they have been adopted.

Emphasis on—and the adoption of—curriculum packages have also proved detrimental to optimal curriculum and instructional improvement. Such a practice commonly focuses on separate course-content improvement with relatively little attention given to necessary interrelationships between and among the various subjects that constitute the total school curriculum. In contrast to the segmental curriculum model, the aggregate model focuses on the total school curriculum with various courses, learnings, and goals treated as they interrelate.

Some Considerations for a Comprehensive Evaluation

The curriculum and instructional program can be evaluated in the fullest sense of the meaning of the word, *evaluation*. To do so, it is necessary both to measure development or status and, also, to determine the worth or value of the growth or status. In this process, the following considerations are necessary in an evaluation of curriculum and instruction. Pertinence is made to the middle school, junior high school, and senior high school.

The first important consideration is that the curriculum and instructional program should be evaluated in light of the goals or objectives that have been set in the particular school. The second consideration is that if the evaluation is to be entire, the determination of growth of the students must be both qualitative and quantitative.[21] Various psychometric devices may be used for qualitative measurements. A variety of means may be used to attain quantitative measurements. The following are but a few: objective and essay classroom tests; standardized tests; checklists, rating scales, inventories, questionnaires; observations, anecdotal records, interviews; sociodramas, autobiographies, and other similar techniques; case studies and case conferences.

Data may be derived about student growth and development, or the status of the curriculum and instructional program, from sources other than the students themselves. The following are included among such other sources of data: (1) opinion polls and/or interviews of graduates, employers, colleges; and (2) judgments of the success of the students in post-levels of education.

> The number of divorces, murders, mental patients, and so forth, among graduates would also give information about the success or failure of a school's program. Because the public schools are instruments of society to preserve itself, any evidence of societal breakdown should be of concern to educators.[22]

If quantitative evaluation is to be valid, it must have the following component parts: "(1) a means of assessing the outward behavioral change in the student; (2) a method of determining inner behavioral change; (3) a process for determining environmental and personal factors that influence, either detrimentally or beneficially, any behavioral change." [23] These component parts may be explained as follows.[24]

Outward Behavioral Change. First, if there has been no change in a student's behavior or tendency toward behavior, no education has taken place. It is not enough, for example, to say that a student can write a theme or a composition with good grammar, spelling, and punctuation. A determination must be made as to how current performance differs from his or her previous performance. There should be a continual annual pattern of behavioral growth in each student. If not, something is wrong. It is the responsibility of the evaluator to discover what it is.

It is to be noted that behavior can be measured, but tendencies toward behavior such as "ideals, attitudes, appreciations, and feelings except through the medium of measuring behavior" cannot be measured.[25]

Inner Behavioral Change.   Second, a student's inner behavior affects his or her scholastic achievement. For example, a positive attitude towards school should help to promote academic achievement. A student's inner behavior not only affects academic achievement, but also other aspects of the student's life; and it will continue to affect his or her life in the future. Therefore, it is important to know whether the student's inner behavioral development is progressing satisfactorily. However, the measuring of any mental process can only be approximated from outward behavior. "Modern psychological techniques make it possible to estimate inner behavior with some degree of confidence." [26]

Environmental Factors.   Third, many environmental factors affect students' behavioral changes. "Among them are type of neighborhood, socioeconomic status of the family, mental status of parents, church affiliation, companions, recreational activities, and home atmosphere." [27] Actually, a student is under the influence of any particular teacher or segment of the program a relatively short period of a day. Before it can be said that a particular school activity, or course, or segment of a school program has been the sole contributor to some specified success of a particular student, it must first be ascertained whether some environmental factor(s) have/has produced the results.

Personal Factors.   Fourth, personal factors also affect students' behavioral changes. Learning is affected by physical condition, mental health, previous learnings, attitudes—and skills and habits of working, studying, and thinking. Though these factors may not be apparent in casual observation, devices can be used for their assessment. If little or no annual growth is occurring, it may not be attributable to the curriculum and instructional program. The lack of adequate growth might well be the result of personal factors. In summary, all factors must be considered before it can be said that it is the curriculum and instructional program that is influencing change.

Teachers.   The role of the classroom teacher is not to be underestimated in all of the above considerations for the determination of student progress and the status of the curriculum and instructional program. Indeed, teachers are in encounter with students daily in teaching-learning experiences. It follows that teachers are important and excellent persons for assessing student progress and the status of the program.

Evaluative Criteria.   The *Evaluative Criteria* for secondary schools, first printed in 1940 and revised periodically, is an excellent means of determining the quality and quantity of the school's program. It also provides for the evaluation of the school plant and the school administration. An *Evaluative Criteria for Junior High Schools* was published by the same evaluation group in 1963. The application of the *Evaluative Criteria* involves first a self-evaluation on the part of the staff of the school. Since teachers are probably the best informed and the most concerned about the quality of a school program for student growth and development, it is recommended that the teachers themselves have a major share in planning and carrying out the self-evaluation. The self-evaluation is followed by a visiting committee that is composed of professional personnel from other schools.

Tools and Techniques

As stated in chapter 1, logical and quantifiable tools and techniques are available for analyzing school programs, monitoring educational projects, collecting feedback (evaluating educational outcomes), and making educational decisions. The following are but a few of these tools and techniques: standardized testing, task analysis, diagnostic or prescriptive teaching, behavioral objectives, criterion-referenced performance, management by objectives (MBO), planning-programming-budgeting system (PPBS), program evaluation review technique (PERT), and operations research (OR). It is not the purpose of this book to teach the use of these tools and techniques and the situations under which they are most pertinent. The reader is referred to the references listed in chapter 1 for detailed information.

Evaluation of Objectives

Some disagreement exists regarding the evaluation of educational goals and objectives. Many books on evaluation ignore the subject of assessing goals and objectives. Some books incorporate the assessment of goals and objectives as a part of the evaluation of the curriculum and instructional program. This author has focused on the formulation and validation of objectives in chapter 3. It is apparent, therefore, that this author places with the majority of writers who advocate that goals and objectives be assessed when formulated—and not delayed for assessment until the time that the curriculum and instructional program is evaluated.

Cybernetic Principle in Evaluation

Cybernetics Defined. Cybernetics is defined as the comparative study of the human or biological control system and the mechanoelectrical control systems and devices, such as computers, thermostats, and photoelectric sorters. Cybernetics regards the human brain, nervous system, and muscular system, as a highly complex servomechanism—an automatic goal-seeking machine which "steers" its way to a target or goal by use of feedback data and stored information, automatically correcting course when necessary. The term *cybernetics,* thus defined, alludes to the principle of feedback control. In general, the term *feedback* refers to a kind of reciprocal interaction between two or more actions in which one activity generates a second activity, which in turn redirects the first activity.

Perhaps a simpler way to look at feedback is to refer to the earlier statement that it represents a process of sampling a portion of the output and comparing that sample to the input. This comparison would, in turn, indicate the effects of the system. It is through this monitoring process that the system "managers" can adjust or readjust the system to produce the desired output.

This writer considers the concept of feedback to be a major construct in the systems approach to curriculum design and improvement. In an attempt to insure that the reader fully understands this concept as a vital part of a regulated system, the following discussion of servomechanisms is presented.

Servomechanisms. Since World War II the feedback principle has been identified especially with control systems known as servomechanisms. An explanation of servomechanisms proceeds thus:

> Servomechanisms are divided into two general types: (1) where the target, goal, or "answer" is known, and the objective is to reach it or accomplish it, and (2) where the target or "answer" is not known and the objective is to discover or locate it. The human brain and nervous system operate in both ways.
> An example of the first type is the self-guided torpedo, or the interceptor missile. The target or goal is known—an enemy ship or plane. The objective is to reach it. Such machines must "know" the target they are shooting for. They must have some sort of propulsion system which propels them forward in the general direction of the target. They must be equipped with "sense organs" (radar, sonar, heat perceptors, etc.) which bring information from the target. These "sense organs" keep the machine informed when it is on the correct course (positive feedback) and when it commits an error and gets off course (negative feedback). The machine does not react or respond to positive feedback. It is doing the correct thing already and "just keeps on doing what it is doing." There must be a corrective device, however, which will respond to negative feedback. When negative feedback informs the mechanism that it is "off the beam" too far to the right, the corrective mechanism automatically causes the rudder to move so that it will steer the machine back to the left. If it "overcorrects" and heads too far to the left, this mistake is made known through negative feedback, and the corrective device moves the rudder so it will steer the machine back to the right. The torpedo accomplishes its goal by going forward, making errors, and continually correcting them. By a series of zigzags, it literally gropes its way to the goal.[28]

An electronic brain, in operation, is an example of the second type of servomechanism. A great deal of data are fed into the machine. These stored, or recorded, data constitute the memory of the machine. When a problem is posed to the machine, it scans through its memory until it locates the only answer that is consistent with—and meets all of the conditions of—the problem.

Great feats that are attributed to automation have been made possible through the use of computers. Computers can be programmed to collect enormous amounts of data, to detect errors, to decide on the appropriate action to be taken, and to make adjustments in the system, so that the actual output and the expected output are as similar as possible.

Application of the Cybernetic Principle. If the cybernetic principle is to be effective, information—especially about errors or dysfunctions—must be fed back into the system, so that corrective action can be taken. All of the components of a cybernetic system exist in most schools. Implications exist for a school system.[29] Objectives which specify the path that the educational process will follow are usually stated. Individuals, or groups of individuals, are available for making adjustments that are needed in the process. A process of evaluation is followed to judge the extent to which objectives are attained.

A cybernetic system requires that all pertinent data be fed back into the system. When data are not fed back, the cybernetic system ceases to function. School systems need "a systematic program for gathering data for measurement and evaluation, analyzing data to identify discrepancies between the actual output and the expected output, and feeding this information back into the system so that adjustments can be made in the process." [30]

Certain weaknesses exist, however, in most educational feedback systems.[31] One weakness is found in that a number of tests are given and scores are recorded, but the results are not used for making adjustments in the educational process. A second weakness is found in that the evaluation program is limited to the curriculum and instructional process. However, in a systems context, the total system must be considered. All of the subsystems must also have objectives to provide direction, and an evaluation program must identify dysfunctions that can be fed back through the cybernetic system for solution. In conclusion, it is to be emphasized that a cybernetic system depends not only on the collection of data but also on the appropriate routing and careful analysis of evaluative data to identify dysfunctions and errors.

Diagnosis and the Cybernetic System

As explained earlier, the cybernetic system depends, for effectiveness, on identifying problems, diagnosing their causes, and prescribing solutions to the problems. The curriculum and instructional system which is based on the cybernetic principle depends, for effectiveness, on the diagnosis of problems by means of the measurement and evaluation program—and the feeding back of the problem into the system for solution and redirection.

In the instructional process, diagnosis of problems occurs at the unit or instructional package level and the bisystem, subsystem, and curriculum levels. An explanation of the diagnostic process follows.[32]

Procedure and Package (or Unit) Levels. At the procedure and package (or unit) levels, the teacher functions as the control unit of the feedback system in a classroom. The diagnosis of problems at this level is mainly concerned with regard to individual students. The questions basic to the diagnosis are these: "Which students have learning problems? What are the strengths and weaknesses in their achievement? What factors have caused their unsatisfactory achievement?" [33] It is recommended that teachers use the variety of means that are available to them for identifying learning problems and strengths and weaknesses—e.g., quizzes or tests, assignments, class projects. The instrument does not have to be a written test. Specific observations by the teacher may serve. The objectives should help to determine the type of evaluation that should be adequate and appropriate. The diagnostic tools that are used may not only provide insight into the nature of the problems but also insight into the possible causes of the problems. The teacher should not only be able to identify problems and their possible causes but also apply remedial techniques for the solution of problems.

Bisystem, Subsystem, and Curriculum Levels. At the bisystem, subsystem, and curriculum levels, the management system functions as the control unit of the feedback system.[34] The supervisory system collaborates in this operation. The management systems that are presented and explained in this book for decision making and problem solving include feedback systems. They are designed to work toward the attainment of specific objectives, and provide for the detection of problems in the instructional system through a comparison of actual output with expected output. Data needed for the location of dysfunction and correction of dysfunction are derived primarily from tests, other evaluative instruments, and feedback from teachers. The basic difference between diagnosis of problems and their causes and prescription of possible solutions—at the bi-system, subsystem, and curriculum levels, and the classroom level (or instructional procedure or unit or package levels)—is one of scope.

System Regulation in Curriculum and Instructional Improvement

Now that it is safe to assume that the reader has a grasp of some rudimentary cybernetic constructs, it seems important to insure that the connection between these concepts and curriculum and instructional improvement is clear. This book represents an attempt to apply insights developed in the systems discipline to the discipline of education. It has been noted that the basic systems model has three elements—input, process (thruput), output. Throughout this book, considerable detail has dealt with these three elements.

It has been noted in previous chapters that systems concepts provide an excellent framework within which the curriculum and instructional worker can gain insight regarding the performance of his or her function. The need to identify and specify inputs, the understanding that all parts of the system are interrelated, and the realization that the interaction between the input and all of the system elements produces the output are important and helpful guides to practice.

In this writer's judgment, the art and science of curriculum and instructional improvement would be enhanced greatly through the application of the principles stated in the previous paragraph. Many texts applying system concepts to education do not go beyond these concepts. Throughout this text, however, reference has been made to the need to collect feedback. This chapter has been written to help the reader understand the regulation function performed by feedback.

Unless a continuous sample of output is systematically collected and compared to the input, no one is really in a position to evaluate the effects of the system per se. The collection and comparison of output to input must also be followed by system adjustment if correction (regulation) is to result. This regulation function is critical. Discrepancies must be evaluated in terms of system modifications required to produce desired output. There is no automatic way to do this in curriculum and instruction. As it has already been suggested, it is the output committee's major objective constantly to monitor output, describe discrepancies, suggest system modification, and report the same to the appropriate decision-making person(s) and/or group(s).

Accountability Defined

The term *accountability* appears in the literature with a variety of meanings. Accountability is "the requirement on the occupant of a role, by those who authorize that role, to answer for the results of work expected from him in the role." [35] The term *accountability* has been used to refer "to the process of expecting each member of an organization to answer to someone for doing specific things according to specific plans and against certain timetables to accomplish tangible performance results." [36] The assumption is that "everyone who joins an organization does so presumably to help in the achievement of its purposes; . . . [and] individual behavior which contributes to these purposes is functional and that which does not is dysfunctional." [37]

Accountability is to be distinguished from responsibility. Responsibility is "an essential component of authority which cannot be delegated." [38] It is, for example,

> the responsibility of a board of education to insure the effective education of the children of its community. Board members cannot pass this responsibility on to principals and to teachers. But they can hold teachers and principals accountable for the achievement of tangible educational effects provided they define clearly what effects they expect and furnish the resources needed to achieve them.[39]

Methods of Accountability

One approach encompasses intervention at three levels of the school organization structure—viz., the top, the middle, and the base.[40] Intervention at the top consists basically of establishing organizational goals. These goals may be established by using a technique referred to as management by objectives (MBO).[41] Figure 21 schematizes the MBO concept.

Most administrators, supervisors, and teachers have had no experience with an accountability program. In most cases, they have no preparation for the tasks that are involved. A development program must be provided to meet their needs. The program must begin at the top with the superintendent, assistant superintendent(s), and principal(s). The development program for supervisors must not only disseminate information but, more importantly, impart skills—especially the skill of conducting accountability interviews with subordinates. The program must include the development of specific instruments and techniques for evaluating how well individual members of the school system are performing their assigned roles. In this last aspect, the teachers are touched most directly.

In another approach, performance contracting is held to be the best example to "assure the achievement of results." [42] In performance contracting, a public or private agent enters into a contractual agreement to perform a service for which the agent "will be held answerable for performing according to agreed-upon terms, within an established time period, and with a stipulated use of resources and performance standards." [43]

In a challenging viewpoint, the doubt is expressed that persons can be evaluated and held accountable for consistent behavior in line with their objectives when the fact is that goals continually change and emerge.[44] It is further observed that preexistent objectives do not really exist any more often than they do not.

Nature of an Effective Evaluation Program

An effective evaluation program is characterized by "(1) clearly stated objectives, (2) a regular and systematic program, (3) an integrated, coordinated, and

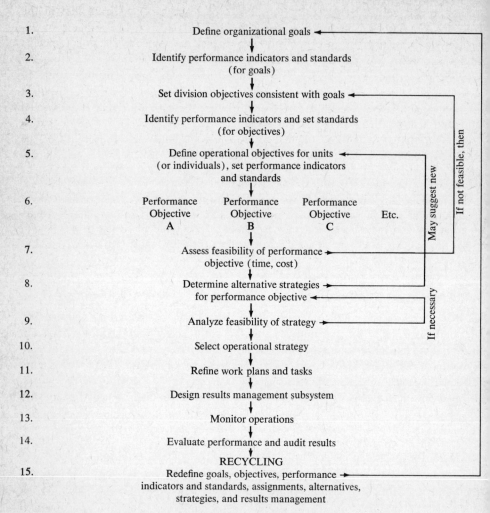

FIGURE 21.   General Systems MBO/R Model

SOURCE: American Association of School Administrators, *Management by Objectives and Results* (Arlington, Va.: The Association, 1973), p. 27. Reprinted by permission.

continuously planned program, (4) an information-storage-retrieval system, (5) continuous in-service education of the staff." [45] The effectiveness of a cybernetic system depends on the quality and quantity of data that are fed into it. Some discussion of the characteristics of an effective evaluation program follows.

First, clearly stated objectives must exist for the total system, and for each of its subsystems and components. The subject of objectives is given extensive explanation in chapter 5. Additional references are given where pertinent. Second, an effective evaluation program is characterized by comparable, rather than a variety of, tests that are administered at regular intervals, preferably at the beginning and end of each year. The tests should be used over a period of years, and only those changes should be made that are justified by obsolescence of the tests or the publication of improved instruments. Third, an integrated and coordinated program will incorporate the expertise of supervisors, and the preferences of teachers for certain evaluative instruments and procedures. Fourth, necessary data, in needed quantity and quality, are on hand and are retrievable without exorbitant cost, time, or effort. Sixth, and last, needed knowledge and skills are imparted to the teachers so that they may participate—and participate intelligently —in the evaluation program.

Summary

Curriculum and instructional improvement, viewed in terms of a systems approach, includes four stages. The fourth and last stage is an evaluation of program outcomes. This chapter explains stage four.

Evaluation is variously defined. It is sometimes used as though it were synonymous with measurement. It is not. Measurement may be said to involve the collection and analysis of data—by means of, for example, an achievement test. Evaluation uses the data that are derived from both measurement and non-measurement procedures and arrives at a value judgment.

A distinction is made between formative evaluation and summative evaluation. Formative evaluation is concerned with the merits of the curriculum and instructional program. Summative evaluation is concerned with the results of instruction.

It should be recalled that the input of a school system is an uneducated individual, and the output is an educated individual. Most schools restrict their evaluation program to a measurement of the output of the system. Benefits result from the measurement of both the input and output of the system. All information that is provided should feed back into the system, thus enabling the staff to take action for improvement.

A survey of the literature reveals that interest favors a broad type of evaluation of curriculum and instruction. Several models are available as approaches to the evaluation. The chapter presents and discusses three such models.

Most efforts to improve curriculum and instruction have been based, over the years, on a segmental curriculum model. Innovations have been adopted, in most cases, without consideration for implications to the rest of the program. In contrast to the segmental curriculum model, the aggregate model focuses on the total school curriculum with various courses, learnings, and goals treated as they interrelate.

This author prefers to interpret the evaluation of the curriculum and instructional program of a middle school, junior high school, or senior high school in the fullest sense of the meaning of the word *evaluation*. Thus, to evaluate the curriculum and instructional program, it is necessary both to measure the development or status and, also, to determine the worth or value of the growth or status. Certain considerations are necessary in such an evaluation of a curriculum and instructional program. The chapter presents and discusses the considerations.

Some disagreement exists regarding the evaluation of educational goals and objectives. Many books on evaluation ignore the subject of assessing goals and objectives. This author places with the majority of writers who advocate that goals and objectives be assessed when formulated, and not delayed for assessment until the time that the curriculum and instructional program is evaluated.

The definition of cybernetics alludes to the principle of feedback control. In general, the term *feedback* refers to a kind of reciprocal interaction between two or more actions in which one activity generates a second activity, which in turn redirects the first activity. All of the components of a cybernetic system exist in most schools. Implications exist for a school system.

The cybernetic system depends, for effectiveness, on identifying problems, diagnosing their causes, and prescribing solutions to the problems. The curriculum and instructional system which is based on the cybernetic principle depends, for effectiveness, on the diagnosis of problems by means of the measurement and evaluation program, and the feeding back of the problem into the system for solution and redirection. In the instructional process, diagnosis of problems occurs at the unit or instructional package level—and, the bisystem, subsystem, and curriculum levels.

The term *accountability* appears in the literature with a variety of meanings. Accountability is to be distinguished from responsibility. The chapter presents a brief discussion of definitions of accountability. Discussion includes selected methods of accountability.

The effectiveness of a cybernetic system depends on the quality and quantity of data that are fed into it. An effective evaluation program is characterized by certain features. The chapter concludes with a discussion of these features.

NOTES

1. K. V. Feyereisen, A. J. Fiorino, and A. T. Nowak, *Supervision and Curriculum Renewal: A Systems Approach* (New York: Appleton-Century-Crofts, 1970), p. 301. Reprinted by permission.

2. Ibid., p. 302.

3. Ibid.

4. Michael Scriven, "The Methodology of Evaluation," in *Perspectives of Curriculum Evaluation,* ed. Robert E. Stake (AERA Monograph Series on Curriculum Evaluation), (Chicago: Rand McNally, 1967), pp. 40–43. Copyright 1967, American Educational Research Association, Washington, D.C.

5. J. Galen Saylor and William M. Alexander, *Planning Curriculum for Schools* (New York: Holt, Rinehart and Winston, 1974), pp. 302–303. Reprinted by permission.

6. Feyereisen, Fiorino, and Nowak, *Supervision and Curriculum Renewal,* p. 310.

7. Ibid.

8. Ibid.

9. Robert B. McIntyre, "Out of the Classroom," *Exceptional Children* 37 (November 1970): 213. Reprinted with permission of The Council for Exceptional Children.

10. Ibid.

11. Ibid.

12. Ibid., pp. 215–17.

13. Ibid., p. 216.

14. R. M. W. Travers, *An Introduction to Educational Research* (New York: Macmillan Co., 1964); cited in McIntyre, "Out of the Classroom," p. 216. Reprinted by permission.

15. McIntyre, "Out of the Classroom," p. 217.

16. Ibid., p. 219.

17. Robert E. Stake, "Language, Rationality, and Assessment," in *Improving Educational Assessment and an Inventory of Measures of Affective Behavior,* ed. Walcott H. Beatty (Washington, D.C.: Association for Supervision and Curriculum Development, 1969); cited in Saylor and Alexander, *Planning Curriculum,* p. 304. Reprinted by permission.

18. Saylor and Alexander, *Planning Curriculum,* pp. 304-7.

19. Ibid., p. 304.

20. Stephen Klein, Gary Fenstermacher, and Marvin C. Alkin, "The Center's Changing Evaluation Model," *UCLA Evaluation Comment* 2 (January 1971): 9-12. Reprinted by permission.

21. Leonard H. Clark, Raymond L. Klein, and John B. Burks, *The American Secondary School Curriculum* (New York: Macmillan Co., 1972), pp. 564-68. Reprinted by permission.

22. Ibid., p. 568.

23. Ibid., p. 565.

24. Ibid., pp. 565-66.

25. Ibid., p. 565.

26. Ibid.

27. Ibid., p. 566.

28. From the book, *Psycho-Cybernetics* by Maxwell Maltz, M.D., pp. 19-20. Copyright © 1960 by Prentice-Hall, Inc. Published by Prentice-Hall, Inc., Englewood Cliffs, New Jersey.

29. Feyereisen, Fiorino, and Nowak, *Supervision and Curriculum Renewal,* p. 304. Reprinted by permission.

30. Ibid.

31. Ibid.

32. Ibid., p. 306.

33. Ibid.

34. Ibid.

35. A. D. Newman and R. W. Rowbottom, *Organization Analysis* (Carbondale, Ill.: Southern Illinois University Press, 1968), p. 26. Reprinted by permission.

36. Felix M. Lopez, "Accountability in Education," *Phi Delta Kappan* 52 (December 1970): 231. Reprinted by permission.

37. Ibid.

38. Ibid.

39. Ibid.

40. Ibid., pp. 232-34.

41. Ibid., p. 232.

42. Leon M. Lessinger and Ralph W. Tyler, eds., *Accountability in Education* (Worthington, Ohio: Charles A. Jones, 1971); cited in Thomas J. Sergiovanni, ed., *Professional Supervision for Professional Teachers* (Washington, D.C.: Association for Supervision and Curriculum Development, 1975), p. 68. Reprinted by permission.

43. Ibid.

44. Sergiovanni, *Professional Supervision,* p. 70.

45. Feyereisen, Fiorino, and Nowak, *Supervision and Curriculum Renewal,* p. 314.

Related Readings

Ashby, W. R. *Introduction to Cybernetics*. New York: John Wiley and Sons, 1963.

Beatty, Walcott H., ed. *Improving Educational Assessment and an Inventory of Measures of Affective Behavior*. Washington, D.C.: Association for Supervision and Curriculum Development, 1969.

Brown, G. S., and Campbell, D. P. *Principles of Servomechanisms*. New York: John Wiley and Sons, 1948.

Clark, Leonard H.; Klein, Raymond L.; and Burks, John B. *The American Secondary School Curriculum*. New York: Macmillan Co., 1972.

De Young, Chris A., and Wynn, Richard. *American Education*. New York: McGraw-Hill, 1972.

Doll, Ronald C. *Curriculum Improvement: Decision Making and Process*. Boston: Allyn and Bacon, 1974.

Feyereisen, K. V.; Fiorino, A. J.; and Nowak, A. T. *Supervision and Curriculum Renewal: A Systems Approach*. New York: Appleton-Century-Crofts, 1970.

Klein, Stephen; Fenstermacher, Gary; and Alkin, Marvin C. "The Center's Changing Evaluation Model." *Evaluation Comment* 2 (January 1971): 9–12.

Lessinger, Leon M., and Tyler, Ralph W., eds. *Accountability in Education*. Worthington, Ohio: Charles A. Jones, 1971.

Lopez, Felix M. "Accountability in Education." *Phi Delta Kappan* 52 (December 1970): 231–35.

Saylor, J. Galen, and Alexander, William M. *Planning Curriculum for Schools*. New York: Holt, Rinehart and Winston, 1974.

Silvern, Leonard C. "Cybernetics and Education K-12." *Audiovisual Instruction* 13 (March 1968): 267–72.

Smith, Karl U., and Smith, Margaret Foltz. *Cybernetic Principles of Learning and Educational Design*. New York: Holt, Rinehart and Winston, 1966.

Stake, Robert E., ed. *Perspectives of Curriculum Evaluation*, AERA Monograph Series on Curriculum Evaluation. Chicago: Rand McNally, 1967.

Wick, John W., and Beggs, Donald L., eds. *Evaluation for Decision Making in the Schools*. Boston: Houghton Mifflin, 1970.

Wiener, N. *Cybernetics, or Control and Communication in the Animal and the Machine*. Cambridge: Massachusetts Institute of Technology Press, 1961.

———. *Cybernetics and Society*. Garden City, N.J.: Doubleday and Co., 1954.

Wilhelms, Fred T., ed. *Evaluation as Feedback and Guide*, 1967 Yearbook. Washington, D.C.: Association for Supervision and Curriculum Development, 1967.

Work Sheet 8A
Questions for Class Dialogue

Student's Name ————————————————————————
Date ————————————————————————

Directions: Study chapter 8 with the following questions in mind. Prepare responses for each question, so that you can intelligently participate in class dialogue. Space is provided with each question, so that you can record any notes that will aid you in the dialogue.

1. Distinguish between evaluation and measurement.

2. Distinguish between formative evaluation and summative evaluation.

3. Is decision making a part of the evaluative process? Explain.

4. Give the components of a model that would symbolize the steps in evaluation for providing data for decision making.

5. (a) Comment on the soundness of using quality as a base for evaluating a school program.

(b) Comment on the soundness of using effectiveness as a base for evaluating a school program.

6. Give the components of one of the evaluation models that are presented in chapter 8 of the text.

7. Evaluate efforts to improve curriculum and instruction based on aggregate or segmental curriculum models.

8. Explain the importance of qualitative and quantitative measurements in determining the growth of students.

9. (a) How may qualitative measurements be obtained?

   (b) How may quantitative measurements be obtained?

10. Specify the component parts of quantitative evaluation if it is to be valid. Explain each component part.

11. Name a few of the logical and quantifiable tools and techniques that are available for analyzing school programs, monitoring educational projects, evaluating educational outcomes, and making educational decisions.

12. Comment on incorporating the assessment of goals and objectives as a part of the evaluation of the curriculum and instructional program.

13. Define cybernetics.

14. What is meant by the cybernetic principle?

15. (a) Do the components of a cybernetic system exist in most schools?

    (b) Draw implications of the cybernetic principle for the school system.

16. (a) On what does the effectiveness of a cybernetic system depend?

(b) On what does the effectiveness of the curriculum and instructional system (that is based on the cybernetic principle), depend?

17. In what way does the teacher function as the control unit of the feedback system in a classroom?

18. (a) Define accountability.

   (b) Distinguish between responsibility and accountability.

19. Discuss some methods of attempting to insure the achievement of desired results.

20. Specify some characteristics of an effective evaluation program.

Work Sheet 8B
School Interview

Student's Name _____

Date _____

Directions:
1. Recall that chapter 8, in the text, specifies that formative evaluation is concerned with the merits of the curriculum and instructional program, and that summative evaluation is concerned with the results of instruction.
2. Interview a curriculum coordinator or a principal in a middle school, junior high school, or senior high school. In the interview, learn the procedure by which both formative evaluation and summative evaluation are conducted in the school. If possible, obtain a copy of the evaluative instruments that are used.
3. Ascertain whether the school uses a systems approach to curriculum and instructional improvement.
4. Be prepared to report your findings to the class. Use the space below for notes that you may want to make.

Work Sheet 8C
Evaluation Meeting

Student's Name _____

Date _____

Directions:
1. Visit a curriculum evaluation meeting in a middle school, junior high school, or senior high school. Ascertain the following:
   a. School personnel in attendance at the meeting—and the role of these individuals in curriculum evaluation in that particular school.
   b. Goals of the meeting.
   c. Attainments of the meeting.
2. Record your findings below.
3. Attempt to attend such a meeting in a school where a systems approach is used in curriculum and instructional improvement, and a school where such an approach is not used. If you attend two different meetings, draw comparisons regarding each of the 3 points mentioned in number 1 above.

Work Sheet 8D
Model Study

Student's Name _____

Date _____

Directions:
1. Study the following model. It is known as the EPIC model, or Evaluative Programs for Innovative Curriculums model.

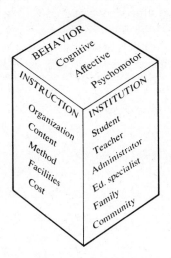

2. Refer to:

> Doll, Ronald C. *Curriculum Improvement: Decision Making and Process.*
> Boston: Allyn and Bacon, 1974, pp. 374–75. (The above model is taken from this reference.)

3. Discuss the concept that is symbolized by the model above. Record your discussion below.

Work Sheet 8E
Test Distinctions and Samples

Student's Name _____
Date _____

Directions:
1. Go to the library and use reference materials to distinguish between:
   a. Achievement and diagnostic tests.
   b. Objective and standardized tests.
   c. Prognostic tests and attitude scales.
   d. Interest inventories and aptitude tests.
   e. Tests of general ability and special abilities.
2. Obtain a sample of each of the above types of instruments.
3. Use the space below to record the distinctions that are requested above.

Work Sheet 8F
Evaluative Criteria

Student's Name _____

Date _____

Directions:
1. Obtain a copy of the *Evaluative Criteria,* a publication of the National Study of Secondary-School Evaluation. Select one section of it, and obtain information for this section as a school would do if it were conducting a self-study.
2. Be prepared to discuss your findings in class. Use the space below for any notes that you would like to make to aid you in class discussion.

Work Sheet 8G
Synthesis of Learnings

Student's Name _____

Date _____

Directions:

1. Recall that chapter 8, in the text, includes an explanation regarding the cybernetic principle in evaluation.
2. Read the following article:

    Silvern, Leonard C. "Cybernetics and Education K-12." *Audiovisual Instruction* 13 (March 1968): 267–72.

3. In the space that is provided below, record a synthesis of your learnings from the above-mentioned article and chapter 8 in the text, regarding cybernetics.

Work Sheet 8H
Book Report

Student's Name _____

Date _____

Directions:
1. Read the following book:
    Wilhelms, Fred T. *Evaluation as Feedback and Guide.* Washington,
    D.C.: Association for Supervision and Curriculum Development, 1967.
2. Write a book report in which you raise the questions and give the solutions
    that are presented in the book.

Work Sheet 8I
Accountability Misconceptions

Student's Name _____

Date _____

Directions:

1. Consider the following statement:

    A careful examination of efforts to establish accountability programs suggests some underlying misconceptions that explain the many failures.

2. Refer to:

    Lopez, Felix M. "Accountability in Education." *Phi Delta Kappan* 52 (December 1970): 231–35. (The above statement is taken from this reference.)

3. Identify (on the basis of the preceding article) the misconceptions that explain the many failures of accountability programs. Write your identifications below.

Work Sheet 8J
Library Search

Student's Name _____

Date _____

Directions:
1. Read the following statement:
    The National Assessment for Educational Progress, sponsored by the Education Commission of the States, is an ambitious effort to gather normative data from a national sample of students' achievements, which provides schools with data which will permit comparison of the effectiveness of the curriculum and instruction with national norms. (De Young, Chris A., and Wynn, Richard. *American Education.* New York: McGraw-Hill, 1972, p. 363.)
2. Conduct a library search of further information regarding the National Assessment for Educational Progress, sponsored by the Education Commission of the States. Especially note any practical applications that have been made— or are being made—in your own state. Record your findings below.

Work Sheet 8K
Process Evaluation

Student's Name _____

Date _____

Directions:
1. Note:
   Criteria are recommended for use in evaluating the curriculum evaluation process itself.
2. Refer to:
   Clark, Leonard H.; Klein, Raymond L.; and Burks, John B. *The American Secondary School Curriculum.* New York: Macmillan Co., 1972, pp. 570–71.
3. From the above reference, identify the criteria that are recommended for use in evaluating the curriculum evaluation process itself. Record the criteria in the space that is provided below.

Work Sheet 8L
Extension of Learning

Student's Name _____

Date _____

Directions:
1. Choose one of the following readings, or one of the readings at the end of chapter 8, to extend the learnings that you have attained from the chapter.
2. Read critically.
3. Synthesize your learnings for class dialogue.
4. Space is provided at the end of this work sheet for notes that you may want to make.

Readings:
1. Smith, Karl U., and Smith, Margaret Foltz. *Cybernetic Principles of Learning and Educational Design.* New York: Holt, Rinehart and Winston, 1966.
2. Wick, John W., and Beggs, Donald L., eds. *Evaluation for Decision-Making in the Schools.* Boston: Houghton Mifflin, 1970.
3. Wilhelms, Fred T., ed. *Evaluation as Feedback and Guide,* 1967 Yearbook. Washington, D.C.: Association for Supervision and Curriculum Development, 1967.

PART III

CONVERSION TO A
SYSTEMS APPROACH

9

Conversion to a Systems
Approach in Curriculum and
Instructional Improvement

The systems approach that has been presented in the preceding chapters for curriculum and instructional improvement is not only suitable for a new school system but also appropriate for an established one. Certain principles and considerations are basic for successful conversion to a systems approach. This chapter presents and discusses these principles and considerations.

Motivation for Conversion

A desire for change should help to expedite conversion to a systems approach in curriculum and instructional improvement. Some persons will favor change for the sake of change. Others may favor change because they are discontent with the current program. Still others may be stirred to favor change if it can be shown to them that another approach should prove more beneficial than the present one.
Equipped with a desire for change,

a small team of selected persons in the school system could familiarize themselves with the basic ideas of systems approaches and, with the help of consultants, could design a model for a curriculum and instruction system. . . . Upon determination of the components and the design of the . . . system, the roles and services of needed personnel could be delineated prior to the actual selection or assignment of key people to man the posts.[1]

Subsequent steps in a systems approach to curriculum and instructional improvement would follow. It must be noted, however, that a staff development program should prepare the staff for involvement in the process.

Staff Development Programs

A staff that is qualified to engage in systems design is a prerequisite to successful curriculum design using the systems approach. If a conversion is to be made to a systems approach for curriculum and instructional improvement, staff development programs should be conducted to prepare the staff for participation in the process. When the staff has been prepared, curriculum and instructional improvement can proceed as described in the preceding chapters.

Staff development programs are focused on equipping personnel for their roles as perceived in a systems approach. Roles and processes differ from those of a bureaucratic organizational structure. The teacher, for one, functions in a different role in a systems organization. In a systems organization, the role of the teacher in a curriculum and instructional system is one of problem identifier, decision maker, and evaluator of the instructional process. The teacher is a cooperative member of the system. As such, the teacher's interest is, among other things, that the goals and objectives of the system be attained. The staff development program should not only involve the participants in developing a knowledge of systems concepts in school settings and in curriculum and instructional processes, but should, also, provide assistance in the application of knowledge in curriculum and instructional improvement.

Predispositions to the Systems Approach

"The systems approach is likely to flourish where certain conditions prevail." [2] Some of the conditions are these: (1) Educational objectives are stated in performance terms. (2) An awareness exists for possible alternate means for utilizing resources for attaining objectives. (3) Adequate staff development is provided for conveying a knowledge of systems concepts and the application of these concepts. (4) Personnel with needed expertise are available.[3]

School Location and Size

Systems, regardless of size and location, have inputs, processes, and outputs. All systems have "interacting components which are mutually dependent and constrained toward accomplishment of organizational goals. All can be divided into any number of subsystems as they are needed. And all subsystems are interactive with a larger structure or suprasystem." [4]

School systems, regardless of size and location, have all of these properties—as do all systems. Systems concepts are applicable to school organizations of any size and location.

It is true that small school systems may seem to have less need than large ones for a systems approach. For one reason, the smaller size allows for easier communication within the organization. For another, "they are less complex." Last, they are "closer to the community with which they interact." [5]

Cost

Argument can be given that a systems approach will save money. Some of the arguments follow. The time that is needed to plan and implement programs, construct instructional packages, and so forth, in conversion from a bureaucratic curriculum organization to a curriculum and instructional system should produce a saving in the long run. Changes, packages, and so forth, are devised for the attainment of objectives that are more precisely formulated, and, consequently, can be evaluated more carefully, than in usual current practice. Such a condition promotes expeditiousness in teaching-learning experiences and, thereby, conserves time, effort, and resources on the part of teachers and students. A systems approach provides for an integration of materials and resources and, consequently, helps to promote optimal use of materials and resources. Last, the purchase of new materials and equipment is justified in light of definitive system objectives that have been formulated.

Opposing arguments are advanced to those who contend that a systems approach will save money. The following are numbered among these opposing arguments.[6] New systems procedures are not designed to reduce spending per se. What happens in some cases is that a focus on cost shifts from materials and equipment to be bought, to programs to be accomplished. Increasing evidence supports the observation that computers can be erratic and easily made inoperative, even by a speck of dust. Computer errors can be very costly and difficult to remedy.

Subsystem Conversion

It must be emphasized that curriculum is a system, and not an activity or a course. Therefore, such activities as revising content, adding new courses, and writing new curriculum guides do not change the system. Systems analysis "subsumes an outlook, or mode of thinking, by which a particular organization may be defined, examined, evaluated, and improved." [7] The process starts with objectives and builds from there.

In redesigning a curriculum and instructional program, the implementation of the system is not delayed until the total system is designed. For one reason, a school system could not be expected and could not afford to maintain the current total program until the new program, including every procedure, is designed and ready for use. For another reason, the conversion of a total program is much too complex and, thus, doomed to failure if a total conversion is attempted.

In redesigning a curriculum and instructional program, a sounder approach is to try out experimentally one subsystem at a time, and, on the basis of the results of each trial, to adjust the dysfunctions of each separate subsystem before that subsystem is adopted. The knowledge that is gained from each experience is valuable for future reorganizations. In each instance, the design extends to the unit or instructional package level. If the staff of the school is large enough, more than one subsystem can be redesigned and implemented at one time.

Paradigms for Instructional Systems

Prior to the implementation of the systems approach—whether at the instructional package or unit level, or for restructuring an entire curriculum—the realization must be made that there may be more than one system or approach that will work. Initially, the decision must be made as to what it is that the system is wanted to perform. Subsequently, a system must be selected, adopted, adapted, or produced to do the job that needs to be done. Care should be given to a consideration of the time and the cost that will be involved. The following are but a few of the paradigms for instructional systems that have been advanced.

Kaufman includes the following as steps in the systems approach as he sees it: define "what is," define "what is required," select an appropriate process for achieving "what is required," implement the process, determine validity of solution, re-do if necessary. In order to synthesize a system using these steps, these additional major-level tasks must be performed: selecting solution strategy, implementing solution strategy, determining performance effectiveness, and revising and correcting as necessary.[8]

Major components of Merrill's system are the learner, the environment, and the instruction. Inputs to the system environment include learner traits, library input (all instructional materials), objectives, and feedback. Outputs from the system are knowledge of results, response record, and display to the learner.[9]

Eraut clearly demonstrates the relevance of the systems approach to the process of instructional design, particularly as applied to course development. His view considers a course as an instructional system, the components being the learners, the instructors, the materials, the machines, and the technicians. Input is the learner's initial knowledge, and output is the learner's final knowledge.[10]

Churchman points to a philosophical consideration by using the term "house-keeping approach" to characterize the part-to-whole method of system design as opposed to the whole system principle which examines the whole problem for whole costs and whole benefits.[11]

Promise for a New Approach

Many of the Seven Cardinal Principles of Education that were issued by the Commission on the Reorganization of Secondary Education in 1918 are as evident today as they were so many years ago. Only a few advocated innovations find their way into the school and the classroom. Schools, as social institutions, "often behave like individuals in that they develop customary ways of behaving to insure an orderly progress towards institutional goals." [12] Schools, as social institutions, resist change.

Many experimental programs fail because "the change or innovation is perceived as creating too much disequilibrium in the system, thus preventing it from meeting its obligations in a well-ordered manner." [13] Small-scale and fragmented changes, such as many of those that are being currently tested, are not advocated. Instead, a coordinated approach to educational reform is needed. Strategies must be coordinated for bringing about desired changes. Innovations must be discussed not only in terms of the change that is desired to be brought about, but also in terms of how the change is to take place. Heretofore, attempts to introduce innovations have often failed to cope with the complexity of the change process.[14]

It must be remembered that when a change occurs within some segment of an institution, the entire system must change. The complexity of change is illustrated in the following statements:

A change in teacher-pupil relationship is likely to have repercussion on teacher-pupil interaction, on parent-principal contacts, on pressure groups operating on the superintendent, on board members' chances for re-election, etc. Any estimate of resistance which considers only the persons primarily and centrally concerned will be inadequate. . . . [15]

The systems approach promises to be a new approach for "arraying goals and strategies which can assist decision-makers in analyzing choices open to them and preparing better ways of coping with the change process." [16] The preceding chapters rest on such a promise. They discuss the systems approach as the approach that is deemed necessary for curriculum and instructional improvement in middle schools, junior high schools, and senior high schools.

Systematically Designed Schools of the Future

The nature of systematically designed schools of the future is envisioned as strikingly different from the nature of most, if not all, of the schools of the present and the past. One description of systematically designed schools of the future encompasses the following aspects.[17]

Such schools will be learning centers of flexible construction, and flexible curriculum and schedule. School hours will be longer than 9:00 A.M. to 3:00 P.M. Schools will open early in the morning, possibly 7:00 A.M., and close late at night, possibly 10:00 or 11:00 P.M. Schools will be open twelve months of the year, and programs and schedules will be suited to the needs of individual students. If, for example, a student holds a part-time job, his or her classes, lectures, and self-study commitments will be organized in such a way that they do not conflict with the job. Furthermore, it is envisioned that classes will be coordinated with a job, so that a student will obtain experience outside of the school, thus perceiving a relationship between himself or herself and the community.

Schools will strive to intermesh academic and vocational education. All work that helps students to master new skills or develop new potentialities, and all work that helps students to prepare to assume adult lives in their communities, will be considered to be a part of their education. Technical experts will come to the schools to offer instruction in the various trades and industries. In some cases, such classes will actually be held in a shop or an industrial plant.

By intermeshing academic and vocational education, the schools will hope that students will see the value of studying material that otherwise they might think unnecessary. For example, involvement in the world of work will cause students, in some instances, to see the relevance of science and mathematics to certain occupations, and the need to study these subjects for entrance and advancement in these occupations.

A variety of techniques, materials, and equipment will be used to allow students to proceed at their own pace. Among these will be the following: programmed instruction, educational television, computer-managed instruction, single-concept films, games, testing machines, and so forth.

Study will proceed not only on an individual basis but also in groups. Though students will sometimes study alone, specific times will be set aside for students to meet as a group with teams of teachers intended to help with learning activities that have given the students difficulty. Older students from more advanced classes will be encouraged to join these groups as tutors.

Teachers will evaluate each student in regard to goals that he or she has selected with the help of the professional staff. A student's standing at any time will be an evaluation of the quality of work that the student has done to that point—e.g., the level of skill shown, the factual knowledge learned, and so on. Teachers will compare a student's present accomplishment with that of past accomplishment as a basis for defining the next quota of work and, possibly, upgrading the student's aspirations. Student success will not be measured by comparing a student's performance with that of the other students.

Examinations will be given upon student request. When a student has completed any designated set of learning activities, and judges that he or she has attained the learning intended, he or she will go to the achievement center to ask for an evaluation of progress. On the basis of the evaluation, the student will or will not proceed to the next stage of study. Such an examination plan is intended to increase the individualized nature of courses of study.

Students will not be given passing or failing grades at the end of the year. Instead, they will confer periodically with counselor-teachers regarding their progress. The counselor-teachers will have available to them, for the conference, up-to-date records that they obtain from the computer. Periodically, the student's teachers will record on tape their subjective impressions of each student's abilities and attitudes. Evaluations of the student's learning progress will be recorded on the same tape. All of this information will be a part of the student's master profile. Furthermore, a record of teacher observations will be available to parents who will periodically receive printed reports.

The above-given practices and programs are envisioned to characterize systematically designed schools of the future. In short, these schools will provide students with greater freedom of choice and self-determination of goals and instructional procedures. At the same time, they will retain the teacher in "the all-important role of catalyst in that complex process called learning"—at the crux of curriculum and instructional improvement.[18]

Summary

The systems approach that has been presented in the preceding chapters for curriculum and instructional improvement is not only suitable for a new school but also appropriate for an established one. Certain principles and considerations are basic for successful conversion to a systems approach. This chapter presents and discusses these principles and considerations.

A desire for change should help to expedite conversion to a systems approach in curriculum and instructional improvement. A staff development program, however, should further prepare the staff for their involvement in the process. Though small school systems may seem to have less need than large ones for a systems approach, systems concepts are applicable to school organizations of any size and location.

In redesigning a curriculum and instructional program, the implementation of the system is not delayed until the total system is designed. A sounder approach is to try out experimentally one subsystem at a time, and on the basis of the results of each trial, to adjust the dysfunctions of each separate subsystem before the subsystem is adopted.

The chapter includes a discussion of the following: (1) the cost factor in a systems approach to curriculum and instructional improvement, (2) the conditions that are conducive to a systems approach, and (3) some paradigms for instructional systems. Also discussed is the nature of systematically designed schools of the future.

The systems approach is emphasized as the approach that is deemed necessary for curriculum and instructional improvement in middle schools, junior high schools, and senior high schools.

NOTES

1. K. V. Feyereisen, A. J. Fiorino, and A. T. Nowak, *Supervision and Curriculum Renewal: A Systems Approach* (New York: Appleton-Century-Crofts, 1970), p. 323. Reprinted by permission.

2. Stephen J. Knezevich, *Administration of Public Education* (New York: Harper and Row, 1969), p. 560. Reprinted by permission.

3. Ibid.

4. Feyereisen, Fiorino, and Nowak, *Supervision and Curriculum Renewal,* p. 322.

5. Ibid.

6. Harry J. Hartley, "Limitations of Systems Analysis," *Phi Delta Kappan* 50 (May 1969): 515-19.

7. Ibid., p. 516.

8. R. A. Kaufman, "A System Approach to Education—Derivation and Definition," a paper presented to the California Teacher's Association Staff Conference on Problem Solving (January 1968); cited in A. Maughan Lee, "Instructional Systems: Which One?" *Audiovisual Instruction* 15 (January 1970): 30. Reprinted by permission.

9. M. D. Merrill, "Components of a Cybernetic Instructional System," *Educational Technology* 8 (April 1968): 5-10; cited in Lee, "Instructional Systems," p. 30. Reprinted by permission.

10. M. R. Eraut, "An Instructional Systems Approach to Course Development," *AV Communication Review* 15 (Spring 1967): 92-101; cited in Lee, "Instructional Systems," p. 30. Reprinted by permission.

11. C. W. Churchman, "On the Design of Educational Systems," *Audiovisual Instruction* 10 (May 1965): 361-65; cited in Lee, "Instructional Systems," p. 31. Reprinted by permission.

12. David S. Bushnell, "A Systems Approach to Curriculum Change in Secondary Education," *Educational Technology* 10 (May 1970): 46. Reprinted by permission.

13. Ibid.

14. Ibid.

15. Goodwin Watson, "Resistance to Change," in *Concepts for Social Change,* ed. Goodwin Watson (Washington, D.C.: National Training Laboratories, 1967), p. 20; cited in Bushnell, "A Systems Approach," p. 46. Copyright 1967 NTL Institute for Applied Behavioral Science. Reproduced by special permission.

16. Bushnell, "A Systems Approach," p. 46.

17. Ibid., pp. 47-48.

18. Ibid., p. 48.

Related Readings

Arnstein, George E. "Schoolmen: Don't Boggle at the Systems Concept—You've Probably Been Using It by a Different Name." *Nation's Schools* 80 (October 1967): 76–77.

Bushnell, David S. "A Suggested Guide for Developing a Systems Approach to Curriculum Improvement." *Education* 90 (April 1970): 351–62.

————. "A Systems Approach to Curriculum Change in Secondary Education." *Educational Technology* 10 (May 1970): 46–48.

Carter, D. G. et al. "Caution: Cult of Solution Seekers." *Clearing House* 49 (April 1976): 373–75.

Feyereisen, K. V.; Fiorino, A. J.; and Nowak, A. T. *Supervision and Curriculum Renewal: A Systems Approach*. New York: Appleton-Century-Crofts, 1970.

Koch, L., and French, J. R. P., Jr. "Overcoming Resistance to Change." *Human Relations* I (1948): 512–33.

Kong, S. L. "Education in the Cybernetic Age: A Model." *Phi Delta Kappan* 49 (October 1967): 71–74.

Miles, Matthew B., ed. *Innovation in Education*. New York: Horace Mann—Lincoln Institute of School Experimentation, Teachers College, Columbia University, 1964.

Watson, Goodwin. "Resistance to Change." In *Concepts for Social Change,* edited by Goodwin Watson. Washington, D.C.: Cooperative Project for Educational Development, National Training Laboratories, N.E.A., 1967.

Work Sheet 9A
Questions for Class Dialogue

Student's Name _____

Date _____

Directions: Study chapter 9 with the following questions in mind. Prepare responses for each question, so that you can intelligently participate in class dialogue. Space is provided with each question, so that you can record any notes that will aid you in the dialogue.

1. How can a desire for change be promoted in the professional personnel of a school where a conversion is planned to a systems approach in curriculum and instructional improvement?

2. Describe the nature of staff development that should be conducted if a conversion is to be made to a systems approach for curriculum and instructional improvement?

3. Under what conditions does the systems approach flourish the best?

4. Are systems concepts applicable to school organizations of any size and location? Explain.

5. (a) What arguments can be given that a systems approach will save money?

(b) What opposing arguments can be given to those who contend that a systems approach will save money?

6. In redesigning a curriculum and instructional program, is the implementation of the system delayed until the total system is designed? Explain.

7. What are some of the paradigms for instructional systems that have been advanced?

8. What promise lies in the systems approach for curriculum and instructional improvement?

Work Sheet 9B
School Visit

Student's Name _____

Date _____

Directions:

1. Visit a middle school, junior high school, or senior high school that has instituted a systems approach for curriculum and instructional improvement, to learn:
   a. The preparations that were made in the school for instituting the approach.
   b. The staff development programs that are conducted, if any, to help insure the effectiveness of the approach.
2. Report your learnings below.

Work Sheet 9C
Model Study

Student's Name _____

Date _____

Directions:
1. Study the following model:

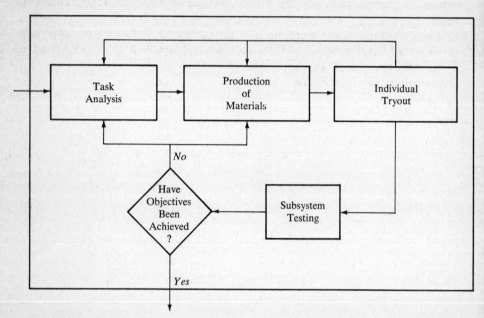

2. Refer to:

> Eraut, Michael R. "An Instructional Systems Approach to Course Development." *AV Communication Review* 15 (Spring 1967): 92–101. (The above-given model is taken from this reference.)

3. Explain the concept that is symbolized by the model.
4. Synthesize the concept with pertinent concepts that are presented in chapter 9 in your text.
5. Use the space below for your writing.

Work Sheet 9D
Systematically Designed Schools

Student's Name _____

Date _____

Directions:

1. Some periodical articles present descriptions of systematically designed schools of the future. Chapter 9 of the text presents one such description. Obtain at least one periodical article that describes systematically designed schools of the future.
2. Synthesize your learnings from the periodical article(s) that you find with those from chapter 9 of the text.
3. Record your synthesis below.

Work Sheet 9E
Learning in a Cybernetic Age

Student's Name _____

Date _____

Directions:

1. Study the model below. It represents a projected pattern of learning in a cybernetic age.

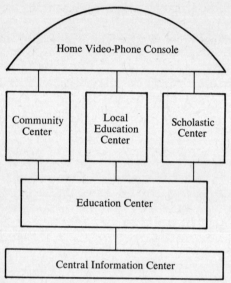

2. Refer to:

> Kong, S. L. "Education in the Cybernetic Age: A Model." *Phi Delta Kappan* 49 (October 1967): 71–74. (The model above is taken from this reference.)

3. Discuss the model above. Record your discussion in the space that is provided below.

Work Sheet 9F
Frequency of Systems Concept

Student's Name _____

Date _____

Directions:
1. Note:
   > The observation is made that schoolmen sometimes use the systems concept without knowing it.
2. Refer to:
   > Arnstein, George E. "Schoolmen: Don't Boggle at the Systems Concept— You've Probably Been Using It by a Different Name." *Nation's Schools* 80 (October 1967): 76–77.
3. Using your learnings from the above article, expound upon the observation that is stated above. Record your statements below.

Work Sheet 9G
Class Speaker

Student's Name _____
Date _____

Directions:
1. Note:

    A principal of a middle school, junior high school, or senior high school where a systems approach is used in curriculum and instructional improvement will be invited to come to the class to discuss the use of the system in his or her school.
2. List the questions that you would like to ask the speaker, based on his or her experiential background, regarding the use of a systems approach in curriculum and instructional improvement. List your questions in the space that is provided below.

Work Sheet 9H
Extension of Learning

Student's Name _____

Date _____

Directions:
1. Choose one of the following readings, or one of the readings at the end of chapter 9, to extend the learnings that you have attained from the chapter.
2. Read critically.
3. Synthesize your learnings for class dialogue.
4. Space is provided at the end of this work sheet for notes that you may want to make.

Readings:
1. Carter, D. G. et al. "Caution: Cult of Solution Seekers." *Clearing House* 49 (April 1976): 373–75.
2. Koch, L., and French, J. R. P., Jr. "Overcoming Resistance to Change." *Human Relations* I (1948): 512–33.
3. Miles, Matthew B., ed. *Innovation in Education.* New York: Horace Mann—Lincoln Institute of School Experimentation, Teachers College, Columbia University, 1964.

Index